edexcel

Edexcel GCSE

History A: The Making of the[illegible]odern World

Unit 1 Pe[illegible]e and War: International Relation[illegible]900–91

Revised ed[illegible]on

Student Boo[illegible]

Robin Bunce • Laura Gallagher • Nigel Kelly
Series editors: Nigel Kelly • Angela Leonard

Contents: delivering the Edexcel GCSE History A (The Making of the Modern World) specification Unit 1

Welcome to the course

Welcome to Modern World History! Studying this subject will help you to understand the world you live in: the events of the last 100 years can help to explain the problems and opportunities that exist in the world today.

There are four units in the course and each is worth 25% of the whole GCSE. Those units are:

- **Unit 1** Peace and War: International Relations 1900-91
- **Unit 2** Modern World Depth Study (Germany 1918-39; Russia 1917-39; or USA 1919-41)
- **Unit 3** Modern World Source Enquiry (First World War and British Society 1903-28; Second World War and British Society 1931-51; or the USA 1945-70)
- **Unit 4** Representations of History (your controlled assessment task).

Introduction to Unit 1

This book covers Unit 1: Peace and War: International Relations 1900-91. Depending on which sections you study in this unit, you might look at why Europe was plunged into war in 1914 and why, despite determined efforts to avoid further conflict, another war broke out just 20 years later. You might also discover that although there has been no major international war since 1945, in 1962 the world came within minutes of a devastating nuclear conflict.

How to use this book

There are six sections in Unit 1 and these are all covered in this book. You will study **three** of these:

- **Section 1:** Why did war break out? International rivalry 1900-14
- **Section 2:** The peace settlement 1918-28
- **Section 3:** Why did war break out? International relations 1929-39
- **Section 4:** How did the Cold War develop? 1943-56
- **Section 5:** Three Cold War crises: Berlin, Cuba and Czechoslovakia *c.* 1957-69
- **Section 6:** Why did the Cold War end? The invasion of Afghanistan (1979) to the collapse of the Soviet Union (1991).

Key terms are emboldened in the text, and definitions can be found in the glossary.

We've broken down the six stages of revision to ensure you are prepared every step of the way.

Zone in: How to get into the perfect 'zone' for revision.

Planning zone: Tips and advice on how to effectively plan revision.

Know zone: The facts you need to know, memory tips and exam-style practice for every section.

Don't panic zone: Last-minute revision tips.

Exam zone: What to expect on the exam paper.

Zone out: What happens after the exams.

ResultsPlus

These features help you to understand how to improve, with guidance on answering exam-style questions, plus tips on how to remember important concepts and how to avoid common pitfalls.

There are three different types of ResultsPlus features throughout this book:

ResultsPlus
Top Tip

The sources in this book contain evidence of how people thought about the Cold War at the time. You do not have to memorise these sources. However, if you can summarise their information in one sentence you may be able to use this in the exam.

Top Tips provide handy hints on how to apply what you have learned and how to remember key information and concepts.

ResultsPlus
Watch out!

Do not confuse Cominform with Comecon. Remember Com<u>econ</u> is <u>econ</u>omic, and Cominform is political.

Watch out! These warn you about common mistakes and misconceptions that students often make.

ResultsPlus
Build Better Answers

Exam question: Describe the key features of Cominform.

(6 marks)

You need to make developed statements that answer the question and describe why the features mentioned in the answer are important.

■ **A basic answer (level 1):**
One key feature of Cominform was that it allowed Stalin to control Eastern Europe.

● **A good answer (level 2):**
One key feature of Cominform was that it allowed Stalin to control Eastern Europe. At Cominform's first conference, leaders of Eastern European countries agreed with Stalin to boycott Marshall Aid.

△ **An excellent answer (full marks)** fully describe two or three key features.

Build Better Answers give you an opportunity to answer exam-style questions. They include tips for what a basic ■, good ● and excellent △ answer will contain.

The Know Zone Build Better Answers pages at the end of each section include an exam-style question with a student answer, examiner comments and an improved answer so that you can see how to improve your own writing.

ResultsPlus
Build Better Answers

Question (b)

Tip: Part (b) questions will usually ask you to describe the 'key features' of a major policy or event. This question is worth 6 marks, so you need to write a bit more than for Question (a). Make sure that when you describe you don't just tell the story: think about the information and organise it as if you were putting it under headings. Let's look at an example.

Decribe the key features of the détente. (6 marks)

Student answer	Examiner comment
In the 1960s there were a few times when it looked like Russia and America would start a nuclear war, such as the Cuban Missile Crisis of 1962. However, after this, Russian and American leaders decided that this was too dangerous and therefore they would have a different relationship, which was called détente. At first, détente went really well and the two countries made a treaty called SALT I. They also had a space mission together, which was very different to the space race to the moon. However, by 1980, détente had broken down and the two countries started the Second Cold War.	This answer shows a lot of knowledge about détente. However, this knowledge is not organised and therefore does not effectively answer the question. A better answer would contain two or three points with supporting evidence.

Let's rewrite the answer to make three points and provide accurate examples to develop them. So that you can spot them easily we will put the points in bold.

The first key feature of détente was co-operation between the superpowers to limit nuclear weapons. For example, they signed the Nuclear Non-Proliferation Treaty in 1968 and SALT I in 1972. Both of these treaties restricted the number of nuclear weapons that each country could control. **A second key feature of détente was co-operation in space.** The Outer Space Treaty of 1967 said that neither superpower could place nuclear weapons in space, and the Apollo-Soyuz mission marked a highpoint of the superpowers working together. **Finally, a third key feature of détente was co-operation in Europe.** At the Helsinki Conference of 1975, Russia and America agreed to work together to fight terrorism in Europe.	This answer makes three points and backs them up with examples. It would therefore receive full marks.

Section 1: Why did war break out? International rivalry 1900–14

At 11 a.m. on 11 November 1918, French and German representatives signed an armistice, bringing the 'Great War' to an end. The war had resulted in destruction and loss of life on a scale which few people had even dreamed was possible. On average, around 6000 lives were lost every day in the war.

What had driven the Great Powers to the point where they thought that the only solution to their rivalry was mass slaughter of each other's soldiers? The sad truth is that when war broke out in August 1914, no one imagined that it would last so long or result in so many deaths. In fact, it was generally thought that 'it would all be over by Christmas'. Men rushed to join the army to make sure they did not 'miss the fun'.

But this was not 'fun'. The war was widespread, lengthy and appallingly costly in human lives. International rivalry in the period 1900–14 was fierce; as a result there were too many scores to be settled for the conflict to be a short one.

In this section you will study:

- the alliance system and international rivalry between the Great Powers 1900–14
- the struggle for control in the Balkans 1900–14
- the growth of tension in Europe 1900–14.

The world in 1900

In 1900, the world was a very different place from the one you know today. If you could go back to 1900, you would see a time when there were no computers, no email, no mobile phones or texting (telephones had only recently been invented), no television, no aeroplanes and very few cars! People at the time would not have believed that a journey to the other side of the world could be completed in less than a day.

Europe in 1900.

The Great Powers

At this time, Europe contained the most powerful countries in the world and was dominated by six 'Great Powers': Britain, Germany, France, Austria-Hungary, Russia and Italy. Each of those powers wanted to control as much of the world's trade and become as wealthy as possible. This meant they were rivals.

During the nineteenth century, Britain had become rich through selling its manufactured goods around the world, particularly to its colonies. But in the early twentieth century, this British dominance came under threat as each of the Great Powers tried to outdo the others by producing more manufactured goods and selling them overseas. The country that made and sold the most goods would become richer and more powerful than the others. In particular, British dominance was being challenged in Europe by both Germany and France.

The United States

British dominance was also under threat from the 'new' power, the United States of America. By 1900 immigration into the USA meant the country had a higher population than Britain and France put together. It was only a matter of time before it produced and sold more manufactured goods and became richer and more powerful than Britain.

So there was rivalry between Britain, France and Germany – and a challenge from the USA. There was also bitter rivalry between Austria-Hungary and Russia in Eastern Europe.

ResultsPlus
Build Better Answers

Exam question: Describe one way in which British dominance in 1900 was being challenged by other powers. (2 marks)

You need to make a developed statement: a statement that both answers the question and provides some detailed support.

■ **A basic answer (level 1):** *British power was being challenged by Great Powers such as Germany.*

● **A good answer (level 2):** *British power was being challenged by the Great Powers, such as Germany. Each of those powers wanted to control as much of the world's trade and become as wealthy as possible. This meant they were rivals.*

The Ottoman Empire (based on modern-day Turkey) controlled large areas of land in Eastern Europe. But the Ottoman Empire was growing weaker, and both Austria-Hungary and Russia wanted to take land from the **Ottomans**.

So, with so many countries in competition, you can understand that there was a real possibility of disagreement and armed conflict in the future.

The Alliance system before 1900

Learning objectives

In this chapter you will learn about:

- how the alliance system developed up to 1914
- the role of Germany in creating tension in Europe.

The rise of Germany

By 1900, the Great Powers in Europe were beginning to divide themselves into two separate groups. A major cause of this had been the growth in power of Germany and its rivalry with other powers, particularly France.

Before 1871, Germany was a collection of small, independent states. On 18 January 1871, these states were brought together as a single country by its famous chancellor, Otto von Bismarck. As part of the unification of Germany, the king of Prussia, Wilhelm I, was crowned emperor (or *Kaiser* in German). Also in 1871, Germany defeated France in war. The Germans made France pay 200 million francs compensation and give the border territories of Alsace and Lorraine to Germany.

A French picture of the Kaiser. Wilhelm II had a withered left arm and was often shown from a flattering angle to disguise this. In German pictures he sometimes held gloves in his left hand to make his arm appear longer. Note that the French artist has not done this.

Isolating France

The Germans knew that France would look for revenge as soon as possible. To prevent this, Bismarck made agreements with other countries so that France would have no allies with which to fight against Germany in the future. In 1882 Germany signed an agreement with Austria-Hungary and Italy, known as the Triple Alliance. In 1887 they also signed an **alliance** with Russia.

Thus, by 1887 Germany had made alliances with three of the other major powers. The only possible ally for France if it wanted to attack Germany was Britain. But Britain had no interest in war in Europe. What it wanted was to maintain peace so that its huge empire was not threatened. It looked like Bismarck had successfully isolated France and kept Germany safe from attack.

Examination question

Describe one action taken by Kaiser Wilhelm II to increase German power between 1900 and 1914.

(2 marks)

Kaiser Wilhelm (William) II

One of the reasons Bismarck's plans came undone was the character of the new Kaiser, Wilhelm II (Wilhelm I died in 1888). Wilhelm II was an intelligent man, but also very moody and he lacked diplomatic skills. Bismarck had worked hard to keep France isolated, but Wilhelm II quarrelled with Bismarck and dismissed him from office. Then he failed to renew the agreement with Russia in 1890. So Russia turned to France, and in 1894 the two countries signed the Dual **Entente** (understanding). France had found an ally.

British fears

Britain was concerned about the growth in German industrial power and the new Kaiser's ambitions to build an empire like those of Britain and France. Wilhelm also planned to build huge numbers of new battleships and cruisers to make a 'great navy', and this worried the British especially. Britain had the world's strongest navy and so was safe from invasion from mainland Europe. It also used its navy to protect its empire. What would happen if Germany built a more powerful navy? French and British fears led to secret discussions between them.

The Entente Cordiale and the Triple Entente

The Entente Cordiale between Britain and France was agreed in 1904. The new British King, Edward VII, favoured a French alliance and the new French Foreign Minister, Declassé, wanted a British alliance to isolate Germany. Both countries felt threatened by the growth of the German empire, its rise as an economic power and the alliance with Austria-Hungary and Italy. The French did not seek to avenge themselves for the 1871 defeat, but they were keen to ensure a 'buffer' against further German aggression.

Meaning 'friendly understanding', the Cordiale was an agreement not to quarrel over colonies rather than an agreement to defend each other if attacked. The French did not want to be dragged into a war before they were ready – their armed forces were too weak.

The Triple Entente between Britain, France and Russia developed in stages. After the lapse of its alliance with Germany, Russia felt threatened by Germany's close ties with Austria, one of its rivals. Russia had begun secret talks with France in 1891, leading to the Dual Entente. This Franco-Russian Alliance was finalised in 1894 (**before** the Entente Cordiale).

Britain and Russia had been colonial rivals in Persia, Afghanistan and China, but Britain came to see Germany as more of a threat following Russia's defeat in the Russo-Japanese War (1905). In 1907, Britain and Russia signed the Anglo-Russian Entente. Britain, France and Russia then agreed the Triple Entente which, again, was **not** an agreement to defend each other if attacked.

A divided Europe

So the six Great Powers were divided into two separate groups.

- Germany, Austria-Hungary and Italy had joined in a formal alliance in which they agreed to help each other in time of war.
- To protect themselves from the growing power of Germany, the other Great Powers – Britain, France and Russia – had joined together. Their agreement was more of an 'understanding' not to quarrel rather than a formal military alliance.

ResultsPlus Top Tip

Remember that, in the examination question on page 8, you are being asked only to describe **one** action – and this is a 2-mark question. So you just need to identify the action and give a very brief description. This answer would be ideal:

Wilhelm II said he would increase German power by building a great navy. He began building battleships.

ResultsPlus Watch out!

Students often confuse the members of the Triple Alliance with the Triple Entente. Try this way to remember who is in which group. 'Entente' is a French word, so France must be in that one. The Germans were big rivals with France, so Germany must be in the Alliance, not the Entente. Four left! Austria-Hungary and Italy both have initials ('A' and 'I') in alliance, so they are in the Alliance. So the other two (Britain and Russia) must be in the Entente.

Activities

1 One of the skills a historian needs is to summarise information in a few words.
What one-line answers would you give to the following questions?
- Kaiser Wilhelm, it is 1907. Are you happy with the alliances you have?
- British foreign secretary, why are you worried about Germany?

2 Once you have prepared your answers, ask the person sitting next to you the same questions. If you get different answers, decide whose answer is better.

Great power rivalry: imperial rivalry

Learning objectives

In this chapter you will learn about:

- the importance of colonies to the Great Powers
- how the Kaiser's actions threatened Britain and France.

The race for colonies

One of the issues that led to tension between the Great Powers in the early years of the twentieth century concerned the ownership of land overseas – colonies. Today, almost all countries rule themselves, but in 1914 many people lived in colonies ruled by one of the Great Powers. These colonies were very important to the European nations as they provided cheap raw materials for industry and also a place where the Europeans could sell their home-produced goods. It has been estimated that from just one of its colonies (India), Britain took over £1000 million in tax and goods in the period 1750–1900. Some colonies were also important as military or trading bases. Egypt was an important British possession because its Suez Canal was a shortcut from the Mediterranean to the Red Sea. This meant that British ships did not have to sail around Africa to get to India and the Far East.

An Italian cartoon from the period leading up to the war, showing Kaiser Wilhelm II's greed for an Empire.

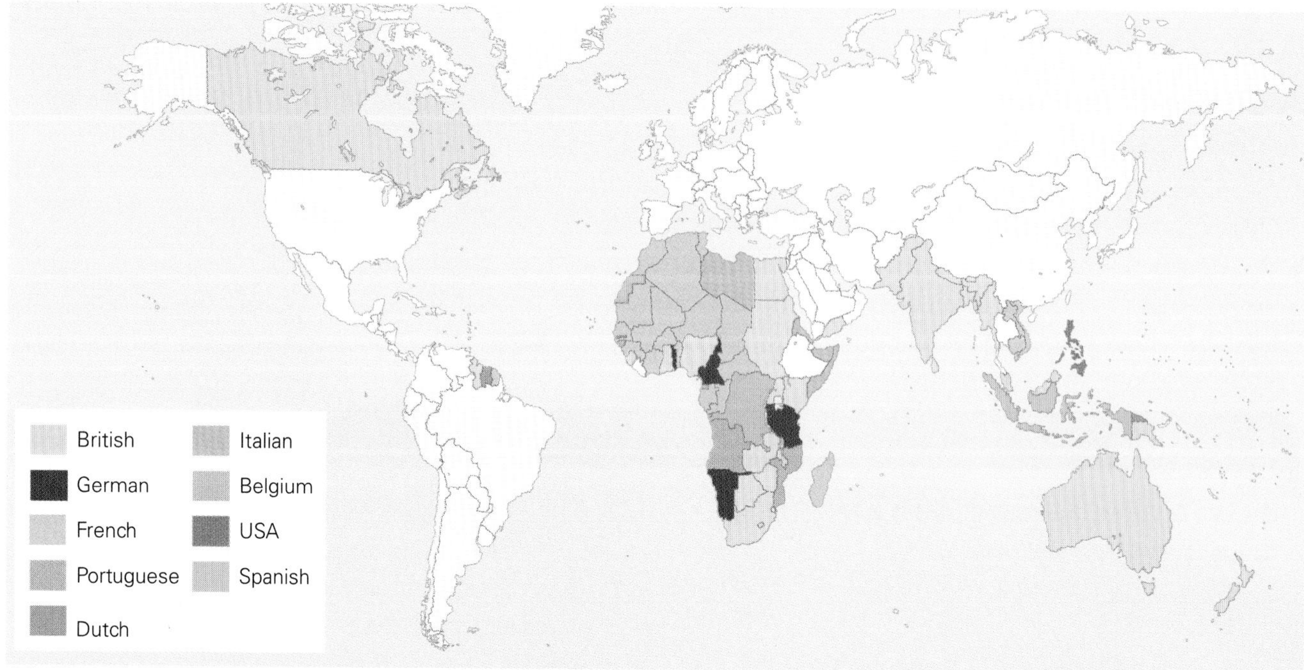

Overseas colonies in 1914.

German threat

Britain and France both had huge overseas empires and they were determined to keep them. This meant protecting their colonies from any country which threatened them.

Kaiser Wilhelm II wanted Germany to also have what he called 'its place in the sun'. He felt that Germany was hemmed in, encircled by the threat of France and Britian. Britain and France knew that any gains Germany made would be at their expense. So, as Germany became more threatening, Britain and France became friendlier to help each other resist German expansion.

Morocco, 1905

In 1904, Britain and France had signed the Entente Cordiale. Kaiser Wilhelm decided to test how strong that agreement was. He knew that France wanted to take control of Morocco, so in 1905 he visited the area and made a speech saying he supported the independence of Morocco. The French were furious but had to agree to hold a conference to discuss the matter at Algeciras in Spain. At that conference Britain and other countries stood by France. They said that although Morocco was independent, France had special rights in the country. Wilhelm had hoped to split France and Britain but all that he had achieved was that Britain and France moved closer together. Britain now agreed to send troops to help France if it was attacked by Germany.

ResultsPlus
Top Tip

Students who do well in this type of question usually do so by finding two or three key points (for example, what the Kaiser wanted, how the French reacted and what the outcome was) and then giving some detail to support each point. Students who do poorly just write all they know.

The Agadir Crisis, 1911

Six years later, there was another crisis in Morocco. In 1911 there was a rebellion against the ruler, the sultan. France sent in troops to put down the uprising and used the rebellion as the opportunity to take over Morocco. The French knew that several countries would complain that their trade would be harmed if the French took control, so they offered compensation. Kaiser Wilhelm was not satisfied with this and sent a gunboat, the *Panther*, to the Moroccan port of Agadir to threaten the French. But, once again, Britain stood by its friend.

The British had the world's most powerful navy and were concerned that Wilhelm was trying to set up a base in Morocco. So the British chancellor of the exchequer, David Lloyd George, made a strong speech threatening to go to war if Germany continued to bully France. The British fleet was put on a war footing to back up Lloyd George's aggressive words. Wilhelm realised that his actions could cause war. He backed down and accepted French control of Morocco. In return, Germany received 100,000 square miles of the French Congo (a French colony in Africa), but this land was mostly worthless swamp and jungle.

Once again, Britain and France had stood firm and Wilhelm had been forced to back down. As one German complained, the Agadir Crisis had 'amused the world and ended by making us look foolish'. Wilhelm was determined that the next contest would not be one in which he looked foolish. Tension between the Great Powers was growing.

Examination question

Describe the key features of the Moroccan Crisis of 1905. (6 marks)

Activities

1 The Great Powers obviously thought that having colonies was a good thing. You are an MP who has been asked to make a speech in parliament explaining why Britain should have colonies. What would you say?

2 **a** Make a list of the Kaiser's actions in Morocco in 1905 and 1911.
 b Now make a list of what he was trying to achieve.
 c Overall, what score out of 10 would you give him for his actions? Why?

Great power rivalry: military rivalry

Learning objectives

In this chapter you will learn about:

- the importance of the navy to Britain
- how Germany was threatening British naval supremacy.

Britannia rules the waves

Britain had defeated the French at the Battle of Trafalgar in 1805 and since that date had controlled the seas with the most powerful navy in the world. Britain's trade was widespread and her huge overseas empire produced great wealth for the country. As long as Britain had the world's strongest navy, it could make sure that none of the other Great Powers would try to seize parts of its empire. It could also use the navy to prevent an enemy from invading Britain. But what if another country wanted to challenge Britain's naval superiority?

In 1898, Kaiser Wilhelm announced that Germany was going to build 41 battleships and 61 cruisers. This was part of a plan to make sure that Germany could defend itself and protect its growing overseas trade. The Kaiser's ambitions caused alarm in Britain. Germany was in central Europe and needed a large army to protect its borders, so why did it need a large navy? It had only a small coastline, but Britain was an island and its power was based on its navy. As the British foreign secretary, Sir Edward Grey, said in 1909:

'There is no comparison between the importance of the German navy to Germany and the importance of our navy to us... it is not a matter of life and death to them as it is to us.'

Britain saw the German naval building programme as part of a deliberate policy to challenge British naval supremacy. We do not know whether this was what Wilhelm was doing; perhaps he was genuinely building a large navy to protect Germany's trade and small empire. Another possible reason for the Kaiser's actions was to frighten the British into reaching an agreement with Germany instead of France.

An 'arms race' develops

Whatever Wilhelm's intentions, Britain saw Germany's shipbuilding programme as a threat. Talks were held to try to limit the size of the British and German navies, but they broke down. Then, in 1906, the game changed. Britain launched the first of a new type of battleship, HMS *Dreadnought*. This ship was so powerful that all previous battleships were immediately out of date. Indeed, the impact of this new type of ship was so great that all battleships built after it were referred to as 'dreadnoughts'. What mattered now was not how many ships the navy had, but how many dreadnoughts it had. So if Germany could build more of these ships than Britain did, it would have a more powerful navy.

A British dreadnought. This battleship was faster, had more powerful guns and was harder to sink than any previous ship.

From 1906, an 'arms race' broke out between Britain and Germany as both countries tried to build the most dreadnoughts. Between 1906 and 1907, Britain built five dreadnoughts, and it was not until 1908 that Germany launched its first. Then, in 1908, Germany built four new ships and Britain just two! Britain considered building either two or four new ships in the years 1910–11, but the British public began demanding eight. There were even times in music halls when the audience burst into a chorus of 'We want eight and we won't wait.' So, eight ships were built between 1910 and 1911. Between 1906 and 1914, Britain built 29 dreadnoughts compared to Germany's 17.

The build-up of armies

In the same way that Britain believed that security came from having a strong navy, so the other Great Powers believed that military strength came from having an army powerful enough to prevent an attack from another country. In the years up to 1914, the Great Powers concentrated on building up their armed forces and ensuring their soldiers were well trained. All the Great Powers except Britain introduced **conscription** (compulsory military service). In France, soldiers had to serve for three years and in Russia for three and a half years. As the graph shows, by 1914 the armies of the Great Powers numbered more than 4 million men, with another 2 million reservists waiting to be called up.

The 'balance of power'

The Great Powers had become involved in an **arms race** to make sure that each of them had armed forces which could win a victory in war. But this did not mean that they intended to fight. Each country knew that it was important to make sure that its forces balanced those of any potential enemy, so that the enemy would be less likely to attack. In this sense, building up armed forces was actually a way of preventing war.

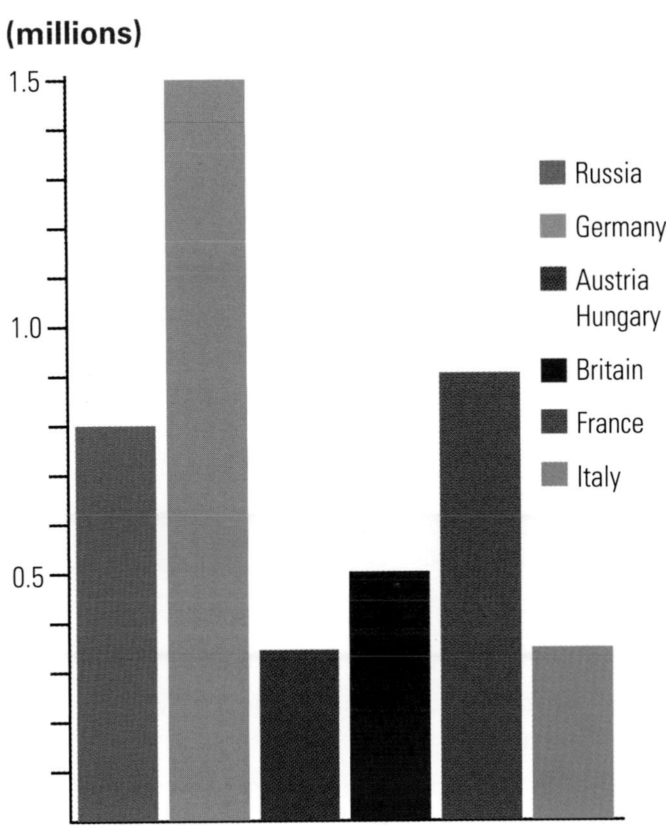

Size of the armies of the Great Powers in 1914.

Activities

1. You are preparing for a debate but don't know which side you will be speaking for! The debate is 'Did the Kaiser build a great navy just to threaten Britain?' As you don't know which side you will be speaking for, make some notes for each side of the argument. Which side would you prefer to speak for? Why?
2. 'We want eight and we won't wait' is a great slogan. Can you think of any other good slogans for the events described on these pages?
3. Consider the statement 'building up armed forces was actually a way of preventing war'. That sounds like nonsense. Explain how making your armed forces stronger could stop war.

Great power rivalry: economic rivalry

Learning objectives

In this chapter you will learn about:

- the economic background to the First World War
- the importance of industrialisation.

The First World War broke out in 1914 because of a series of events and disagreements in that year. But those events were just short-term reasons why war broke out when it did. The real causes of war were long-term and much more deep-seated. They had existed for some time and made war very likely. All that was needed was the short-term reasons to trigger the start of the war.

The battle for economic supremacy

At the beginning of the twentieth century, Britain had been the most powerful country in the world, with the largest empire and the richest trade. However, Germany had overtaken Britain by 1914. It produced more iron, more steel and more cars.

Germany was also showing a keen interest in gaining colonies, which would give it access to cheap raw materials and markets into which to sell its goods. Its interest in colonies had also brought it into conflict with France.

But while Britain was increasingly concerned about the expanding German navy, and France felt threatened by Germany over its colonies, what was really happening was that Germany was building a stronger economy than those of Britain and France and they were trying to stop this. So, to what extent was the First World War really just about money?

Activities

Let's do some statistics. Look at the graphs and answer the following questions.

1. Which country had the most valuable trade in 1913? Why do you think this was?
2. Which country had the second highest? Why might this be a problem to the country with the highest?
3. Why did Britain have a much higher 'overseas population' than other countries?
4. Why do you think figures for steel production are shown? Why does it matter how much steel is produced?
5. Why does it matter how large the population is? Does that mean that Russia must have been the strongest because it had the largest population?
6. What was the combined total for a) the Triple Alliance and b) the Triple Entente for:
   - annual trade
   - steel production?
7. In 1913 the USA had a home population of 91 million, annual trade of £1.8 million and steel production of 23.6 million tonnes. What does that tell you?
8. 'None of these figures matter. All that is important is the size of a country's armed forces.' Explain whether you agree with that statement.

The Great Powers in 1913

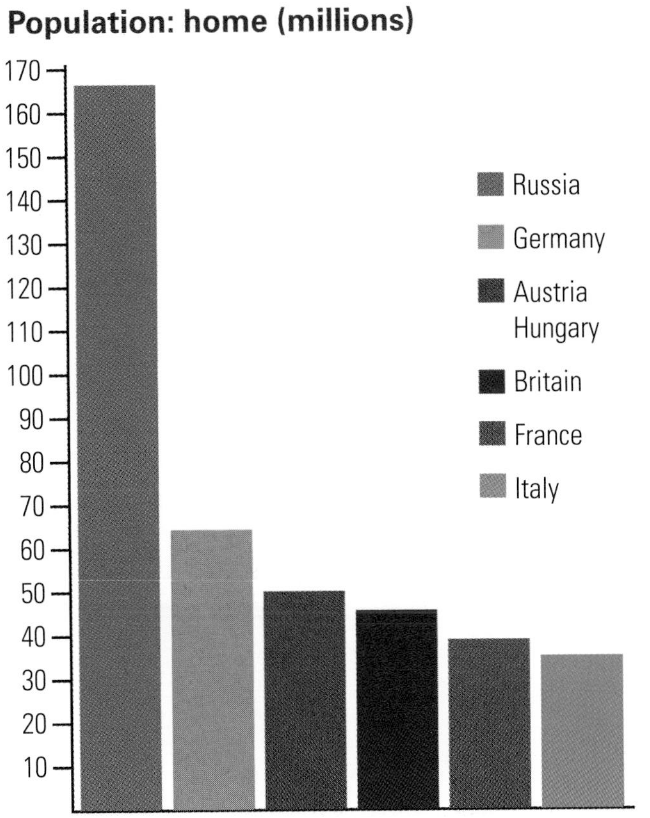

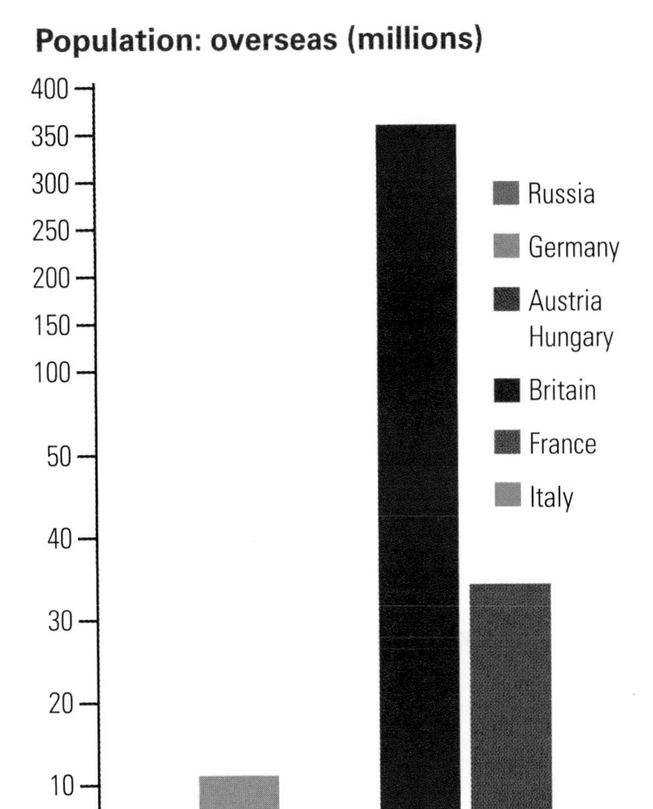

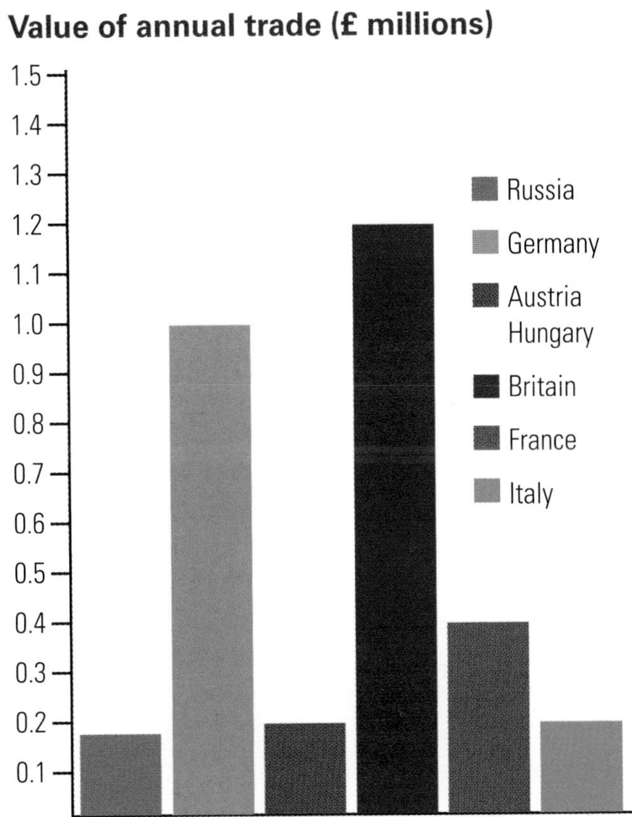

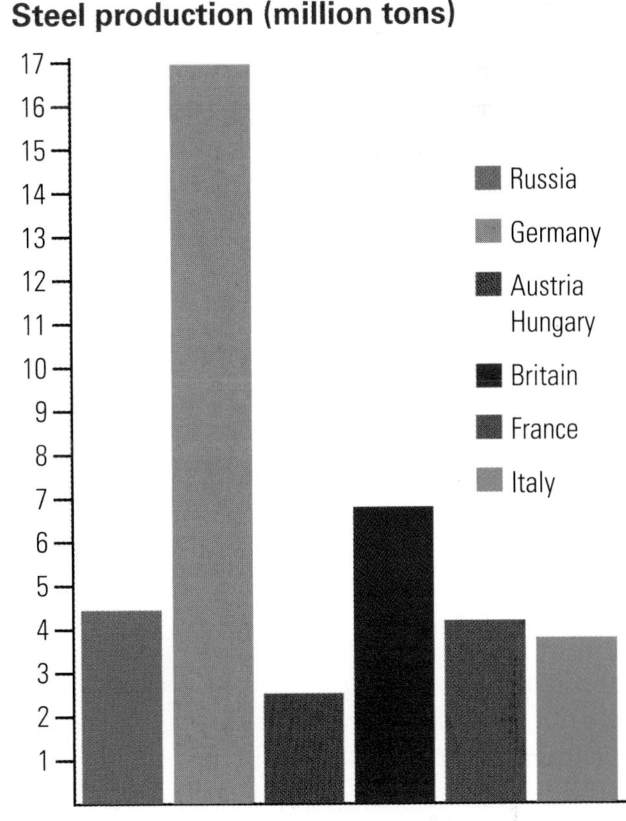

The Balkans: problem area

Learning objectives

In this chapter you will learn about:

- the importance of the decline of Ottoman power
- the importance of the Balkans to different countries.

The Kaiser's plans to expand Germany led to increased rivalry with Britain and France. Two of the other Great Powers, Russia and Austria, had their own dispute to deal with.

The Ottomans

Since the seventeenth century, much of south-east Europe (the Balkans) had been part of the Ottoman Empire. The Ottomans were the Muslim rulers of what is now called Turkey, with their capital in Constantinople (modern-day Istanbul). However, by the nineteenth century Ottoman military power was in decline. In 1832 Greece won its independence from the Ottoman Empire. This marked a gradual weakening of power as other countries within the empire, such as Serbia and Bulgaria, also achieved independence.

What made the Balkans such a controversial area was the fact that the Great Powers all had their own reasons for intervening. Britain, France and Italy had important trade in the eastern Mediterranean and wanted to ensure that this trade was not disrupted. For Austria-Hungary and Russia, however, the 'Balkan Question' was about much more than trade.

The Balkans in 1900. The areas inside the red line were part of the Ottoman Empire, but had their own rulers who were supposed to rule the land for the Ottomans.

Austria-Hungary

Austria-Hungary was a large and scattered empire in central Europe, with its capital in Vienna. It was ruled by the **Habsburg** family and so is often referred to as the 'Habsburg Empire'. The empire had 11 different nationalities in it. The Austrians were Germans and the Hungarians were Magyars, but the Habsburgs also ruled over millions of 'Slav' subjects, such as Czechs, Serbs, Bosnians and Croats. The major aim of the Habsburg emperor, Franz Joseph, was to stop the growth of **nationalism**. This was a belief that different nationalities should rule themselves and it threatened to break up the empire.

Ever since it had gained its independence from the Ottoman Empire in 1878, Serbia had been a problem for Austria-Hungary. There were several million Serbs in southern Austria and they were keen to unite with Serbia. Franz Joseph was very worried by this, and some of his ministers thought it might be better to conquer Serbia to stop the threat. The Czechs in the north and the Croats in the south-west also wanted independence. If the Serbs broke free to join Serbia, the demands of the Czechs and Croats would grow.

Russia

To complicate matters, Russia also had a strong interest in what happened in the Balkans. Russia's only southern port was Sebastopol in the Crimea. To reach the Mediterranean, Russian ships had to sail through a narrow strait called the Dardanelles. This area was controlled by Turkey and could easily be cut off. So Russia was determined to help establish pro-Russian governments in the Balkans, which would allow their ports to be used to transport Russian goods in the Mediterranean.

When Bulgarians rose up against the Ottoman Empire in 1876, Russia saw an opportunity to gain influence in the Balkans and sent troops to fight on the side of the rebels, helping to liberate Bulgaria in 1878. Although Russia's policy in the Balkans involved a 'drive to the Mediterranean', they were able to disguise this ambition by claiming much more noble aims. The Ottomans were Muslims, but many of the people in the region were Christians, and a lot of them belonged to the Russian Orthodox Church. So the Russians were able to portray themselves as protectors of the Christian religion against oppressive Muslim rulers.

The Russians were also Slavs, so were keen to promote Slav nationalism and thus help the Slav people in the region win their freedom from the Ottomans. Of course, if this freedom caused problems for the Habsburgs and threatened the break-up of Austria-Hungary, that would be even better.

So the Balkans was a region where there was enormous potential for the Great Powers to fall out.

- The Ottomans were trying to keep their empire in Europe.
- The Slav people were trying to set up independent countries.
- Austria-Hungary was trying to stop these Slav countries being set up.
- Russia was trying to encourage the Slavs to ensure it had a secure access to the Mediterranean.
- Britain and France wanted to keep Russia out of the Mediterranean to protect their own trade.

Tsar Nicholas II of Russia. He was keen to see his country's influence grow in the Balkans.

Did you know?

After the 1917 revolutions in Russia, Tsar Nicholas, his wife Alexandra and his family were shot by the communists. Their bodies were thrown down a mineshaft and not discovered until the fall of communism in 1991. The bodies were identified by taking DNA samples from Prince Philip of Britain, who is a cousin of Alexandra.

Activity

From what you have read here, explain whether you think the following is likely to happen in the next pages you read on the Balkans. Give reasons to support your answer – and no cheating by looking it up!

a Austria-Hungary and Britain will fall out.

b Serbia and Austria-Hungary will fall out.

c Turkey will take control of Austria-Hungary's eastern territories.

d Russia and Austria-Hungary will fall out.

The Balkans 1900–13: turning up the heat

Learning objectives

In this chapter you will learn about:

- the impact of the Bosnian Crisis
- how the Balkan Wars increased tension.

The weaknesses of the Ottoman Empire in 1900

By 1900, the Ottoman Empire was very weak. This was especially true in the Balkans – the part of the Empire in Europe. Various factors contributed to this:

- The Balkans was made up of many ethnic groups with their own languages and their own sense of nationality. Among these were Bosnians, Serbs and Croats. Added to this, the Ottoman Empire was Muslim and most of the people in the Balkan countries they had taken over were not.
- The Ottoman Empire was too big for the army to keep control everywhere. In the Balkans, different Balkan states wanted their independence. Austria-Hungary and Russia both wanted to increase their influence in the Balkans, and push the Ottoman Empire out of Europe.
- The Ottoman Empire was retreating:
  - it had already given some states their independence
  - some states were semi-independent states within the Ottoman Empire
  - the sultan (ruler) had been forced to let Austria-Hungary 'administer' Bosnia-Herzegovina in his name at a conference in 1878. He could not control it so the alternative was to allow it to be independent.
- The sultans of the Ottoman Empire had long been inefficient and corrupt. The sultan in 1900, Abdul Hamid II, spent most of his time hidden in his palace, drinking heavily and fearing a revolution.

Balkan nationalism

The various Balkan ethnic groups had a strong sense of their own national identities. But they were small and not powerful. Most were ruled by either the Ottoman Empire or Austria-Hungary. Their boundaries were redrawn to suit these rulers. So, for example, several million Serbs (estimates vary from 2 to 6 million) were living in the Austro-Hungarian Empire. Balkan nationalism was encouraged to grow by:

- the fact that Greece (1832), Serbia (1878) and Romania (1878) became independent and other states (e.g. Bulgaria) were given semi-independence within the Ottoman Empire
- the increasing weakness of the Ottoman Empire
- the encouragement of Russia – which would benefit from the Ottoman Empire and Austria-Hungary being weakened.

The Bosnian Crisis 1908

Austria-Hungary did not want to see more independent countries in the Balkans, nor did it want to see the expansion of Russian influence. So it supported the continuation of Ottoman control in the region. However, there were some problems with this policy. At a conference in 1878 it was agreed that Austria-Hungary should 'administer' Bosnia-Herzegovina. This area had been controlled by the Ottomans, but they no longer had the military power to keep control. Austria-Hungary did not want to see the Serbian people in Bosnia-Herzegovina join with Serbia, so it was happy to provide 'peaceful protection' for the country.

However, in 1908, there was a revolution in Turkey. An army group called 'the Young Turks' replaced Sultan Abdul Hamid with his brother, Mohammed V. The Young Turks actually ran the country, however, not the new sultan. They began to introduce reforms to turn the Ottoman Empire into a modern state. It seemed as if they might make the Ottoman Empire stronger. This caused alarm in Austria-Hungary and set off a crisis in the Balkans.

- Austria-Hungary annexed Bosnia-Herzegovina in September 1908 to prevent any Ottoman attempts to recover the territory the Austro-Hungarians had been administering for them since 1878. From now on it would be officially part of the Habsburg Empire.
- The Ottomans considered that their territory had been seized.
- Serbia, which had a very strong nationalist movement, objected to the annexation as it hoped to bring the Bosnian Serbs into Serbia. It could not fight Austria-Hungary alone, so asked its Russian allies to help stop the annexation.
- Russia objected to Austria-Hungary's action and the threatened increase in Habsburg power, and considered war.
- Germany made it clear to Russia that it would help Austria-Hungary if Russia tried to help Serbia take back Bosnia-Herzegovina.

Finally, Austria-Hungary agreed to pay the Turks compensation, which was accepted.

Russia backed down, as the Germans stood by the Triple Alliance, so Serbia had to back down as well. Without Russian support it had to accept the Austrian takeover.

Austria-Hungary's success came at a price. Both Serbia and Russia were determined to make sure they won the next dispute. Another consequence was the formation of a Serbian terrorist organisation, called the 'Black Hand', to fight Austria-Hungary in the Balkans. This organisation would turn out to play a significant role in the outbreak of war in 1914.

The Bosnian Crisis was over, but it had several effects:

- Austria-Hungary began to see the Serbs as a real threat.
- It was the first real test of the Triple Alliance – and Germany had come to the aid of Austria-Hungary; it showed the alliance system could work.
- The formation of the Black Hand was to prove most significant.

Sultan Abdul Hamid II is helpless as parts of the Ottoman Empire are pulled from beneath his feet by Bulgaria and Austria.

The Balkan Wars, 1912–13

The Balkans after the wars of 1912–13.

Despite the reforms carried out by the Young Turks, the Ottoman Empire continued to break up. In 1911 the Young Turks fell from power in Turkey. The Balkan states saw this as an opportunity to attack the Ottomans. Serbia, Greece, Bulgaria and Montenegro came together in an organisation known as the Balkan League, and in 1912, declared war.

In just three weeks the Balkan League pushed the Ottomans back as far as Adrianople – almost out of Europe altogether. The dramatic decline of the Ottomans worried Austria-Hungary, who feared nationalism would rise once more and unsettle its people. It managed to persuade the Great Powers to hold a conference in London to draw up a peace treaty, which ended the First Balkan War.

But, within a month, fighting started again. In the first war the Balkan countries were united in opposition to the Ottomans. But now they argued about what they had won in that war. Bulgaria attacked its former allies because it was unhappy with its gains in the first war. Romania also joined in to try to win land from Bulgaria. Even the Ottomans joined in and took back some of the land which had been lost in the first war!

Results of the Balkan Wars

The wars had been fought over possession of land in south-east Europe, but their importance was much more widespread.

- The Ottoman Empire was now confirmed as ending at Adrianople. In effect, its European possessions were gone.
- Greece, Romania and Serbia received new territories won from Bulgaria.
- Serbia emerged from these wars as the most powerful Balkan country but it was also the most dissatisfied. During the wars it had captured part of the Adriatic coastline and ceased to be a landlocked country. But at Austria-Hungary's insistence, this territory was taken from Serbia. Austria-Hungary did not want Serbia to grow in power and be an even greater threat. Some Serbs became even more convinced that one day they would have to go to war with the mighty Habsburgs.

Activity

How satisfied do you think the following countries were by what had happened in the Balkans in the period 1908–13? Explain your answer.

a Austria-Hungary

b Serbia

c Russia

d The Ottoman Empire

ResultsPlus
Build Better Answers

Exam question: Describe the key features of the Bosnian Crisis in 1908. (6 marks)

You need to identify important points, not simply write all you know. Here, for example, you could choose to describe a cause of the crisis, an event within it and an effect of it.

■ **A basic answer (level 1)** gives simple statements that are accurate, but contain no supporting detail.

● **A good answer (level 2)** gives a statement that is accurate and is developed with specific information.

▲ **An excellent answer (full marks)** gives two or three statements. Each statement picks a relevant key feature and is backed up with specific information.

For this question these would be good features to develop:

- Austrian annexation of Bosnia and rivalry with Russia
- Turkish recovery
- German support for Austria–Hungary
- Serbian determination to succeed, backed by Russia.

Sarajevo

Learning objectives

In this chapter you will learn about:

- the events of the Sarajevo assassination
- the role of chance in history.

By 1914, the rivalry between the Great Powers was becoming so strong that some politicians began to speak openly of their fears that a major war would soon break out. It seemed that all the rivalries and mistrust needed to start a war existed; it was just a reason to begin fighting that was missing. That reason was provided on a sunny summer's morning in Sarajevo, the capital of Bosnia-Herzegovina, although people didn't realise it immediately.

Unpopular marriage

Archduke Franz Ferdinand was heir to the throne of Austria. In 1890 he had married Countess Sophie Chotek. Franz Ferdinand's father, Emperor Franz Joseph, had forbidden the marriage because Sophie was not of royal blood. Kaiser Wilhelm II, Tsar Nicholas II of Russia and even Pope Leo XIII wrote to Franz Joseph asking him to allow the marriage. Eventually he relented, but he did not attend the ceremony nor did government officials or most of Franz Ferdinand's family. Sophie was made Princess of Hohenberg, but the couple had to agree that their children would not inherit the throne and they would limit their public appearances, as it was not considered 'appropriate' for the heir to the throne to be seen with non-royalty.

Archduke Franz Ferdinand and Princess Sophie arrive in Sarajevo on 28 June 1914.

Reviewing the troops

Ferdinand was head of the army, so he was able to attend military reviews with his wife. On 28 June 1914, he and Sophie boarded a train to Sarajevo to inspect the local troops. Early in the morning of a warm, sunny day they inspected a military camp near the railway station. Then they climbed aboard an open-top limousine waiting to take them to their next appointment. Crowds cheered the royal couple as their motorcade made its way through the streets. Franz Ferdinand wore full military uniform including a hat decorated with ostrich feathers. Sophie wore a white dress with a large white hat. They smiled and waved to the crowd.

Conspirators

But not all the crowd was there to cheer the couple. Among the well-wishers were six young Bosnian Serbs who had been given guns and bombs to kill Franz Ferdinand. They were stationed along the route and waited nervously to carry out their assassination.

As the procession continued, it passed two of the conspirators. However, they were too terrified to act. One later claimed that a policeman had approached him just as he was to throw the bomb; the other said that he felt sorry for Sophie. A third conspirator, Nedeljko Cabrinovic, did act. As the car passed, he knocked the cap off a hand grenade and threw it at the Archduke. The grenade bounced off the car and blew up the car behind, killing two officers and injuring about 20 people. Cabrinovic swallowed poison but it failed to work and he was arrested. Franz Ferdinand's car sped to the town hall. On the way it passed three more conspirators. Two had lost their nerve and the other, Gavrilo Princip, could not shoot as the car was going too fast.

An artist's impression of the assassination of the Archduke Franz Ferdinand, painted in 1914.

Second chance

At the town hall, Franz Ferdinand told officials that he wanted to visit the injured bomb victims in hospital. To prevent further attacks, the Archduke would not take the direct route via Franz Joseph Street. Unfortunately, the driver was confused by his instructions and took a wrong turn. That was no real problem – all he had to do was reverse. So he stopped and began to turn the car round. The car reversed right in front of Gavrilo Princip, who had stayed in town after the failed bomb attack. Now was his chance. He stepped forward and fired two shots. There followed a moment's silence before Sophie slumped forward. She had been hit in the abdomen. Franz Ferdinand cried out 'Sophie, Sophie! Don't die. Keep alive for our children!' but she died a few minutes later. Princip's other bullet had pierced the Archduke's jugular vein and he too was dead within minutes.

Did you know?

28 June was the royal couple's wedding anniversary. It was also Serbia's 'National Day', a public holiday to celebrate the day in 1839 when a Serbian hero had assassinated the Ottoman sultans.

Sarajevo: the consequences

Learning objectives

In this chapter you will learn about:

- the impact of the Sarajevo assassination
- how Austria-Hungary intended to take revenge on Serbia.

Despite the horror of the assassination, the days following it were quiet. In 1914 there was no 24-hour news coverage, nor were there radio or television reporters to keep the public informed. Foreign newspapers reported the assassination but few people could have realised that within six weeks Europe would be at war.

Austria-Hungary takes action

In Sarajevo, five of the conspirators were arrested (the sixth had escaped). The organiser of the conspiracy, Danilo Ilic, was also arrested. Although it is not clear exactly who masterminded the assassination, Ilic was in contact with the chief of Serbian military intelligence, Colonel Apis. The conspirators were members of the Black Hand, which also received help from Serbia. So it seems likely that Serbia was involved in the assassination, although at their trial the conspirators claimed to be acting on their own.

The conspirators were found guilty at a trial in October 1914 (by which time Europe was at war). At the trial, the court stated that '*it is proved by the evidence that military circles in the Kingdom of Serbia in charge of the espionage service, collaborated in the outrage*'.

Although Ilic was hanged, both Cabrinovic and Princip were under 20 years old at the time of the assassination and could not receive the death penalty. They received the maximum prison sentence of 20 years. Both died in prison of tuberculosis; neither lived to see the end of the war that their actions had triggered.

Germany offers support

Although it appeared nothing was happening in the days immediately after the assassination, behind the scenes important steps were being taken. The Habsburgs decided that action had to be taken against Serbia. As Russia was likely to give support to Serbia, it was important that Austria-Hungary made sure that its allies would stand by it. On 5 July, Kaiser Wilhelm was informed that Austria-Hungary was about to take action against Serbia. He promised that Germany would stand by its ally – even if that meant war with Russia.

> The Kaiser has authorised me to inform our majesty that we may rely upon Germany's full support. This action must not be delayed. Russia is in no way prepared for war and may think twice before it declares war. If we really feel it necessary to go to war with Serbia, the Kaiser believes we should take advantage of present circumstances.

Part of the report of the Austrian ambassador in July 1914.

The ultimatum

On 23 July, the Habsburg government sent an **ultimatum** to Serbia.

The Royal Serbian Government must agree:

- to stop every publication which shall incite hatred of Austria-Hungary
- to shut down all organisations in Serbia which occupy themselves with **propaganda** against Austria-Hungary
- to remove from educational instruction in Serbia everything that serves or may serve to nourish the propaganda against Austria-Hungary
- to remove from the military and administrative service all officers and officials who have been guilty of carrying on the propaganda against Austria-Hungary, whose names the government of Austria-Hungary will provide
- to carry out a judicial inquiry against every participant in the conspiracy of the 28th June (the Habsburg government will be part of the inquiry team)
- to prevent the participation of Serbian authorities in the smuggling of weapons and explosives across the frontier into Austria-Hungary.

The Imperial and Royal Government awaits the reply of the Royal Government by Saturday, the 25th at 6 p.m., at the latest.

Part of the ultimatum sent by the Habsburg government to Serbia on 23 July 1914.

Appendix:

The crime investigation undertaken at court in Sarajevo against Gavrilo Princip and his comrades on account of the assassination committed on the 28th June this year, along with the guilt of accomplices, has until now led to the following conclusions.

1. The plan of murdering Archduke Franz Ferdinand during his stay in Sarajevo was planned in the capital of Serbia, Belgrade.
2. The six bombs and four Browning pistols along with ammunition – used as tools by the criminals – were given to the conspirators by Serbian officials.
3. The bombs were hand grenades originating from the weapons depot of the Serbian army.
4. To guarantee the success of the assassination, Serbian army members instructed the conspirators in the use of the grenades and gave lessons on shooting Browning pistols.
5. To make possible the conspirators' passage across the Bosnia-Herzegovina border and the smuggling of their weapons, an entire secretive transportation system was organised by Serbian army and customs officials.

The appendix to the ultimatum. It sets out the results of an inquiry held by the Habsburg government.

Activities

When students revise, they sometimes like to summarise large pieces of information into much smaller documents. Read the ultimatum and the appendix sent by Austria-Hungary to Serbia and summarise what it is saying in just a few sentences. Which of the points made do you think the Serbians would have found hardest to agree to? Explain why you made this choice.

The lights are going out all over Europe

Learning objectives

In this chapter you will learn about:

- why war broke out in August 1914
- how the alliances and ententes contributed to the outbreak of war.

The ultimatum which Austria-Hungary sent to Serbia caused dismay in Belgrade.

> The Serbian government has been pained and surprised at the statements, according to which members of the Kingdom of Serbia are supposed to have participated in the preparations of the crime. Serbia cannot be held responsible for the actions of private individuals, such as articles in the press and the peaceable work of societies. It is, however, prepared to hand over for trial any Serbian subject whose part in the crime of Sarajevo can be proved.

The Serbian reply to the ultimatum sent by Austria-Hungary. It was sent on 25 July, just before the deadline for a reply set by Austria-Hungary ran out.

The response was not unreasonable and the Serbian government agreed to co-operate as much as it could. What it absolutely refused to do, however, was allow representatives of the government of Austria-Hungary to enter Serbia to take part in an inquiry.

The road to war

As tension increased, the British foreign secretary, Sir Edward Grey, tried to organise a conference of the Great Powers, but both Austria-Hungary and Germany rejected his suggestion. Austria-Hungary had expected its ultimatum to Serbia to be unacceptable, and after it received the Serbian response, it declared war on 28 July.

The Russians had been expecting this news, and on 30 July Tsar Nicholas agreed to prepare his forces for war.

Germany had promised to support Austria and so told Russia that it must stand its troops down and not help Serbia. When it did not do so, on 1 August Germany declared war on Russia.

Germany had been preparing for war for several years and had drawn up its plan to fight as early as 1905. This 'Schlieffen Plan' was based on the following beliefs:

- When war came, Germany would have to fight Russia and France.
- At the outbreak of war, Austria-Hungary would invade Russia and so Germany need concern itself only with France.

- A full-scale attack on France could result in a quick victory. Then the Germans could help the Austrians fight the huge Russian army (which would take some months to get ready for war).
- Britain may well not enter the war to defend France. If it did, the defeats of both France and Russia would make it reluctant to fight on its own.

So when France **mobilised** its forces for war on 1 August, in anticipation of an attack following German mobilisation, Germany responded by invading France. The Schlieffen Plan involved an attack on France through Belgium. Until this attack on Belgium there was a chance that Britain might stay out of the war. However, Britain now announced that it intended to honour its agreement of 1839 to guarantee Belgium's independence. The agreement had been made in another century and Germany complained that Britain was going to war over a 'scrap of paper'. Whatever the reason, Britain declared war on Germany on 4 August.

Europe was now at war. Grey had told the House of Commons the day before: 'We are going to suffer, I am afraid, terribly in this war, whether we are in it or whether we stand aside.' He was right.

A cheering crowd in Berlin on 3 August 1914, the day Germany declared war on France.

ResultsPlus
Build Better Answers

Exam question: Explain why the Sarajevo assassination led to war in August 1914. (12 marks)

You need to make relevant points, supported by specific examples, with a clear focus on how each factor led to the situation described.

In each level, the number of statements you make will affect your mark. For example, in level 2, a single developed argument is unlikely to get more than 5 marks, whereas three developed arguments will achieve 8 or 9 marks.

■ **A basic answer (level 1)** is correct, but would not have details to support it (for example, *One reason is because Austria blamed Serbia)*.

● **A good answer (level 2)** provides the details as well (for example, *One reason is because Austria blamed Serbia. The conspirators were members of the Black Hand which was helped by Serbia. So they went to war to put Serbia in its place. The other powers then joined in)*.

▲ **A better answer (level 3)** explains how the reasons are inter-linked, or prioritises the reasons (for example, *Austria-Hungary disliked the way that Serbia was becoming more important and thought that the Serbs were trying to break up the Habsburg Empire. So they went to war to put Serbia in its place)*.

▲ **An excellent answer (full marks)** links and prioritises the causes (for example, *The other powers then joined in. But, of course, none of this would have happened if the Great Powers were not so distrustful of each other. That was the main cause because…)*.

Activity

It seems very strange that people should cheer when war has just been declared. How do you explain the behaviour of the crowd in the photograph taken in Berlin on 3 August 1914?

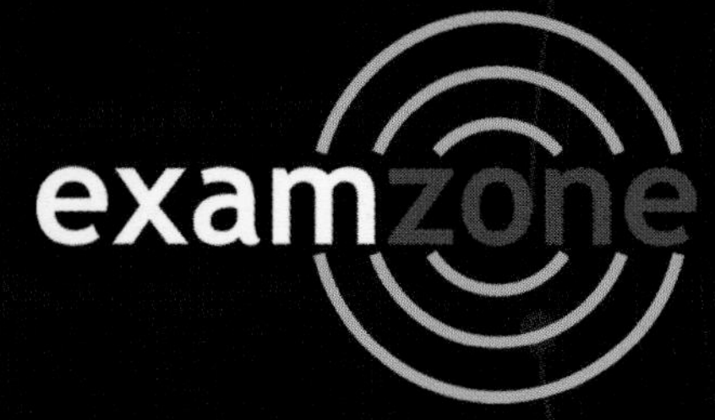

Know Zone Unit 1 - section 1

In the Unit 1 exam, you will be required to answer questions from three sections. In each of those sections you will have to answer three questions: Part (a), Part (b) – where you have to do one of the two questions set – and Part (c).

You have about 25 minutes to answer the three questions on each section. Use the number of marks available for each question to help you judge how long to spend on it and how much to write.

Here we are going to look at questions for Parts (a) and (b).

ResultsPlus
Build Better Answers

Question (a)

Tip: Part (a) questions will ask you to identify an action, decision, cause, way or factor and then give some supporting detail to get the second mark.
Let's look at an example.

Describe one way in which Germany threatened France's control of Morocco. (2 marks)

Student answer	**Examiner comment**
Germany threatened France's attempt to take control of Morocco by saying Morocco should stay independent.	The answer is certainly brief and it does give a way, but we need to do a little more to get the second mark. We need to provide a bit more support for our statement.

Let's rewrite the answer with supporting detail.

Germany threatened France's control of Morocco by saying Morocco should stay independent. This happened in 1905 when the Kaiser visited Morocco and made a speech.	A way identified and supported with knowledge. That's all you have to do for 2 marks.

Question (b)

Tip: Part (b) questions will usually ask you to describe the 'key features' of a major policy or an event. This question is worth 6 marks, so you need to write more than for Question (a). Make sure that when you describe you don't just tell the story: think about the information and organise it as if you were putting it under headings. Let's look at an example.

Describe the key features of the Balkan Wars in 1912–13. (6 marks)

Student answer	Examiner comment
In the Balkan Wars, Bulgaria attacked its former allies because it was unhappy with its gains in the first war. Romania, which had not entered the first war, also joined in to try to win land from Bulgaria. Then the Ottomans joined in and repossessed some of the land which had been lost in the first war.	This tells us some of the facts in the war, although only about the second one. But it doesn't really give the 'features', so would only be rewarded with less than half marks for providing simple statements. There are no 'pegs to hang the facts on', which would help you give a developed description of key features.

Let's rewrite the answer with features added. So that you can spot them easily we will put them in bold.

One of the features of the Balkan Wars was that **the individual countries in the region wanted to throw off Ottoman rule and gain land.** So they joined together and defeated the Ottomans. Turkey was driven almost completely out of Europe. **Another feature was that the Balkan countries did not get on.** You could see this when Bulgaria attacked its former allies because it was unhappy with its gains in the first war.	As you can see, this answer has two developed descriptions of key features and would receive 5 marks. For full marks you would need to provide more detail to support the answer.

Section 2: The peace settlement 1918–28

In 1918 the First World War finally came to an end when German officials asked the Allies (Britain, France, Italy and the USA) to agree to an armistice.

Then began the difficult task of drawing up the peace treaties. The victorious Allies met in the Palace of Versailles in Paris, where it soon became clear that they had different ideas of what should be in the treaties. Some countries, such as France, wanted to punish the defeated nations and weaken them so that they could never start another war. Others, such as the United States, wanted to make sure that the Paris conference created a League of Nations, which would act as a forum for discussion and prevent future warfare by settling disputes between nations in a peaceful manner.

The League of Nations was created at Versailles, but the treaties were so tough on Germany, in particular, that some historians believe that the causes of the Second World War can be traced back to the conference. The Germans hated the Treaty of Versailles as it took land from them, limited the size of their armed forces and made them pay huge sums in compensation. As soon as they had the chance, they would look to reverse the terms of the treaty.

That chance did not come in the 1920s, which was a time when international relations improved dramatically as countries looked to avoid a repeat of the horrors of the war. Even so, when there were disagreements, the League of Nations found it hard to act effectively.

In this section you will study:

- the Paris Peace Conference and the aims of the 'Big Three' (Britain, France and the USA)
- the peace treaties and their impact on the defeated powers
- the creation and peacekeeping role of the League of Nations in the 1920s and the work of its agencies.

The armistice

Learning objectives

In this chapter you will learn about:

- why Germany wanted an armistice
- the terms of the armistice.

Why did Germany want an armistice?

Much of the fighting in the First World War took place along France's eastern border with Belgium, in an area known as the Western Front. By the end of October 1918, the Allies (Britain, France, the USA and Italy) were close to victory. Germany's allies were leaving the war – Bulgaria signed an **armistice** on 30 September, Turkey on 30 October and Austria-Hungary on 3 November. The main German fleet mutinied on 29 October, and this spread to become a revolution in some German cities. Many people were starving because the Allies had **blockaded** Germany's ports to stop supplies.

So on 8 November, a German delegation met the Allied supreme commander, Marshall Foch, near Compiègne in France. The Allies set out tough terms for the German surrender. Finally, at 5 a.m. on 11 November, agreement was reached.

The terms

Germany had to:

- withdraw all its troops from occupied countries in the west and give up any land it had won in the war in the east against Russia
- withdraw its troops 30 miles east (further inside Germany) from the banks of the Rhine, with the Allies' troops on the west bank, ready to cross if the armistice broke down
- surrender huge numbers of artillery, machine guns, aircraft, locomotives and railway wagons – and its entire submarine fleet
- allow its navy to be moved to Allied ports and placed under Allied control.

Ending the fighting

The Germans had asked for fighting to stop on 8 November. Foch refused until the armistice was signed. On 11 November it was agreed the war would end at 11 a.m. – which would mean the fighting ended on the eleventh hour of the eleventh day of the eleventh month. This was nicely symbolic, but some historians have estimated that up to 10,000 troops were killed, missing or wounded in the six hours between the armistice being agreed and the war ending.

Did you know?

The last soldier killed was a German officer, Lieutenant Tomas. Some minutes after 11 a.m. he walked towards some American soldiers to tell them his men would leave the houses they were sheltering in. The Americans hadn't heard the war had ended and shot him.

Did you know?

In 1914 Russia went to war on the side of the Allies. However, in 1917 the Bolshevik Party (later called the Communist Party) seized power. The Bolsheviks had to fight a civil war in Russia and did not want to fight the Germans. So they dropped out of the war in February 1918.

The aims of the 'Big Three'

Learning objectives

In this chapter you will learn about:

- the aims of the 'Big Three'
- how these aims affected the terms of the treaties.

Making peace

With the war over, the Allies met at the Palace of Versailles in France to agree the terms of the formal treaties that would end the war. The Allies made separate treaties with each defeated country, agreed and signed at different times.

The Treaty of Versailles, between the Allies and Germany, was signed in June 1919. It was the most controversial of the peace treaties. One of the problems with this treaty was that the Allies came with widely different views about what should happen to Germany.

The views that mattered most in discussion were those of the most powerful victors – Britain, France and the USA, known collectively as the **'Big Three'**. (Italy, while also a victor, was allowed to join a 'Council of Four', consisting of the Big Three plus Italy. Russia was not invited.) Germany was not invited to the talks – as the defeated nation it had no say in what the terms would be. Later, the Germans were to argue that as they had no say in the terms of the treaty, they were not bound to accept it.

The Big Three frequently disagreed, often strongly. They all had to make compromises to come to any agreement at all.

The Fourteen Points

In January 1918, President Wilson of the USA had proposed Fourteen Points, which he said would be the key to a fair peace. His ideas included:

- a ban on secret treaties and a reduction in arms
- countries should not claim colonies without consulting other countries and the local inhabitants
- **self-determination** (the right of nations to rule themselves) for countries which were once part of the Ottoman or Habsburg Empires. He also said an independent Poland should be created.

What did the 'Big Three' want?

Lloyd George (Britain), Clemenceau (France) and Wilson (USA), discussed three key issues:

- how Germany and its allies should be punished
- how France should be protected against future invasion
- how international relations could be improved – including self-determination.

Unfortunately, each winner had very different aims. This caused tensions across these issues.

A cartoon published in January 1919. The USA, England, France and Italy are making 'peace soup'. President Wilson is adding the ingredient 'sweet oil of brotherhood', but the other countries are just concerned with themselves, so they add 'national sentiment'.

- Lloyd George wanted to punish Germany and had just won a general election in Britain in which he had promised to 'make Germany pay'. He agreed with Clemenceau that Germany was a dangerous neighbour for France and should be weakened. However, he also saw Wilson's point that punishing Germany too hard could lead to another war. What he did not like was Wilson's belief that the setting up of a League of Nations should be the main concern of the conference.
- Clemenceau wanted to take revenge against Germany and to introduce **reparations** – payments to help repair all the damage. France had suffered terribly during the war as much of the fighting had been in France. Huge amounts of farmland had been destroyed and about 2 million French soldiers killed or wounded. Germany had twice the population of France and was more advanced industrially, making it a worrying neighbour. Germany had attacked France in 1870 as well as in 1914, so France wanted to make sure this did not happen again. France had suffered the most during the war and had most to lose if Germany went to war again. Clemenceau wanted the treaty to cripple Germany as a military power and to create a 'buffer zone' between France and Germany as added protection.
- Wilson wanted to make sure the USA did not ever have to 'rescue' Europe from war again. He believed Germany should be punished, but wanted the treaty to focus on improving international relations and preventing another war. Peace could be achieved by making the treaty fair, not vengeful. His major aim was to establish a League of Nations to work for world peace and for all nations to agree to cut down their weapons. He was a strong supporter of self-determination.

The world needed reconciliation and renewed economic ties - renewed integration. President Wilson favoured reconciliation. But, among the Allies, self-righteousness and revenge prevailed – driven by a strong fear of German aggression.

How Germany and its allies should be punished

- Wilson's main aim was to agree a fair peace and get the world economy working again. He wanted:
  1. not to punish Germany and its allies too harshly, as it would neither create world harmony nor help the world economy
  2. to set up a League of Nations to guarantee peace in the future.
- Clemenceau's main aims were to weaken Germany and to take revenge for the war. He wanted:
  1. to take compensation from Germany to rebuild and to support the French injured, widowed or orphaned by the war
  2. to take the Rhineland from Germany to weaken Germany industrially, and to act as a 'buffer zone' between France and Germany to make it harder for Germany to invade France again – France had been invaded by Germany twice in 44 years
  3. to break Germany up into small states
  4. to make sure Germany was stopped from building up a strong army.
- Lloyd George wanted:
  1. to take compensation from Germany – to make Germany 'pay for the war'
  2. to take Germany's colonies
  3. to make sure Germany was stopped from building up a strong navy.

How France should be protected against future invasion

- Wilson's view was that, if a sensible peace was agreed and a strong international organisation put in place to referee international disputes, then France would be safe. He felt there was no real need for other safeguards.
- Clemenceau's view was based on distrust of Germany. He felt that no international organisation could make any country behave in a certain way. The only way to keep France safe was to make Germany too weak to attack again.
- Lloyd George's view was that an international organisation might work, but it might not. He thought Germany was a dangerous neighbour, so France did need a 'buffer zone'.

How international relations could be improved

Setting up an international organisation for world peace was Wilson's main focus at the conference. He could exert a lot of pressure at the conference because the USA was providing military aid and, more importantly, food and other supplies to the Allies. He tried to avoid arguments, but he threatened to leave the conference over France's proposal to break Germany up into smaller states. He wanted to co-operate and compromise so he could create his dream: the League of Nations.

Clemenceau and Lloyd George had important differences with Wilson:

- They did not have as much faith as Wilson in an international organisation for peace – they did not think many countries, including their own, would want an international organisation telling them what to do.
- They had problems with the idea of self-determination. Firstly, if it was followed all over the world, they would lose their colonies (the USA had none to lose). Secondly, they felt that lots of small nations would be easy targets for larger nations and so make war more likely (as had happened in the Balkans before 1914).

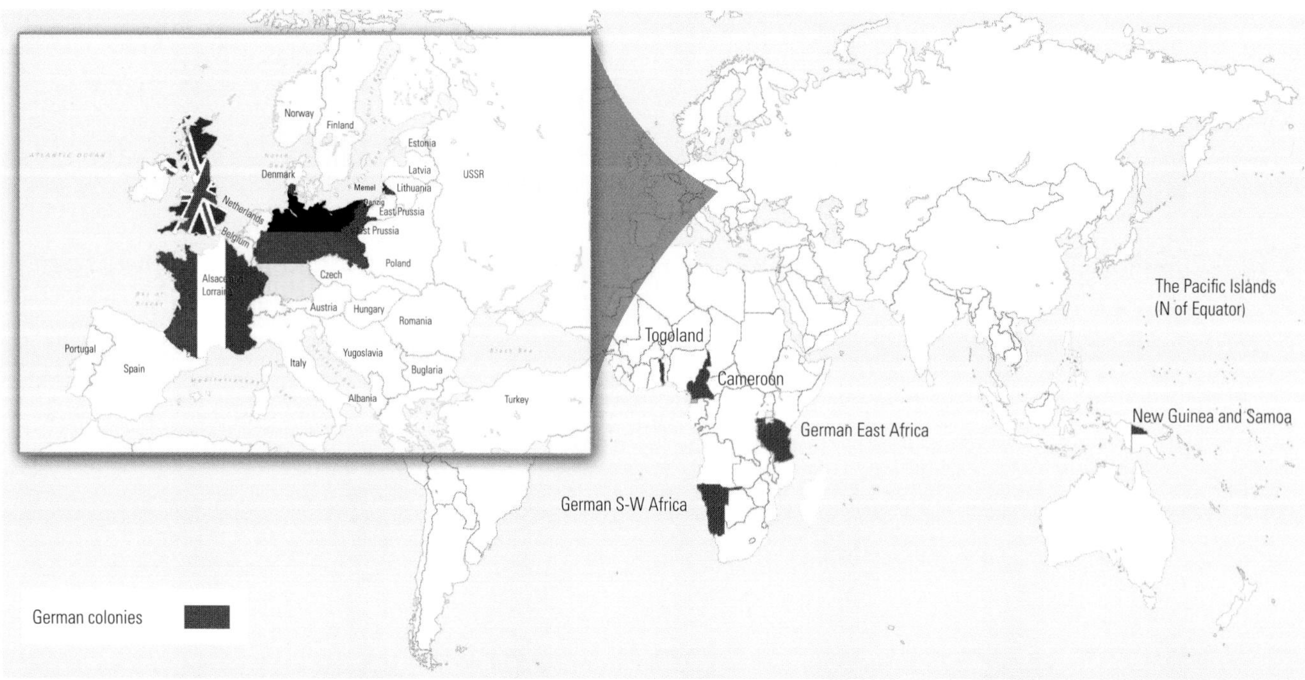

Germany and its territory at Versailles.

Italian demands

The 'Big Three' also had to consider their other ally's demands. Italy wanted the rewards it had been expecting for having entered the war - lands at the expense of what had been the empires of Austria-Hungary and the Ottomans - regardless of ethnic distributions. Italy also wanted the port of Fiume, not minding that this would be punishing South Slavs for the sins of Austria-Hungary. But Italy was overshadowed by the 'Big Three'.

Prime Minister Lloyd George (Britain)

Prime Minister Clemenceau (France)

President Wilson (USA)

Activities

Who do you support?

1 For each of the 'Big Three' :
   - **a** summarise in two sentences what they wanted out of the Treaty of Versailles
   - **b** explain why they wanted that.
2 Wilson seemed to be thinking about what was good for the world rather than just what was good for his country. Does that mean that Lloyd George and Clemenceau were just being selfish? Explain your answer.

ResultsPlus

Watch out!

It is easy to confuse who was who in the Big Three. Here is an easy way to remember. In alphabetical order the countries are France, Great Britain and the USA. The leaders follow the same alphabetical order – Clemenceau, Lloyd George and Wilson.

The Treaty of Versailles

Learning objectives

In this chapter you will learn about:

- why the European powers were so determined to punish Germany in the peace treaty
- the terms of the Treaty of Versailles.

Background

The First World War brought about casualties on a previously unknown scale. It was these horrifying losses which help explain why Britain and France went to the Paris Peace Conference determined to 'make Germany pay.'

The Paris Peace Conference

When the Paris Peace Conference started in Versailles in January 1919, it was agreed that decisions would be made by the Council of Four – the leaders of Britain, France, the USA and Italy. However, Orlando, the Italian leader, left the conference over Italian claims to the Hungarian port of Fiume, after it was given to the newly created state of Yugoslavia and not Italy. This meant that the 'Big Three' were able to agree the treaty among themselves.

Table A

Casualties of the main participants in the First World War. The number of casualties is calculated by adding up those killed, wounded, missing or taken prisoner.

Country	Total forces	Killed	Wounded	Prisoners and missing	Total casualties
Austria	7,800,000	1,200,000	3,620,000	2,200,000	7,020,000
British Empire	8,904,000	908,000	2,090,000	191,000	3,189,000
France	8,410,000	1,358,000	4,266,000	537,000	6,161,000
Germany	11,000,000	1,777,400	4,216,000	1,152,800	7,146,200
Italy	5,615,000	650,000	947,000	600,000	2,197,000
Russia	12,000,000	1,700,000	4,950,000	2,500,000	9,150,000
Turkey	2,850,000	325,000	400,000	250,000	975,000
United States	4,355,000	117,000	232,000	4,500	353,500
Other countries	4,105,000	493,600	468,000	315,700	1,277,300
Total	65,039,000	8,529,000	21,189,000	7,751,000	37,469,000

Table B

Debts that the Allies had at the end of the war. They had borrowed from each other to pay for the costs of the war. There was a revolution in Russia in 1917 and the new government said it would not pay the debts run up by the old government.

	Owed to (in £ million)	
	Britain	USA
France	626	652
Italy	590	357
Russia	757	41
Belgium	110	76
Britain		931

Activity

Use the information in Table A and Table B to create a Powerpoint presentation explaining which countries were most affected by the war. You need to think carefully about how you present this information. For example, would using percentages be a good idea; what type of graph might show these figures best?

The 'Diktat'

Twenty-seven nations were represented at Versailles, but the defeated countries were not allowed to attend. In Germany, the peace treaty was called the ***'Diktat'*** because it was dictated not negotiated. The Germans saw it as an 'imposed' settlement – not something they had agreed to.

The Treaty of Versailles

The Germans were told the terms of the peace treaty on 7 May 1919. They were so tough that the German chancellor resigned rather than agree to them. However, there was no alternative because the Allied armies controlled Europe. On 28 June the treaty was signed in the Palace of Versailles; its main terms are described below.

Territorial terms

- Germany lost territory in Europe (see map on page 67 in Section 3).
    - o Alsace and Lorraine were given to France.
    - o Eupen and Malmedy were given to Belgium.
    - o In Schleswig there were two **plebiscites** (public votes). Northern Schleswig voted to become Danish and Central Schleswig voted to stay German.
    - o In the east, Poland became a country for the first time since 1815. It was given West Prussia and Posen, as well as the 'Polish Corridor', which linked Poland to the sea and split East Prussia from the rest of Germany.
    - o Danzig, the main port in the Polish Corridor, became an independent city under the care of the League of Nations.
    - o Memel was also to be independent under the League.
- Germany was not allowed to unite with Austria (**Anschluss**).
- Germany also lost all of its overseas colonies. These were given to the victorious powers as 'mandates'.
    - o Togoland and Cameroon were assigned to Britain and France.
    - o German South West Africa (now Namibia) was assigned to South Africa.
    - o German East Africa was assigned to Britain.
    - o New Guinea was assigned to Australia.
    - o Samoa was assigned to New Zealand.
    - o The Pacific islands north of the equator were assigned to Japan.

Did you know?

British Empire forces included soldiers from countries such as Australia, New Zealand and Canada. They fought with great honour during the war. India, alone, provided over one million soldiers.

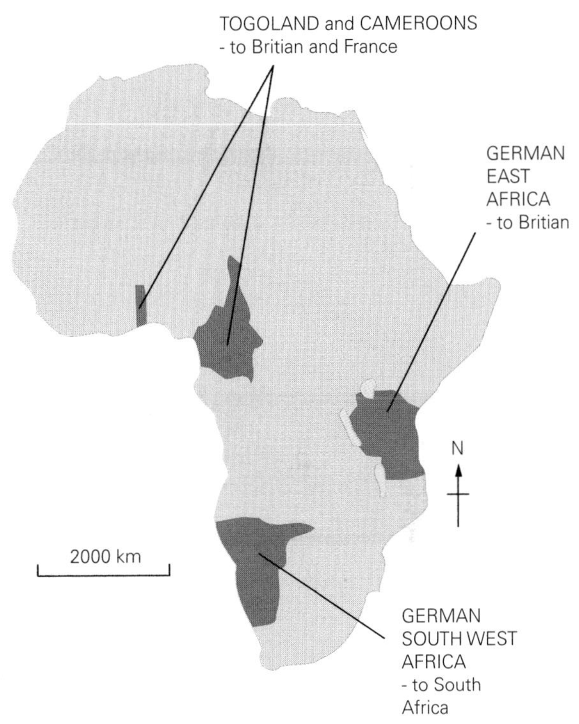

Territorial terms of the Treaty of Versailles: German colonies in Africa.

Did you know?

The League of Nations established 'mandates' when handing over control of the defeated powers' colonies to the victors. The new rulers had to accept certain obligations to the mandate's population and restrictions on what they could do there. There were three types of mandate, based on how much control was required to run the country.

Economic terms

- In Article 231, the 'war guilt' clause, Germany was forced to admit it was responsible for starting the war.
- As the war was Germany's fault, it had to pay reparations – money to compensate the Allies for the damage and losses caused by the war. A commission was set up to agree the final figure, and in 1921 it decided on £6,600 million.

Many of the terms of the Treaty of Versailles hit the German economy hard. Reparations clearly took money from Germany. However, other terms also hit the German economy hard, making it even more difficult for Germany to raise the £6,600 million reparation payments.

- The industrial area of Germany called the Saar (which had huge coalfields) was to be run by the League of Nations until 1934, with all profits it made going to France.
- Germany lost all its colonies, which affected its ability to trade.
- It lost all the land it had taken from Russia in the Treaty of Brest Litovsk that ended the war between Germany and Russia. The land taken had been one of the most industrialised areas in Russia.
- The military terms of the treaty had economic effects too, creating unemployment in the armed services and in the industries that supplied them.

Did you know?

Article 246 of the treaty said that Germany agreed to 'hand over to the British Government the skull of the Sultan Mkwawa which was removed from the Protectorate of German East Africa and taken to Germany.'

Military terms

- The German army was reduced to 100,000 men. (At the start of the war there had been about 11 million men in the army and navy.)
- It could have no tanks at all.
- The German navy could only have 15,000 men, six battleships, some smaller ships and no submarines.
- Germany could not have an air force.
- The Rhineland was demilitarised. This meant that Germany was not allowed to send any troops at all into the Rhineland. This created the buffer between Germany and France that France had wanted, because it would be much harder for Germany to invade France if it didn't have troops in the Rhineland, and easier for France to invade Germany, if the Rhineland was undefended.

Other terms

- The former Kaiser and other German leaders were to be tried for war crimes.

The League of Nations

The League of Nations was set up as an alternative way of solving disputes between countries. However, although it was hoped that the League would prevent the need for armed conflict between nations, none of the other countries were restricted in the size of their military forces as Germany was.

Examination question

Describe one action taken in the Treaty of Versailles to limit Germany's armed forces.
(2 marks)

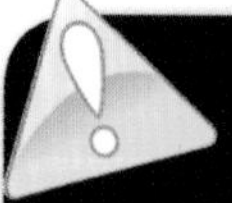

ResultsPlus
Watch out!

It is easy to say that the people who drew up the Treaty of Versailles were foolish and were far too hard on Germany. You need to think about why they did what they did and whether their behaviour was reasonable at the time. It is easy to be critical years later!

German reaction

Almost all Germans resented the terms of the Treaty of Versailles enormously. The way the war had ended, with an armistice and not with an overwhelming military defeat, meant they were not convinced they had lost the war. They had never been told how badly Germany was doing in the war. Many felt those in control had just given in. There were several points that caused huge resentment.

- The fact that Germany had not been allowed to take part in the talks.
- The 'War Guilt' clause. No country had ever been expected to take sole responsibility for a war before.
- The fact the profits from the Saar were to go to France.
- The reduction of the armed forces.
- The demilitarisation of the Rhineland was seen as ignoring German sovereignty.

Why this was a problem for the Weimar government

The Weimar government had signed the treaty – there had been no option. But German resentment created huge political problems for the Weimar government.

- Almost all Germans felt the reparations demanded were unfair. So any payments the Weimar Government made, no matter how small, were seen as giving in.
- The government did not want to do too much before the constitution was set up and a new government was elected. It saw itself as a provisional government only. But this made it look very weak to most Germans.

Various political groups saw a chance to seize power because the Weimar government was weak and unpopular.

German protest against the Treaty of Versailles. The main banner reads "Day of Versailles, Day of Dishonour".

The other peace treaties

Learning objectives

In this chapter you will learn about:

- how Europe was politically divided after the war
- the terms of the various treaties other than Versailles.

Problems

The Big Three had found it very difficult to agree on the terms of the Treaty of Versailles. They found it even harder to agree on the terms of the treaties for the other defeated powers.

Whatever the Allies wanted, some of the results of the war could not be reversed. The peacemakers drew up a series of treaties based on the following principles:

- self-determination should be given where possible
- reparations should be paid
- there should be restrictions on the armed forces.

The break-up of the Habsburg Empire

The once-powerful Habsburg Empire in Austria-Hungary had broken up by 1918 into several small individual states. The new states of Austria, Hungary, Czechoslovakia and Yugoslavia had declared their independence from the **Habsburgs** during the last few months of the war. Other peoples also wanted the self-determination Wilson had called for.

Negotiating with Turkey

Turkey was ruled by a sultan in 1918, but many Turks feared the Allies would abolish his position. The Allies kept the Sultan and he signed the Treaty of Sèvres in 1920, agreeing to the terms decided by the Allies. The Turkish parliament refused to agree to the treaty as it gave away too much Turkish land. Then the Sultan was overthrown in a revolution and the new leader, Kemal Ataturk, negotiated a new treaty (Lausanne) with less harsh terms.

The problem of Russia

Russia was a particular problem to the Allies. In 1914 it had joined the war on the side of the Allies. However, in 1917, two revolutions had overthrown the Tsar and brought in a new 'Bolshevik' government, which immediately faced a civil war when supporters of the Tsar tried to bring him back. The Bolsheviks could not fight a civil war and a war against Germany at the same time. So Russia made peace with Germany in the Treaty of Brest-Litovsk in March 1918. Russia was forced to hand over large areas of land in return for peace.

After the war, the Allies were not going to let Germany keep its gains. However, they did not accept the Bolshevik government in Russia, so they were not keen to return the land Russia had given up.

Solutions

Russia's losses at Brest-Litovsk consisted largely of distinct national groups. So by following Wilson's idea of self-determination, Estonia, Finland, Latvia and Lithuania were made independent states at the Treaty of Versailles. In addition, parts of Russian territory were given to Poland. Only Ukraine was returned to Russia.

Examination question

Describe the aims of the peacemakers at Versailles in drawing up the treaties of St Germain, Neuilly and Trianon. (6 marks)

ResultsPlus
Top Tip

Students who just list the terms of the treaties will do poorly on the exam question on the left. It is not enough to know a lot about each treaty – you need to say why the terms were drawn up as they were. Students who do well will link terms to aims, for example: *'The Habsburg Empire was formally broken up because Wilson wanted to bring about self-determination'*

All the treaties

The terms of the treaties varied, but they all had the following clauses which limited the defeated countries' choices about their future.

- All military restrictions were to be supervised by an allied commission.
- As well as having their military forces reduced, they were banned from the weapons trade.
- Reparations were to be set by an allied commission.
- Boundaries were to be decided by an allied commission.
- They had to sign the Covenant of the League of Nations.
- Those that had colonies abroad lost them.

The Treaty of St Germain

Signed between: the Allies and Austria

10 September 1919

The Allies' main aims in this treaty were to break up the Austrian Empire, reduce Austria's military strength, take reparations and make sure that Austria and Germany never re-united.

Political and economic terms

- o Austria's empire was divided. Czechoslovakia, Hungary, Yugoslavia and Poland became new countries, with borders set out by the treaty.
- o Austria had to agree not to re-unite (politically or economically) with Germany without the agreement of the League of Nations.
- o Reparations were never set.

Military terms of the treaty

- o Austria could only have 30,000 troops.
- o Its weapon holdings were limited and it was only allowed one weapons factory.
- o It could not have a navy or an air force. It was allowed three small boats to patrol the Danube.

Effects of the treaty

- o Austria lost a huge amount of farmland and industry. It could only produce a fraction of the goods it had produced before.
- o The road and rail networks of the old empire did not work well for the new Austria – nor for the new nation states.
- o Austria now had to pay duty to trade with places once part of its empire. Its economy failed. The Bank of Vienna collapsed. No reparations were paid.
- o The new nation states were weak. Most of them had groups that were unhappy with the boundaries drawn up by the treaty and also disagreed over how they should be governed.

The break-up of the Habsburg Empire under the terms of the Treaty of St Germain, September 1919.

The Treaty of Neuilly

Signed between: the Allies and Bulgaria

27 November 1919

The Allies' main aims in this treaty were to reduce Bulgaria's military strength, settle its borders and take reparations. However, they did not want to punish Bulgaria as heavily as Germany and Austria, where they felt the main blame fell.

Terms of the treaty

- Bulgaria lost land to Greece and Yugoslavia. It had to agree that people living in these lands could choose their citizenship and move freely to the country of their choice until 1921.
- Bulgaria's army was limited to 20,000 troops.
- Bulgaria's weapon holdings were limited and it was only allowed one weapons factory.
- It could not have a navy or an air force. It was allowed ten small boats to patrol the Danube.
- Reparations were set at £100 million.

Effects of the treaty

- Despite gaining land from Turkey, Bulgaria resented the loss of land.
- Many people disliked the boundaries drawn up by the treaty, and ethnic rivalries were created in some areas.
- Bulgaria resented the restrictions on its forces.
- Bulgaria also resented the fact that it was the only country to actually pay reparations, a huge burden for its economy.

The Treaty of Trianon

Signed between: the Allies and Hungary

4 June 1920

The Allies' main aims in this treaty were to reduce Hungary's military strength and take reparations. However, they did not want to punish Hungary as heavily as Germany and Austria, where they felt the main blame fell.

Terms of the treaty

- Hungary was made a separate country, no longer part of the Austro-Hungarian Empire.
- Hungary lost land to Czechoslovakia, Romania, Yugoslavia and even Austria.
- Hungary's army was limited to 35,000 troops.
- Hungary's weapon holdings were limited and it was only allowed one weapons factory.
- It could not have a navy or an air force. It was allowed three small boats to patrol the Danube.
- Reparations were set at over £400 million.

Effects of the treaty

- Hungary lost about two-thirds of its land and three million people.
- Romania took more land on its border in 1919. The Allies could not get Romania to agree to the border it had set. Its government resigned.
- Hungary became communist.
- It never paid reparations.

ROMANIA
160 km
N
BULGARIA
YUGOSLAVIA
Black Sea
TURKEY
Constantinople
GREECE
Western Thrace
TURKEY
Aegean Sea

Land lost by Bulgaria in the Treaty of Neuilly.

Land lost by Hungary in the Treaty of Trianon.

The Treaties of Sèvres and Lausanne

Signed between: the Allies and Turkey
Sèvres: 10 August 1920
Lausanne: 24 July 1923

The Allies' main aims in this treaty were to break up the Ottoman Empire, reduce Turkish-held land in Europe, free the Straits (the Dardanelles, the Sea of Marmora and the Bosphorus) from Turkish control and reduce Turkish forces.

Terms of the Treaty of Sèvres

- In Europe, Turkey lost Eastern Thrace and Smyrna to Greece. It lost land to Bulgaria. So the only European land it kept was Constantinople and a small amount of land around it.
- Arabia became independent. Two new independent nations were set up: Armenia and Kurdistan. Syria, Palestine, Transjordan and Iraq were to become mandates of Allied countries, working towards independence.
- The Straits were no longer to be controlled by Turkey. Ships could pass through 'in war or peace' and the forts controlling them were not manned by Turkish forces.
- Turkey's army was limited to 50,000 troops.
- Turkey's weapon holdings were limited and the military commission was to set the number of weapons factories.
- It could not have a navy or an air force. It was allowed 13 small boats to patrol its coast.
- Allied troops were to stay in Turkey to enforce military provisions.
- There were no reparations, but the Turks did have to pay the costs of foreign troops in Turkey.

Effects of the Treaty of Sèvres

The people of Turkey were outraged by the terms of the treaty. There was an uprising, led by Mustapha Kemal, and the Sultan's government was overthrown. Rather than fight Kemal's forces, the Allies agreed to renegotiate the Treaty of Sèvres.

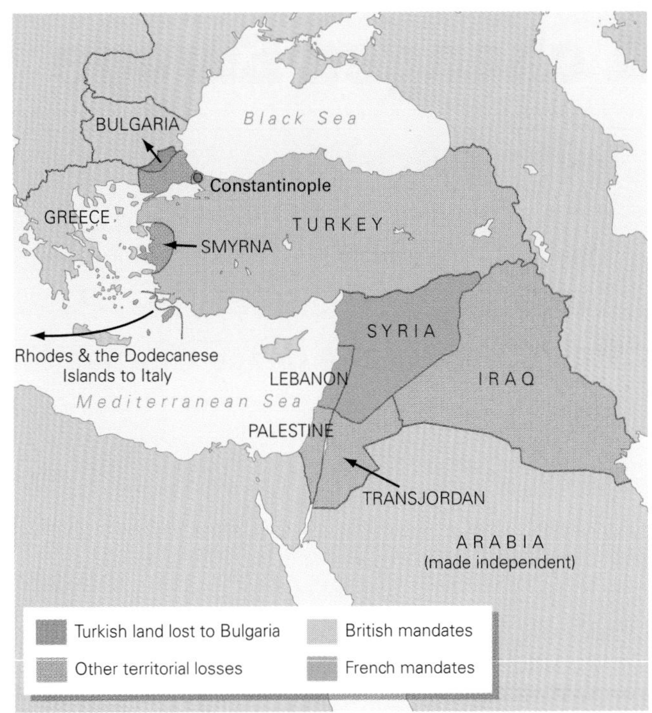

Land taken from Turkey in the Treaty of Sèvres, 1920.

Changes made by the Treaty of Lausanne

- In Europe, Turkey regained Eastern Thrace and Smyrna from Greece.
- Turkey regained control of the forts that controlled the Straits, but ships were still to pass freely.
- No limits were placed on Turkey's armed forces.
- There were no reparations, but the Turks did have to pay the costs of foreign troops in Turkey.

Activity

1 Did the Allies get what they wanted? Complete the table below.

Treaty	Allies got	Allies didn't get
St Germain		
Neuilly		
Trianon		
Sèvres/Lausanne		

2 Prepare notes for a debate between Bulgaria and Austria about which country was treated more harshly in the treaties. Make short notes about the argument for and against each one.

A changed Europe

Learning objectives

In this chapter you will learn about:

- the new Europe in 1926.

The impact of the peace treaties on Europe by 1926

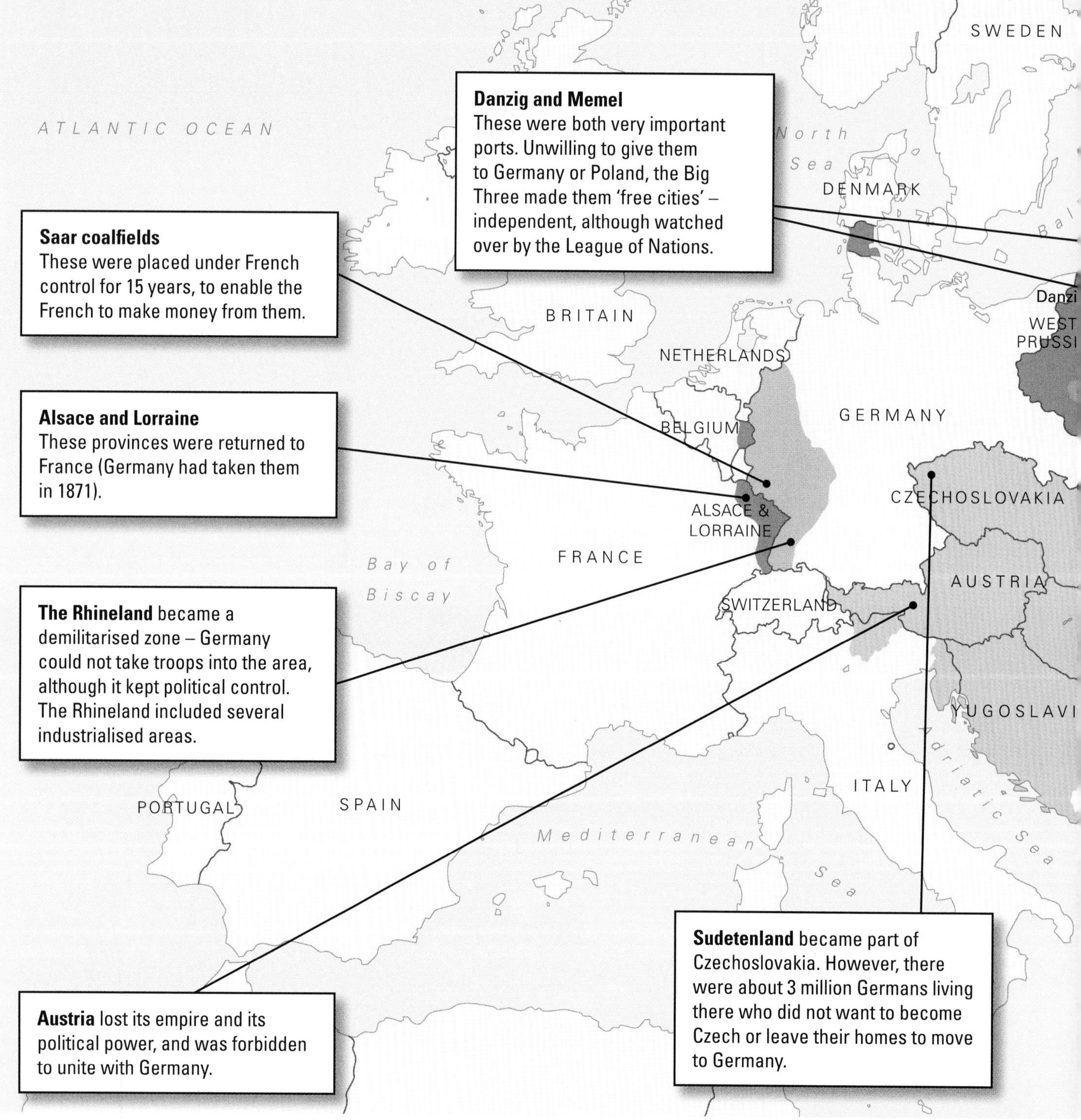
ATLANTIC OCEAN
NORWAY
SWEDEN
North Sea
DENMARK
BRITAIN
NETHERLANDS
BELGIUM
GERMANY
ALSACE & LORRAINE
FRANCE
CZECHOSLOVAKIA
AUSTRIA
SWITZERLAND
YUGOSLAVI
ITALY
Adriatic Sea
Bay of Biscay
PORTUGAL
SPAIN
Mediterranean Sea
Danzi
WEST PRUSSI
Danzig and Memel
These were both very important ports. Unwilling to give them to Germany or Poland, the Big Three made them 'free cities' – independent, although watched over by the League of Nations.
Saar coalfields
These were placed under French control for 15 years, to enable the French to make money from them.
Alsace and Lorraine
These provinces were returned to France (Germany had taken them in 1871).
The Rhineland became a demilitarised zone – Germany could not take troops into the area, although it kept political control. The Rhineland included several industrialised areas.
Austria lost its empire and its political power, and was forbidden to unite with Germany.
Sudetenland became part of Czechoslovakia. However, there were about 3 million Germans living there who did not want to become Czech or leave their homes to move to Germany.

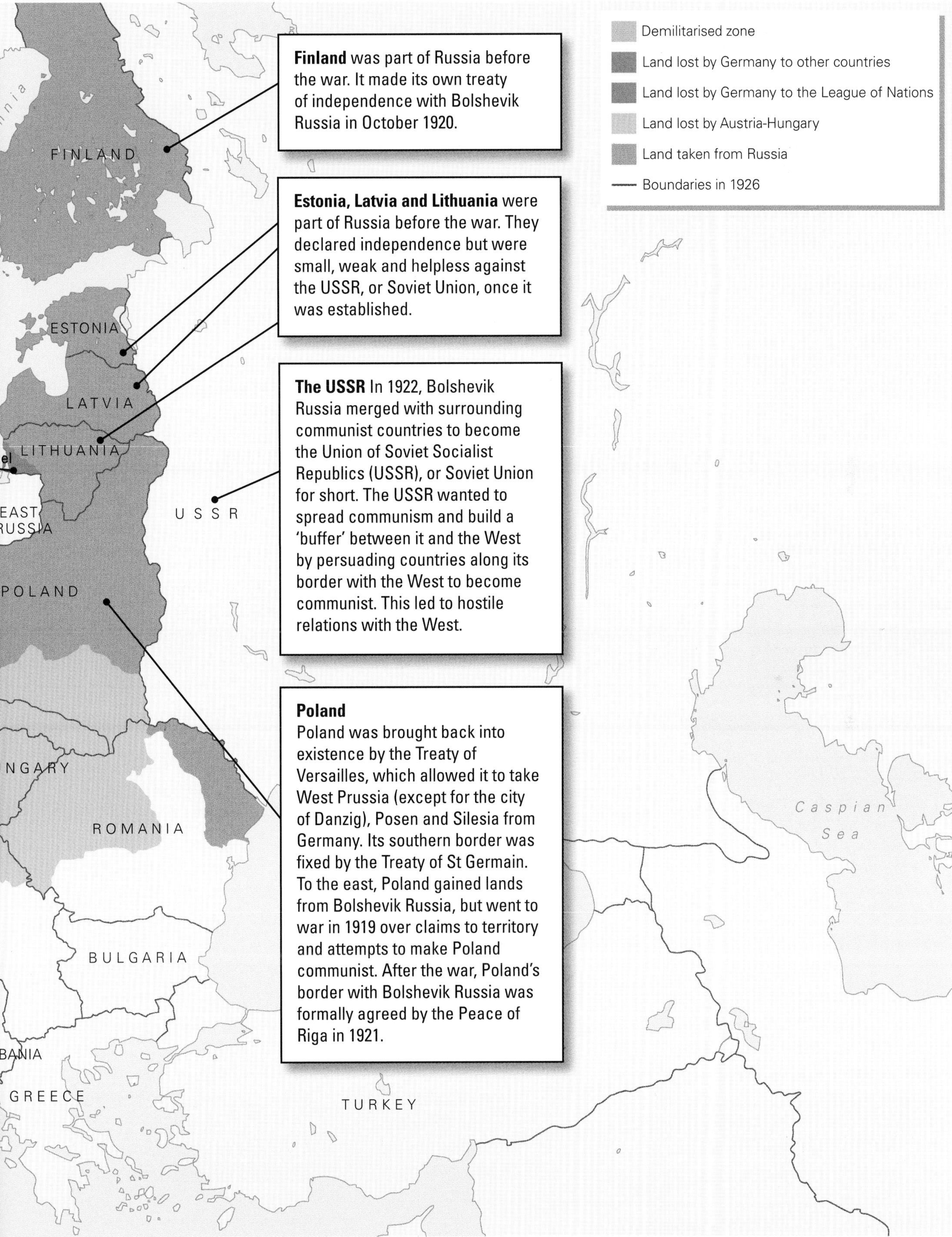
Demilitarised zone
Land lost by Germany to other countries
Land lost by Germany to the League of Nations
Land lost by Austria-Hungary
Land taken from Russia
Boundaries in 1926
Finland was part of Russia before the war. It made its own treaty of independence with Bolshevik Russia in October 1920.
Estonia, Latvia and Lithuania were part of Russia before the war. They declared independence but were small, weak and helpless against the USSR, or Soviet Union, once it was established.
The USSR In 1922, Bolshevik Russia merged with surrounding communist countries to become the Union of Soviet Socialist Republics (USSR), or Soviet Union for short. The USSR wanted to spread communism and build a 'buffer' between it and the West by persuading countries along its border with the West to become communist. This led to hostile relations with the West.
Poland
Poland was brought back into existence by the Treaty of Versailles, which allowed it to take West Prussia (except for the city of Danzig), Posen and Silesia from Germany. Its southern border was fixed by the Treaty of St Germain. To the east, Poland gained lands from Bolshevik Russia, but went to war in 1919 over claims to territory and attempts to make Poland communist. After the war, Poland's border with Bolshevik Russia was formally agreed by the Peace of Riga in 1921.
FINLAND
ESTONIA
LATVIA
LITHUANIA
EAST
RUSSIA
USSR
POLAND
UNGARY
ROMANIA
BULGARIA
BANIA
GREECE
TURKEY
Caspian Sea

Reactions to the Treaty of Versailles

Learning objectives

In this chapter you will learn about:

- how the Big Three felt about the decisions made at Versailles
- the German reaction to the Versailles treaty.

The Big Three

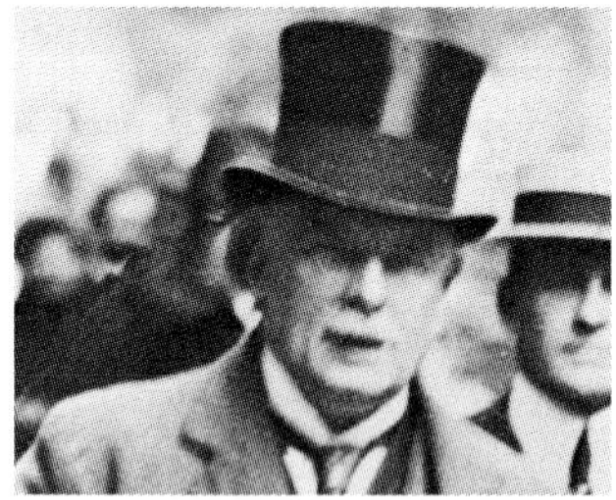

Prime Minister Lloyd George Britain

Lloyd George felt that the treaty was too harsh. He feared it might lead to another war, and he worried that the German government would become so unpopular that communists could stage a revolution. He understood the French need for greater security, and would have preferred to put even more limits on Germany's armed forces while lowering reparations. He thought this would help France and still allow the German economy to recover. But he could not go too far in pressing for a 'fair deal' for Germany, because he had won the election promising to be hard on Germany.

Prime Minister Clemenceau France

Clemenceau wanted Germany to pay heavily. He was not concerned with fairness. He felt the German lands lost were not enough, and that the Rhineland should have been permanently demilitarised. He felt the Germans should be punished for the war and for ruining large parts of France where the fighting was. He thought the Germans had got off lightly, and his people agreed. Clemenceau was voted out of power in January 1920, largely because he was blamed for too soft a peace. However, Marshal Foch, who had negotiated the armistice in 1918, said: '*This is not Peace. It is an armistice for twenty years.*' He thought the Germans would soon be ready for revenge.

President Wilson USA

Wilson thought the treaty was too harsh. He called it a treaty of revenge that made future peace unlikely. He also felt reparations were too high and would cause economic problems. His hope was that the League of Nations could put things right. His main problem, however, was that his own people wanted nothing more to do with the war. Wilson protested that he could '*predict with absolute certainty that within another generation there will be another world war*' unless the USA signed the treaty, but he was ignored. The USA did not sign the treaty and did not join the League of Nations.

German reaction

- The German delegation arrived in Paris at the end of April 1918 and was given the terms of the treaty on 7 May. The head of the delegation, Count Minister Ulrich Graf von Brockdorff-Rantzau, complained about Article 231, saying: '*We are required to admit that we alone are guilty of the war. Such a confession in my mouth would be a lie.*' So he resigned rather than sign, as did the chancellor of the German government.
- Under the terms of the armistice, 74 ships of the German fleet had been sent to a British naval base. The German crews were still on board and they sank all the ships rather than give them to the British.

- The newly formed Weimar government in Germany agreed to sign the treaty. There was no real choice: the Allies could begin the naval blockade again and Germany would starve. The German National Assembly voted to accept the treaty, and two politicians were sent to Versailles for the signing ceremony on 28 June. In Germany, the Weimar government was blamed for accepting the treaty. Critics of Weimar spread the idea that the army had not actually been defeated in the war. Their story was that Germany had lost the war because the liberals and socialists had undermined the war effort – 'stabbed it in the back'. The Weimar politicians who accepted and signed the peace became known as the 'November Criminals'. It was this hatred of the Treaty of Versailles which was to be the driving force behind Hitler's foreign policy in the 1930s.

A vast crowd, mainly made up of Germans from Alsace and Lorraine, demonstrating against the Versailles Treaty proposals, 12 June 1919.

A German cartoon headed 'Versailles', published on 3 June 1919. Wilson stands on the left while Clemenceau prepares the guillotine; Lloyd George stands to the right. The caption reads 'You too have the right to self-determination: would you like your pockets to be raided before or after your death?'

ResultsPlus

Build Better Answers

Exam question: Describe one way in which Clemenceau's aims were carried out in the Treaty of Versailles. (2 marks)

You need to make a developed statement; a statement that both answers the question and provides some detailed support.

■ **A basic answer (level 1):** *Germany was punished.*

● **A good answer (level 2):** *Germany was punished. The Rhineland became a demilitarised zone – Germany could not take troops into the area.*

Activity

The publisher of a GCSE history textbook has asked you to pick a picture which best shows the feelings of the German people for the Treaty of Versailles. The choice has been narrowed down to the two images on this page. The publisher expects a list for and against each picture, plus a recommendation of which you suggest and why.

A troubled Europe

Learning objectives

In this chapter you will learn about:

- how international relations deteriorated in 1923
- the importance of the Locarno and Kellogg–Briand Pacts.

Between 1921 and 1923, Germany suffered a series of economic problems. It was seriously in debt from the war and its industry was destroyed. It also had to make crippling reparations payments. In July 1922, Germany, already behind with its reparation payments, said it could not make any payments in 1923 and 1924. By 1923, the Allies had already twice reduced the huge amount set at Versailles, realising that Germany would never be able to pay. However, it was also true that Germany resented every penny that it did pay and was deliberately paying as little as possible.

Poland's shifting boundaries

The Treaty of Versailles, as part of its principle of self-determination, had said that Eastern Prussia, occupied by Germany at the end of the war, should hold a plebiscite to decide whether to join Germany or Poland. This was held on 11 July 1920. Although there were Allied observers there, the plebiscite was held by German officials. They announced that over 87% of people had voted. Of those, over 90% had voted to join Germany. In 1922, Poland also lost Posen to Germany. On 15 March 1923, Poland's boundaries were finally fixed.

The occupation of the Ruhr

In 1923, France and Belgium lost patience. On 11 January 1923, their armies marched into Germany and occupied the Ruhr, the heart of Germany's industry. Their intention was to run the industries for themselves and take the goods in place of unpaid reparations. German workers responded with passive resistance – by going on strike, working slowly or deliberately making faulty goods. France and Belgium gained very little for their trouble and the German economy collapsed.

The German government printed more money to try to pay reparations but this just caused hyperinflation – money became worthless. A loaf of bread which had cost 4 marks in 1921 cost 1,500,000 marks in 1923. The occupation quickly became unpopular in France as well as in Germany.

Various countries tried to intervene to help settle the matter. In 1924, the Dawes Plan was set up by the United States to restructure reparations. Germany's payments were again reduced and the German economy was to be helped by US loans – but Germany still had to make payments. The Dawes Plan made it possible for the last occupying troops to leave the Ruhr in August 1925.

In August 1923, Gustav Stresemann had become chancellor of Germany. He was determined to fix the economy and to develop less hostile relations with other countries. It was Stresemann who had persuaded the USA to set up the Dawes Plan in 1924. Now that Germany had restarted paying reparations, it could begin to build better relations with other nations.

The Locarno Pact (1925)

This **pact** paved the way for Germany to join the League of Nations (which it did in 1926). It was a collection of seven treaties between Britain, France, Italy, Belgium, Czechoslovakia, Germany and Poland, signed in Locarno, Switzerland, on 16 October 1925 – though not all countries signed all the agreements. The countries agreed to respect their common borders and to go to the League of Nations if there were disputes.

- All agreed that the borders between Belgium and Germany, and between France and Germany, would not change from those set by the Treaty of Versailles. Britain, France and Germany all pledged to declare war on any country trying to change these borders. This made all countries feel safer – no power would want a war in which they were one against two great powers. Britain and France felt less mistrust of Germany and even withdrew their troops from the Rhineland ahead of the schedule agreed at Versailles.

- Specifically, Germany agreed that Alsace-Lorraine would be French, whilst France agreed not to occupy the Ruhr again.
- All agreed that the borders of the countries on Germany's eastern border could be revised 'by peaceful means', but there was no guarantee that the signatories would go to war to defend these borders.
- All agreed to settle disputes among themselves peacefully via the League of Nations. Also, if any one country broke the agreement, they would defend the country that had been attacked if the League said that was fair.
- Germany, Belgium and France agreed never to attack each other unless they were defending themselves or acting on a decision made by the League of Nations.
- Germany and Poland agreed to settle all disputes peacefully through the League of Nations.
- Germany and Czechoslovakia agreed to settle all disputes peacefully through the League of Nations.
- France and Poland agreed to support each other if one of them was attacked.
- France and Czechoslovakia agreed to support each other if one of them was attacked.

Problems with the Pact

While the Pact was welcome, it did have problems:

- Eastern European countries were concerned that their borders were not properly protected, but open to renegotiation, even if it was by peaceful means. They feared Germany's refusal to promise to respect their borders. It made them vulnerable to invasion.
- Czechoslovakia and Poland were concerned that Britain did not agree to defend them if they were invaded, as France had done.

The Kellogg–Briand Pact (1928)

This pact was a signed agreement between 62 countries that war was wrong and that they would always seek peaceful solutions to any problems between them. It was signed in Paris on 27 August 1928. The pact was important because it showed how strongly countries supported the League of Nation's desire to maintain peace. It was drawn up between the US secretary of state, Frank Kellogg, and the French foreign minister, Aristide Briand.

The Kellogg–Briand Pact marked the high point of international relations in the inter-war years. There is no doubt that the countries that signed the pact genuinely wanted to avoid war, but when economic problems began from 1929, they found that sometimes they had to put their own interests first.

ResultsPlus
Build Better Answers

Exam question: Describe the key features of the French Occupation of the Ruhr. (6 marks)

You need to identify important points, not simply write all you know. Here, for example, you could choose to describe a cause of the crisis, an event within it and an effect of it.

■ **A basic answer (level 1)** gives simple statements that are accurate, but contain no supporting detail.

● **A good answer (level 2)** gives a statement that is accurate and is developed with specific information.

▲ **An excellent answer (full marks)** contains two or three statements. Each statement explains a relevant key feature and is backed up with specific information.

For the question above the following would be good features to develop:

- the French lose patience
- the reaction of the Germans
- the effects on Germany.

Activities

1 **a** List the international problems that arose between 1919 and 1925. For example, you might say 'France occupied the Ruhr.'

b In pairs, compare lists and make one that records all the problems.

c For each problem, discuss whether it was a result of the Treaty of Versailles. Write a sentence explaining what you decide each time.

The League of Nations: how was it organised?

Learning objectives

In this chapter you will learn about:

- how the League of Nations was organised
- how its work extended beyond peacekeeping.

Collective security

The League of Nations was established in 1919 during the Versailles conference. At the conference, President Wilson of the United States had pushed hard for an international organisation to increase international co-operation and prevent the horrors of the First World War being repeated. The Covenant of the League (a set of 26 Articles that all members agreed to follow) was written into each of the individual treaties drawn up after the war. These articles set out how nations could avoid future war. How was this to be done?

- Nations agreed to work together to protect any member threatened by another country. This was called **collective security**.
- If any member country went to war, other countries would stop trading with it. Military action might also be taken.
- All member countries were encouraged to disarm.
- There was to be increased co-operation between countries in business, trade, and improving the living and working conditions of people across the world.

The organisation of the League

The League was to be based in Geneva, Switzerland. All nations were invited to join, except those which had been defeated in the First World War (including Germany, Austria and Turkey). Russia was also excluded because other countries would not recognise its communist government. Although the League was the idea of President Wilson, his own country, the USA, refused to join. In the 1921 presidential election, the Americans chose Warren Harding, who promised to keep America out of European politics – a policy later called **'isolationism'**. So in its first meeting, the League of Nations comprised 42 nations.

The Assembly

This was the 'parliament' of the League. It met once a year and every member sent a representative. It could recommend (to the Council) actions to do with issues such as membership or the budget. To ensure co-operation, its decisions had to be unanimous (agreed by all members).

The Council

The Assembly was too large and met too infrequently to react quickly to international events, so a Council was also set up. It met five times a year, had four permanent members (Britain, France, Italy and Japan) and between four and nine temporary members elected by the Assembly for three years. The Council was the part of the League which considered international disputes and also supervised the special commissions. It, too, required a unanimous vote before decisions could be taken.

The Permanent Court of Justice

This part of the League was based in the Hague in the Netherlands. It was formed to settle disputes by having them heard by a team of judges from member countries. It did not, however, have a way to force members to accept its rulings.

The Secretariat

Like any large organisation, the League needed a group of civil servants to prepare papers, keep records and help organise its work. This was the Secretariat.

The International Labour Organisation (ILO)

This existed to bring about the League's aim of improving working conditions around the world. Representatives of governments, workers and employers met annually to set minimum standards and persuade member nations to adopt them.

The aims of the ILO included:

- reasonable working hours (an 8 hour maximum working day; a 48 hour maximum working week)

- reasonable working conditions (e.g. safe machinery, clean factories/workplaces)
- reasonable workers' rights (e.g. owner liability for accidents, the right to form trade unions, equal pay for women)
- an end to child labour.

The ILO acted by setting up a framework of rules and regulations that member states were asked to adopt. It also worked by campaigning and carrying out inspections in member countries. Some countries did adopt its working hour restrictions. Within member countries it did improve working conditions and reduce child labour in some industries, especially by observing the minimum ages that children could start work in various jobs.

The main weakness of the ILO was that it could only give advice. It set out various rules and regulations, but had no power to make countries, or businesses within those countries, adopt the policies it suggested.

The Commissions

As well as its main organisations, the League also had a large number of commissions to carry out specialist work. Some of these commissions existed for a short term; for example, the Refugees Commission was tasked with helping First World War **refugees** return to their home country. Other commissions were more permanent, such as those set up to deal with slavery or health.

Activities

1 Below is a list of problems for the League to deal with. Explain which organisation within the League you think would deal with that problem.
   - **a** There are still millions of people dying of malaria.
   - **b** Country A has complained that Country B has invaded it and is calling for action.
   - **c** A trade union organisation has complained that its members are not being given their rights.
   - **d** The president of one of the member countries wants to be sent details of a recent discussion in the Assembly so that he can discuss it with his government.
   - **e** One of the member states has complained that the League is spending too much on dealing with the problem of world health.
   - **f** A member country says it is being forced to pay unfair duties on goods it sells to another member country.

2 If in 1919 you had to pick one part of the League which you thought was most likely to be successful, which part would you chose? Explain your choice.

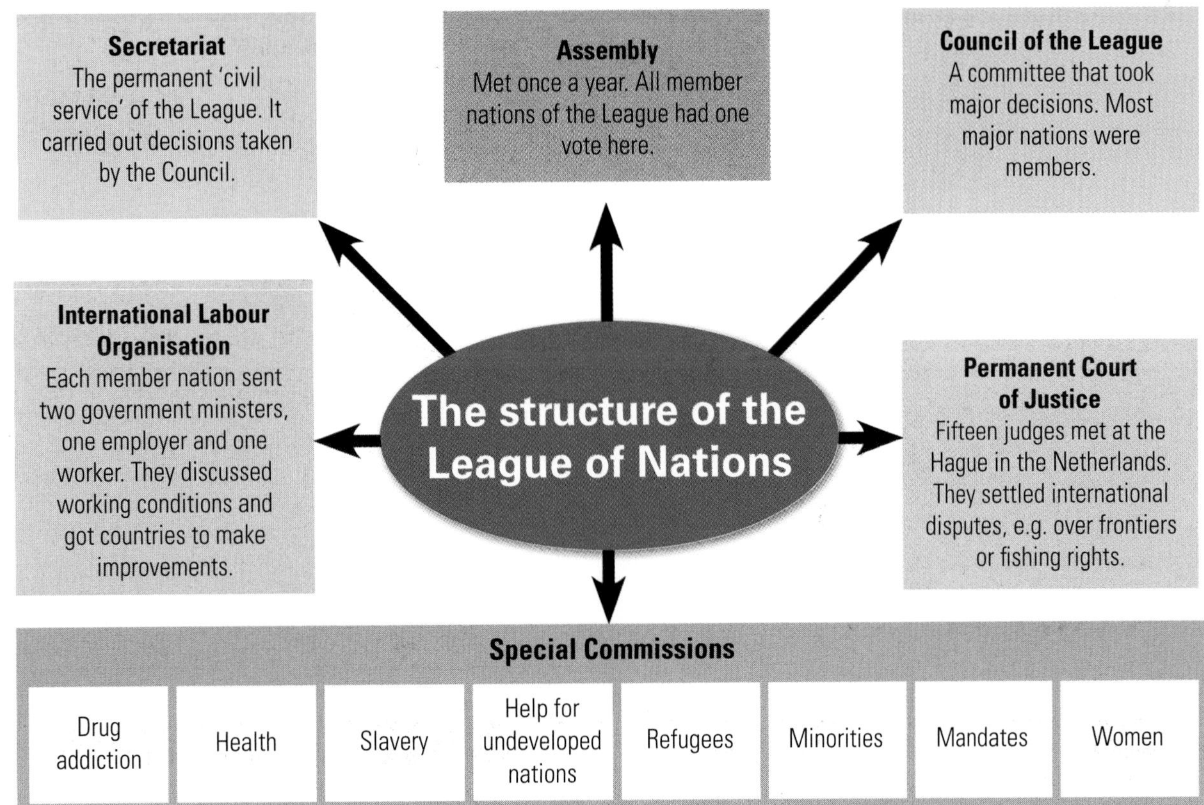

The League of Nations in action

Learning objectives

In this chapter you will learn about:

- the political actions of the League in the 1920s
- the valuable work of the commissions.

Settling disputes

During the 1920s the League became involved in a number of disputes around Europe. In some of these the new international peacekeeper seemed to be doing really well. In others, it looked weak and ineffective.

1 Vilna, 1920
This city was claimed by both Lithuania and Poland. It had been given to Lithuania at Versailles but had a majority Polish population. In 1920, Poland invaded Lithuania and occupied Vilna. This was an act of aggression that the League should have stopped. But League members were not prepared to take action, and Britain and France wanted to keep Poland as an ally against Russia. So Poland kept Vilna.

2 Upper Silesia, 1921
Upper Silesia had large numbers of Poles and Germans. At Versailles it was decided that there should be a plebiscite (public vote) to see which country should own it. The plebiscite was in favour of Germany but the League split the territory between them. Both countries accepted the decision.

3 The Aaland Islands, 1921
Control of these islands was disputed between Sweden and Finland. The League decided they should go to Finland. Both countries accepted the decision.

4 Corfu, 1923
Following a dispute in which five Italian surveyors were killed by Greek soldiers, the Italian leader, Mussolini, occupied the Greek island of Corfu. This was an act of aggression by a major member of the League. However, Britain and France did not want to take action against Mussolini. The Greeks were forced to apologise to Mussolini and pay compensation; only then did Italian troops leave Corfu.

5 Greek–Bulgarian dispute, 1925
In 1925 the Greeks invaded Bulgaria, with whom they were having a border dispute. The League condemned the Greek action and told them to withdraw from Bulgaria. They did.

The League of Nations at work in Europe in the 1920s.

The commissions

The Slavery Commission

Although slavery had been illegal for many years, it was still practised in a number of countries, particularly in Africa. The Slavery Commission was set up to abolish slavery and also the practice of forcing women into prostitution. Its main successes were in the mandated countries, where it pressured the administering governments to end slavery in those countries.

- Ethiopia had to commit to ending slavery as a condition of joining the League of Nations.
- 200,000 slaves were freed in Sierra Leone.
- The Commission worked with Liberia to abolish forced labour and inter-tribal slavery.
- Records were kept to control slavery, prostitution and the trafficking of women and children.

The Commission for Refugees

After the First World War, there were around 500,000 prisoners of war who needed to be returned to their homelands. The Council of the League appointed Fridtjof Nansen, a famous Norwegian explorer, to organise this work.

Nansen was extremely successful: in less than two years almost all the prisoners were sent home. He also established the Nansen Passport as a means of identification for stateless people, and later became high commissioner of the Commission for Refugees, set up in 1921. After his death in 1930, the commission became known as the Nansen International Office for Refugees and continued to help refugees, in particular those fleeing from Nazi policies.

The Mandates Commission

After the First World War, 14 territories which had previously been governed by the defeated powers were placed under the control of one of the victorious powers. The territories were divided into three classes:

Class A mandates were considered sufficiently advanced to be able to achieve independence after guidance from the governing power. All Class A mandates, such as Lebanon, had reached full independence by 1949.

Class B mandates were the former German-ruled African colonies of Tanganyika, parts of Togoland and the Cameroons, and Ruanda-Urundi. These were to be administered by Britain, France and Belgium.

Class C mandates were German-held territories that were absorbed into other countries. The most important of these were South West Africa (now Namibia) assigned to South Africa; New Guinea, assigned to Australia; and Western Samoa (now Samoa) assigned to New Zealand.

In theory the League supervised the running of these mandates, but in reality it had no way of enforcing its will on the controlling powers.

Other commissions

There were many other commissions carrying out very valuable work.

- A Permanent Central Opium Board worked to control the use of opium (an addictive drug).
- A Health Organisation Commission focused on trying to end leprosy and launched a huge mosquito extermination campaign to try to end malaria and yellow fever. It distributed medical information around the world and played a major part developing vaccines.
- A Disarmament Commission was set up and was successful in winning agreement from Britain, France, Japan and Italy to limit the size of their navies. It also helped set up the Kellogg–Briand Pact (see page 49). It is true, however, that in the end disarmament failed.

Activities

1 From what you have read on these pages, explain whether you agree with the following statements:
   a The League settled all the political problems well in the 1920s.
   b The best work the League did in the 1920s was through its commissions.
2 What mark out of 10 would you give the League for its work up to 1928? Explain why you gave this mark.

The League of Nations: doomed to failure?

Learning objectives

In this chapter you will learn about:

- the weaknesses of the League of Nations
- how those weaknesses hindered the work of the League.

The League had some successes in the 1920s, but some historians have argued that it was doomed to failure from the start. You may have noticed in the last chapter that there were times when the League's actions seemed to go against its principles of taking steps against countries which carried out acts of aggression. This is partly explained by looking at the weaknesses which existed in the League – and which were eventually to lead to its failure as an international peacekeeping organisation.

Reputation

The League of Nations was the idea of President Wilson of the USA. It was formed as a result of the Versailles conference and its rules were incorporated into each of the treaties agreed at the conference. The defeated nations had no say in the treaties and were not invited to join the League. So these countries saw the League as in some way connected to the hated peace treaties.

Membership

It was not only the defeated nations who were not members of the League. Russia was also excluded because it was a communist country and the other powers feared communism. Most importantly, however, the United States chose not to join. By 1919 the USA was the most powerful and richest nation in the world. Without it the League was a much weaker organisation. Although there were 42 members in the League and that number grew over the years, the League was never an organisation of all states. Indeed, some people called it 'the league of some nations'.

Organisation

The League's organisation made it difficult for it to act effectively. Each country, no matter how large or small it was, had a vote in the Assembly, and all decisions had to be unanimous. The Council was a smaller body of more important nations, but here, too, decisions had to be unanimous. All it took was for one country to say 'no' and a policy could not be implemented.

'Self-first' policies

A major weakness of the League was that it was dominated by France and Britain, and each nation had different ideas of how the League should act. France wanted the League to enforce the terms of the Treaty of Versailles. Britain saw the League as a useful place for nations to discuss issues, but didn't believe that it should take real action. Furthermore, whatever Britain and France may have seen as the role of the League, neither was prepared to see it take action which would damage its own interests. So they were happy to see Poland take Vilna and did not oppose Mussolini in Corfu. In the 1930s this 'self-first' policy was to destroy the League.

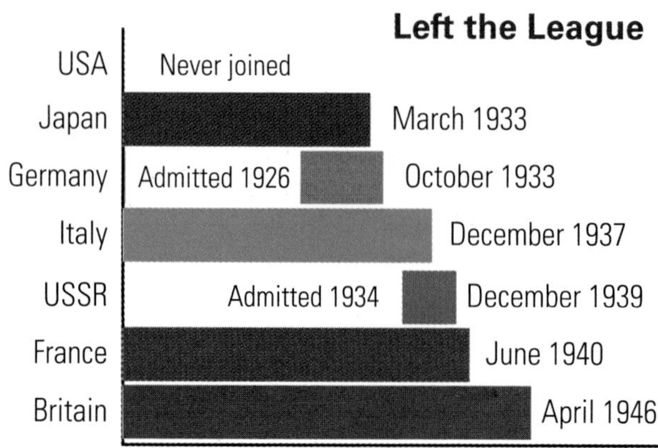

Membership of the League of Nations, 1919–46.

Lack of power

Even if Britain and France had shown full commitment to the League, it still faced the problem that countries could not be forced to accept its decisions. Article 16 of the Covenant said that when a nation refused to accept the League's decision, moral pressure should be applied to try to embarrass it into complying. If that did not work, **economic sanctions** would be applied: no country would trade with the wrongdoer. But during the 1930s, the world went into an economic recession and countries were reluctant to take action that might harm their own economy. The last measure possible was for the members of the League to raise an army and take military action. The major powers were never prepared to do that.

THE GAP IN THE BRIDGE.

A British cartoon from 1920. It shows the League of Nations Bridge with a gap in the middle. That gap represents the most important stone, the key stone. It is the USA which is the key stone and it will not complete the bridge by joining the League.

Activities

You have been asked to explain the art of cartoon drawing. With a partner, explain why the 1920 cartoon on this page is so clever. Here are some ideas to get you started:

- Who does the cartoonist say designed the bridge?
- What is special about the missing stone?
- Who is stopping the missing stone being put in place?
- What will happen to the bridge without the stone?

ResultsPlus
Build Better Answers

Exam question: Explain why the League found it difficult to be fully effective in the 1920s. (12 marks)

You need to make relevant points, supported by specific examples, with a clear focus on how each factor led to the situation described.

In each level, the number of statements you make will affect your mark. For example, in level 2, a single developed argument is unlikely to get more than 5 marks, whereas three developed arguments will achieve 8 or 9 marks.

■ **A basic answer (level 1)** is correct, but does not have details to support it. For example:
One reason is because it didn't have all the countries in it.

● **A good answer (level 2)** provides the details as well:
One reason is because it didn't have all the countries in it. For example, Germany was not allowed to join because it had lost the war.

▲ **A better answer (level 3)** shows the links between reasons or shows why one is more important. For example:
I think a major reason is that some of the great powers were happy to use the League to settle disputes which were only minor, but were not prepared to take measures which might affect them by ruining their relations with each other. So Mussolini was allowed to bully Greece over Corfu.

▲ **An excellent answer (full marks)** shows how three reasons are inter-linked and reaches a judgment about their relative importance.
I think a major reason is that some of the great powers were happy to use the League to settle disputes which were only minor, but were not prepared to take measures which might affect them by ruining their relations with each other. So Mussolini was allowed to bully Greece over Corfu.

In some ways this is linked to the fact that the League was weakened because not everyone was in it. The United States, for example, did not join. How did anyone think the League would solve world problems without the USA? So it became a weak body dominated by Britain and France.

Know Zone Unit 1 - section 2

In the Unit 1 exam, you will be required to answer questions from three sections. In each of those sections you will have to answer three questions: Part (a), Part (b) – where you have to do one of two questions set – and Part (c).

You have about 25 minutes to answer the three questions on each section. Use the number of marks available for each question to help you judge how long to spend on it and how much to write.

Here we are going to look at questions for Parts (b) and (c) of Section 2.

ResultsPlus Build Better Answers

Question (b)

Tip: Part (b) questions will usually ask you to describe the 'key features' of a major policy or an event. This question is worth 6 marks. Make sure that when you describe you don't just tell the story: think about the information and organise it as if you were putting it under headings. Let's look at an example.

Describe the key features of the decisions made about Austria and Hungary in the Treaties of St Germain and Trianon. (6 marks)

Student answer	Examiner comment
In the Treaty of St. Germain, Austria agreed to the break-up of the Habsburg Empire. It accepted Hungary, Poland, Czechoslovakia and Yugoslavia as independent countries. Land was also lost to Italy. Austria's army was limited to 30,000 men and it had to pay reparations. In the Treaty of Trianon, Hungary became an independent country, though it was only one-third of the size that it had been as part of the Habsburg Empire. Land was given to Czechoslovakia, Romania, Yugoslavia and Austria. It had to pay reparations and the Hungarian army was limited to 35,000 men.	This tells us some of the decisions made in the treaties but it doesn't really give 'the features', so would only be rewarded with less than half marks for providing simple statements. There are no 'pegs to hang the facts on', which would help you give a developed description of key features.

Let's rewrite the answer with features added. So that you can spot them easily we will put them in bold.

One of the key features was that the two countries had to pay compensation for damage that had been done. In the Treaty of St Germain, Austria had to agree to pay reparations. In the Treaty of Trianon, Hungary also had to pay. **Another feature was that they lost land.** Austria agreed to the break up of the Habsburg Empire. It accepted Hungary, Poland, Czechoslovakia and Yugoslavia as independent countries. Land was also lost to Italy. Although Hungary became an independent country, it was only one-third of the size that it had been as part of the Habsburg Empire. Land was given to Czechoslovakia, Romania, Yugoslavia and Austria. **A third feature was that their military power was weakened.** Austria's army was limited to 30,000 men and the Hungarian army was limited to 35,000 men.	This answer now has three developed descriptions of key features and would receive full marks.

Question (c)

Tip: Part (c) questions require extended writing. They will ask you to use your knowledge to explain why something happened. You should try to find three reasons and explain them. Remember that you will have only about 15 minutes to answer this question and so you need to get straight to the point.
Let us look at an example.

Explain why international relations improved in the period 1924–28. (12 marks)

Student answer	Examiner comment
International relations improved in the period 1924–28 for a whole variety of reasons. The League of Nations was encouraging co-operation and the Americans were helping boost Germany's economy. But I think the most important reason was the work of Stresemann in building better relationships. Without him, it would not have happened.	This is a disappointing answer. The student has shown a high-level skill in identifying reasons and trying to prioritise them, but has not provided an explanation of why the reasons listed actually improved relations. So for that reason it could not score more than 3 marks for providing 'generalised statements of causation'. Remember that you need to identify the causes, give some historical detail and make a link made between the causes and the question.

Let's rewrite this so that it explains the causes of improved relations.

International relations improved in the period 1924–28 for a whole variety of reasons. The League of Nations was formed during the Versailles Conference. Nations agreed to work together to protect any member threatened by another country. This was called collective security. If any member country went to war, other countries would stop trading with it. All member countries were encouraged to disarm. There was to be increased co-operation between countries in business, trade and improving the living and working conditions of people across the world. When Germany joined in 1926 this helped create a feeling of greater co-operation. During this period, the Americans were helping boost Germany's economy. For example, in 1924, the Dawes Plan was set up by the USA to restructure reparations. Germany's payments were again reduced and it was to be helped by US loans. This took a lot of the 'tension' out of Europe. The French left the Ruhr. That was important. But I think the most important reason was the work of Stresemann in building better relationships. He solved Germany's economic problems by bringing in a new currency, took Germany into the League of Nations and also signed the Locarno and Kellogg-Briand Pacts. So relations improved because Germany was no longer the enemy.	Now we have the three reasons explained and linked to the question. But remember that if you want full marks you have to give three reasons and prioritise them by making links between them. This student seems to think Stresemann's work was the most important reason. Could you finish the answer by explaining why?

Section 3: Why did war break out? International relations 1929–39

By 1929, memories of the First World War were fading and the League of Nations had helped improve relations between the nations of the world. However, tension grew as economic depression hit the industrialised world in 1929. During hard times, countries look to their own affairs rather than international co-operation. The League proved powerless in the face of aggression from Japan, Italy and, especially, Germany.

In this section you will study:

- the failure of the League of Nations: Manchuria (1931–32) and Abyssinia (1935–36)
- Hitler's challenges to the peace settlement, 1933–March 1938
- the failure of appeasement, 1937–39.

You will see how Hitler set about reversing what the Germans saw as the injustices of the Treaty of Versailles. When Hitler rearmed Germany and began to build *Grossdeutschland* (Greater Germany), Britain and France tried to avoid war with a policy of appeasement, making concessions to avoid direct military conflict. By 1939, however, it was obvious that this policy had failed.

The end of prosperity

Learning objectives

In this chapter you will learn about:

- why the Great Depression began in 1929
- how economic depression affected relations between the Great Powers.

Did you know?

Large companies have shares which can be bought and sold in the 'stock market'. Each share is a small part of that company's value. If you buy shares and their price goes up (because the company is worth more money), then you can sell them and make a profit. If the price goes down it's best not to sell, because if you do you will make a loss. In 1929 share prices tumbled. If you had bought 100 shares in Westinghouse (a well-known company) in 1928, you would have had to pay about $30,000. If you had to sell them after the Wall Street Crash, you would have got about $10,000 back!

The Wall Street Crash

In 1929 the American economy collapsed. The first signs came in October when the Wall Street stock market in New York saw a dramatic slump in the value of shares. Soon, thousands of people discovered that those shares were worth only a fraction of what they had paid for them. Confidence in the economy collapsed overnight. Banks stopped giving out loans as they saw their customers struggling to repay existing loans.

Businesses experienced a huge drop in the number of goods that they could sell. Four million cars were sold in the USA in 1929, but only one million in 1932. Companies 'laid off' workers as they cut production. The American economy went into a downward spiral so that by 1933 production of manufactured goods was only 20% of what it had been in 1929.

The world 'catches cold'

Today, the American economy is such a large part of the world's economy that it has been said that 'when America sneezes, the world catches a cold'. This was also true in 1929. The USA had made substantial loans to other countries, such as Germany, to help them rebuild their economies after the First World War and provided economic help via the American Relief Administration. But now that times were hard, they wanted this money back. Since the USA could no longer afford to import (buy in) goods from overseas, the economies of other countries suffered too, because demand for their goods dropped. So the world economy went into a severe decline and it suffered the **'Great Depression'**. Much of the goodwill that had existed between nations in the 1920s also collapsed.

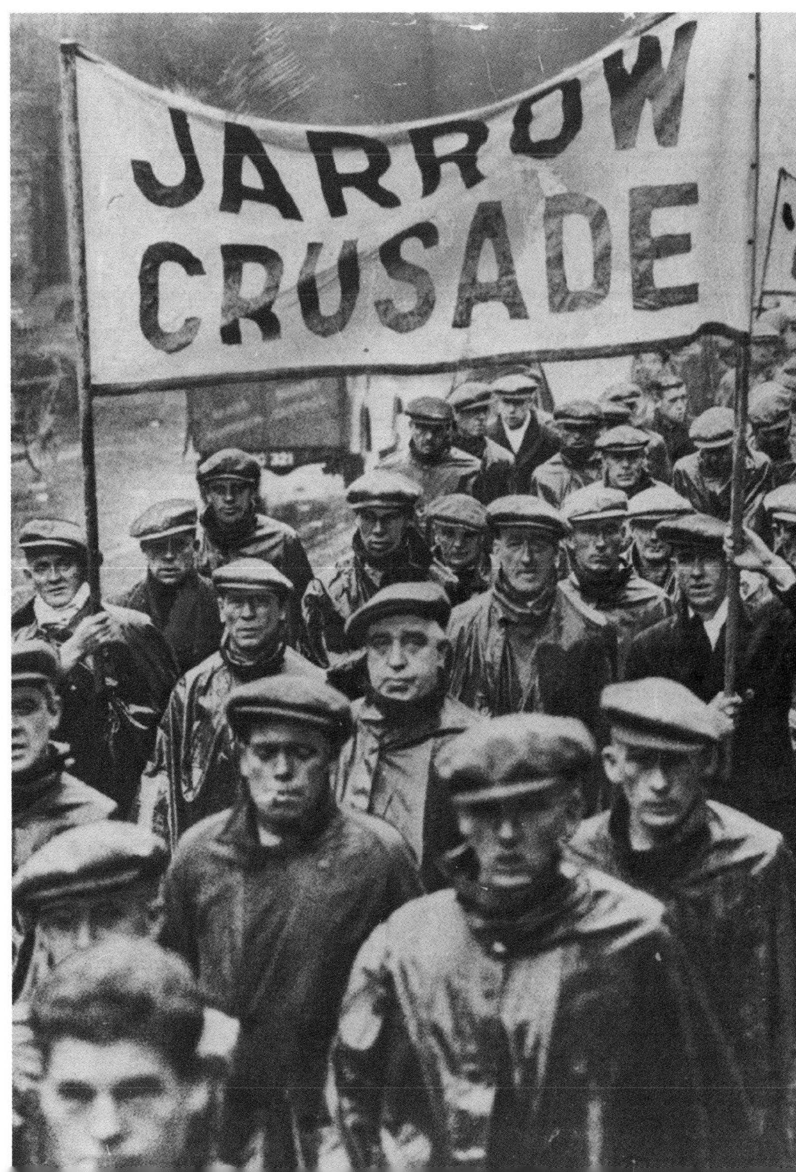

Unemployed shipbuilding workers in England on a protest march for jobs in 1936.

The effects of the Great Depression on Germany

The effects of the Depression on the German economy were worse than in any other European country, simply because Germany lost more aid and had already been weakened by the Treaty of Versailles.

- Many businesses were forced to close. They depended on loans from German or US banks, both of which were calling for their loans to be repaid. Also, there was less demand for most goods, as people could not afford them.
- Many people lost their savings when the banks collapsed and those who could not repay loans on their homes lost those, too.
- Unemployment shot up: in 1929 there were 1.3 million unemployed; by 1932 it was 5.1 million.
- The government cut unemployment payments, to try to cope with having to pay out to so many more people, and then raised taxes to help to pay the benefits.
- The *rentenmark* (Germany's currency) began to lose value. This was particularly significant in Germany. People remembered the inflation of the early 1920s. The introduction of the *rentenmark* in late 1923 had begun a recovery – but they worried that the *rentenmark* was about to collapse in the same way as the *mark* had.

Stresemann, the Chancellor (who had introduced the *rentenmark*), had died. The government could not agree on how to deal with the effect of the Depression. They looked weak. Extremist parties, who had been losing support as the economy recovered, began to gain support again.

Dole queues in Germany in the early 1930s.

- The Communists improved their share of the vote. Many people thought they would have a better life in a country without private ownership of land and business, and with state support for everyone. In the 1929 elections, they won 54 seats. In 1932, they won 89 seats.
- The Nazis made the greatest gains. They ran a clever election campaign that promised the things people so badly needed, such as work and bread. They did not aim at one group in Germany, such as the workers. They targeted the poor and the middle classes, the workers and employers, by playing on their various fears and promising to solve them. In 1929, when the economy was recovering, they only won 12 seats in the German parliament, with about a million votes. In 1932, they won 230 seats and had about 13 million votes.

By exploiting these economic hardships, Adolf Hitler was able to rise to power in Germany: for desperate times brought people to support desperate measures. It was this that gave him the chance to pursue his expansionist ideals on reuniting the German-speakers of Europe.

The Manchurian Crisis

Learning objectives

In this chapter you will learn about:

- the impact of the Great Depression on Japan
- how the League failed to stop Japanese aggression in Manchuria.

The effects of the Great Depression on Japan

Japan suffered more than most countries in the Great Depression. It was a small country with no raw materials (except silk), and its economic well-being depended upon exporting (selling abroad) enough silk to be able to pay for imports of essential items such as coal, rubber and iron for its industries. By 1929 its population had risen to over 65 million and it was having difficulties finding jobs for its people. There were even times when there were food shortages.

When the American economy collapsed in 1929, it put tariffs (taxes) on Japanese goods in order to protect its own industries. As Japan found it more difficult to export its goods, its economy suffered terribly. By 1931, half of its factories had closed and millions were unemployed.

The army's solution

Japan had a very powerful army and its army leaders had great influence. The army leaders had a solution to Japan's problems. Japan needed raw materials, a market for its goods and living space for its surplus population. The solution was obvious: these things could be won by military conquest. The target was obvious as well – since 1904, Japan had held the right to build a railway line through the Chinese province of Manchuria. A Japanese army was based in the area to protect the railway line. Perhaps Japan could extend its influence further into Manchuria? It possessed excellent supplies of coal, iron ore and oil. However, the Japanese government did not approve of such military action.

The Mukden Incident

Then, on 18 September 1931, part of the railway near Mukden was destroyed by a bomb. The Japanese army claimed that the bomb had been set off by Chinese soldiers who had then fired on the Japanese army. According to the army, therefore, it had been 'forced' to invade Manchuria to 'protect' Japanese interests. While it is not known for certain who was responsible for the bombing, it is widely accepted that it was a deliberate attempt by the Japanese army to create a reason for invading Manchuria. Although the Japanese government disapproved of the invasion, the Japanese people greeted the news with enthusiasm and the government was forced to support the army's actions. By February 1932, the Japanese had completed the conquest, renamed the territory 'Manchukuo', and put the last Chinese Emperor, Pu Yi, in control – although he had to do what the Japanese told him.

The Japanese invasion of Manchuria, 1931.

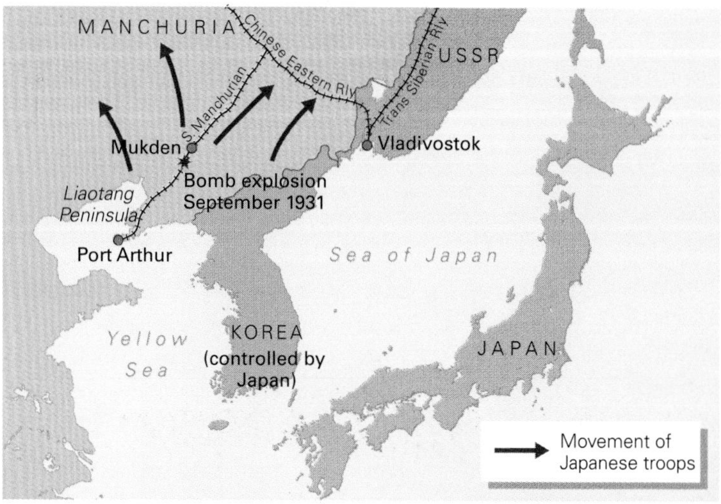

The League's reaction

The Japanese invasion was a test for the League of Nations. The Chinese appealed to the League to act against the Japanese aggression but the League was in a difficult position. It could be argued that Japan was just restoring order in an area where it did have existing rights. There might also be some truth in what Japan was saying about the Mukden Incident. Furthermore, most countries in the League, particularly France and Britain (the two most powerful members), didn't want to take action which meant they had to spend money on their troops, since this would harm their own economies. So what could the League do? Should it apply **economic sanctions**? As Japan's main trading partner was the USA, which was not in the League, they were not likely to work.

The League had to respond to China's appeal, so it set up a commission of inquiry under Lord Lytton. He sailed to China (a journey of several months) and carried out an investigation. In the meantime, the League asked Japan to withdraw its troops from Manchuria. Japan ignored the request.

The Lytton Commission reported in September 1932, one year after the first action. The report said that Japan had acted unlawfully and it should return Manchuria to China. The Japanese response was to ignore the report and leave the League. In 1933 Japan invaded the Chinese province of Jehol. Then in 1937 it began a full-scale invasion of China.

The results of the crisis

In the first major crisis it faced, the League was shown to be powerless. Japan was clearly in the wrong and ignored the League when told to withdraw from Manchuria. However, perhaps the League's reluctance to act was because events in China seemed to pose little threat to world peace – and certainly not to Britain and France. If a similar problem occurred in Europe, people hoped the League would take more decisive action.

Activity

You have been asked to make a short speech on the radio, either criticising the League for its response to the Manchurian crisis, or defending it. Choose which argument you want to give and prepare your speech. It has to last exactly 30 seconds – this is the time the programme has allocated to it.

ResultsPlus
Build Better Answers

Exam question: Explain why the League failed to stop the Japanese invasion of Manchuria. (12 marks)

You need to make relevant points, supported by specific examples, with a clear focus on how each factor led to the situation described.

In each level, the number of statements you make will affect your mark. For example, in level 2, a single developed argument is unlikely to get more than 5 marks, whereas three developed arguments will achieve 8 or 9 marks.

■ **A basic answer (level 1)** is correct, but does not have details to support it. For example:
One reason is because it didn't take very decisive action.

● **A good answer (level 2)** provides the details as well. For example:
One reason is because it didn't take very decisive action. It set up a Commission of Inquiry under Lord Lytton, but it took him several months just to get there. This was an indication to the Japanese that the League didn't really take the matter seriously, so it just carried on with its attack.

▲ **A better answer (level 3)** explains how the reasons are inter-linked or reaches a judgment about their relative importance. For example:
One reason is because it didn't take very decisive action. It set up a Commission of Inquiry under Lord Lytton, but it took him several months just to get there. This was an indication to the Japanese that the League didn't really take the matter seriously, so it just carried on with its attack.

Perhaps the main reason was that the League did not have an army and so was never really going to take military action. It could take economic action and apply sanctions. But there wasn't a whole lot of trade between Western Europe and Japan, anyway, so it would not have much impact. What was needed was support from the USA but it would not agree because it was not in the League. So the lack of an army and the lack of decisive action combined to make the League ineffective in helping China.

The Italian invasion of Abyssinia

Learning objectives

In this chapter you will learn about:

- the ambitions of Mussolini
- how the League failed to stop Italian aggression in Abyssinia.

Italian ambitions

The Italian leader, Mussolini, wanted to build an Italian empire in Africa. Italy already owned Libya, Eritrea and Somaliland. Abyssinia was one of the few independent countries in Africa and Italy had previously tried, unsuccessfully, to conquer it, so it was an obvious target. When 30 Italian soldiers were killed in a border clash with Abyssinian troops in December 1934, Mussolini had the excuse he needed to invade.

The Italian invasion of Abyssinia.

During 1935 Mussolini began preparing his forces for the attack. Britain and France were keen to avoid offending Mussolini as they saw him as a possible ally against Hitler. In April they signed an agreement with him called the Stresa Front. In this, they agreed to stand united against Germany. Mussolini believed that his new friends were prepared to turn a blind eye to what was happening in Abyssinia in return for his friendship.

While Britain and France continued talking to Mussolini in an attempt to avoid an Italian invasion of Abyssinia, a ballot (vote) was held by the League of Nations. It showed that most British people wanted to use military force to protect Abyssinia in the event of an Italian invasion. The ballot made British politicians 'talk tough'. In September, the British foreign secretary, Sir Samuel Hoare, made an impassioned speech to the Assembly of the League calling for collective resistance to Italian aggression. But this seems to have made little difference to events. In fact, in October 1935, Italian forces invaded Abyssinia. Not surprisingly, their modern army, with bomber planes, tanks and poison gas, soon had the Abyssinians, who fought armed only with spears, in retreat.

Activity

Explain whether you agree or disagree with these statements about the League's action during the Italian invasion of Abyssinia.

- **a** They did all they could.
- **b** They should have stopped Mussolini right at the start.
- **c** It didn't work out, but the British and French policy was the best way.

Haile Selassie

Haile Selassie, the Abyssinian emperor, appealed to the League for help. The League had to take measures. It was formed to stop aggression, and Mussolini's invasion was an act of clear aggression. So the League imposed economic sanctions: no weapons were to be sold to Italy and no rubber or iron. It did not ban sales of oil as it thought that Italy could easily buy oil from non-League countries like the USA. However, it agreed to discuss the 'oil issue' further. Even when Mussolini invaded Abyssinia, Britain and France did not close the Suez Canal to Italian ships, which would have caused him great difficulty. They did not want to provoke a war with Mussolini or drive him into an **alliance** with Hitler – nor were they willing to impose sanctions that might threaten their own economic recovery.

Treachery

Behind the scenes, Britain and France worked to find a solution to the problem. The British and French foreign ministers, Samuel Hoare and Pierre Laval, devised a plan to give Mussolini two-thirds of Abyssinia if he agreed to stop fighting. There was uproar when the details of the Hoare–Laval **Pact** were leaked to the press in December 1935. What were the two most important members of the League doing by agreeing to give most of Abyssinia to Italy at a time when the League was supposed to be considering extending sanctions? Both Hoare and Laval were forced to resign but the damage was done. Britain and France had been shown to be putting their own interests first and those of the League second.

Mussolini continued his attack and on 2 May captured the Abyssinian capital, Addis Ababa. A week later he completed the conquest of the country. Haile Selassie fled his country. He travelled to Geneva where he asked the League for help. He told members that they were discussing '*...the value of promises made to small states that their integrity and independence will be respected and ensured*' and that '*God and history will remember your judgments*'.

But it was too late. Abyssinia was in Italian hands and the League was thoroughly discredited. The British and French plan to use Mussolini against Hitler also proved ineffective. In October 1936, Italy and Germany signed an agreement known as the Rome–Berlin Axis in which they agreed to work together more closely. Over the next three years, Hitler's aggressive foreign policy led Europe to war, and the League was powerless to stop it.

Like Manchuria before it, the Abyssinian crisis had proved that the League was ineffective when dealing with the interests of great powers. Over the next three years, Hitler exploited this to the full.

ResultsPlus
Top Tip

A possible examination question about this topic is 'Explain why the League failed to stop the Italian invasion of Abyssinia'. Some students will tell the story of what happened. This is a big mistake. Students who do well will give reasons and then add details. Try adding detail to some of these reasons:

- Britain and France wanted Mussolini as an ally against Hitler.
- Britain and France didn't want to harm their own economies through sanctions.
- The League had no army.
- The British and French governments didn't really care about 'insignificant' Abyssinia – though their people did not necessarily agree.

A British cartoon from 1935, mocking Britain and France – they are shown threatening Mussolini.

Germany and the Treaty of Versailles

Learning objectives

In this chapter you will learn about:

- the impact of the Treaty of Versailles on Germany
- whether the treaty was fair on Germany.

A fair peace?

When the Germans signed the **armistice** at the end of the First World War, they believed that peace would be based on the Fourteen Points put forward in 1914 by President Wilson of the USA. Wilson wanted his Fourteen Points to be the basis of a future in which the horrors of the First World War would never be repeated. Wilson thought Germany should be punished for its role in the war, but not too harshly – if the Germans thought they had been treated unfairly, they might want revenge and start another war.

However, German hopes were soon dashed. Their representatives were not even allowed to attend the peace conference in the magnificent palace of Versailles, near Paris. On 7 May 1919 they were presented with a peace treaty which was much harsher than they had expected. There was no negotiation and the treaty soon became known as a ***'diktat'*** (dictated peace).

A harsh peace?

The treaty said that Germany had to accept full blame for starting the war and, therefore, pay **reparations** (compensation) to the Allies. The amount of compensation was later fixed at £6,600 million. The Germans were also to lose a large amount of territory. All its colonies and over 70,000 square kilometres of land were taken and given to neighbouring countries. Germany itself was split in two by the decision to create a 'Polish Corridor', giving Poland access to the sea.

Germany also had to accept major cutbacks in its armed forces. It was no longer to have an air force and restrictions were placed on the size of its navy and army. No troops were allowed in the Rhineland, the part of Germany on the border with France.

The Germans were stunned by the terms of the treaty and there were mass demonstrations in German cities calling for the treaty to be rejected. But if Germany refused to sign the treaty, it was likely that Allied armies would occupy the country and Germany was not strong enough to restart the war. So on 28 June 1919, two German ministers went to Versailles and signed the treaty.

The German government was immediately blamed by many Germans for its weakness in agreeing to the terms of the treaty. Extremist opponents of the government claimed that it had 'stabbed Germany in the back'. From the start, the German people did not accept the treaty as fair and were prepared to support anyone who promised to reverse its harsh terms.

THE RECKONING.

A British cartoon about the Treaty of Versailles, 1919. It is poking fun at the Germans. Most Germans were complaining that the Treaty of Versailles was too harsh on Germany. This cartoon suggests that Germany would have been harsher on other nations if it had won the war. The German in the cartoon says 'Monstrous, I call it. These reparations are only one-quarter of what we would have made them pay if we had won.'

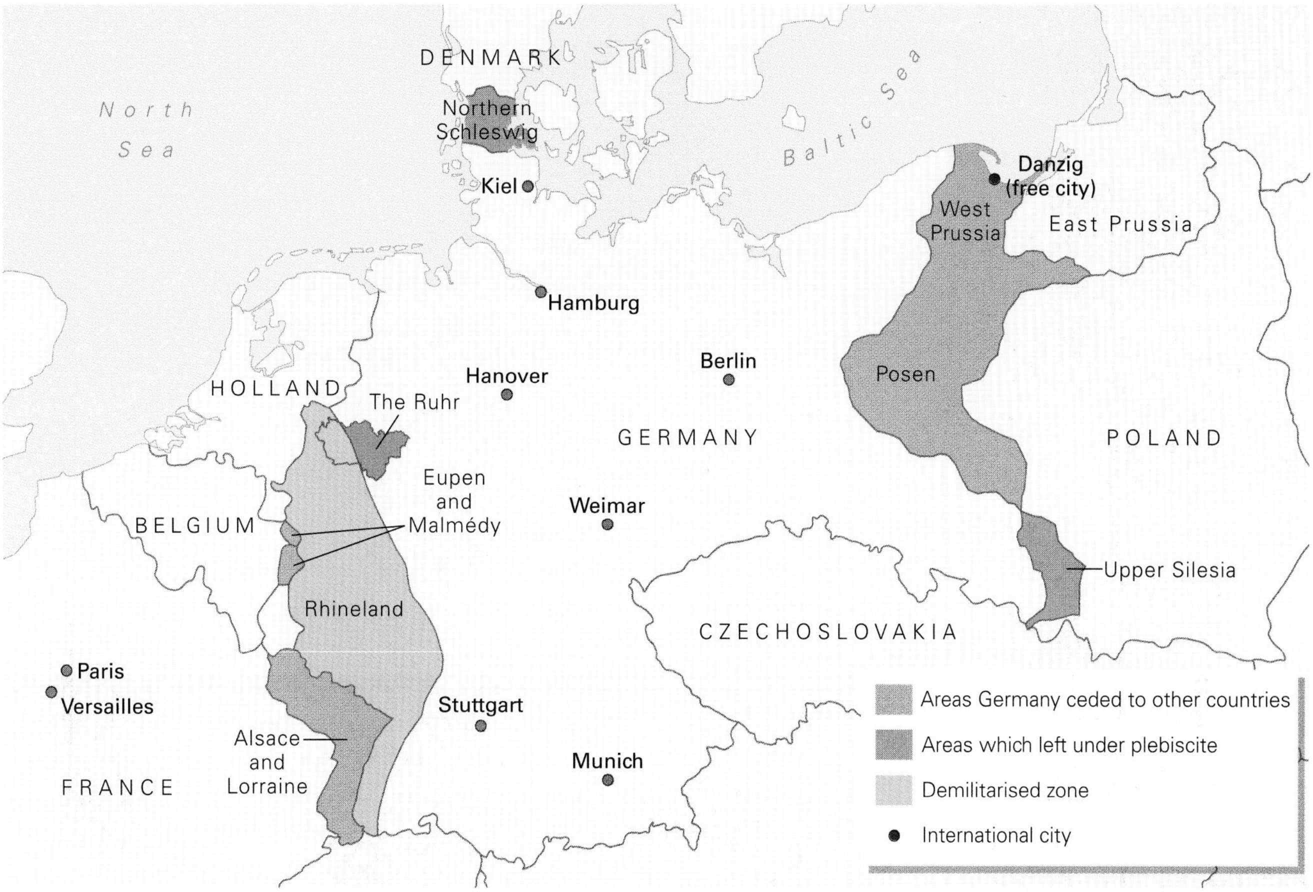

How Germany was affected by the Treaty of Versailles.

> Vengeance! German nation! Today in the Hall of Mirrors at Versailles a disgraceful treaty is being signed. Never forget it! Today German honour is being dragged to the grave. Never forget it! The German people, with unceasing labour, will push forward to reconquer that place amongst the nations of the world to which they are entitled. There will be vengeance for the shame of 1919.

An article in a German newspaper on 28 June 1919.

One of the things you might be asked in the exam is how Hitler broke the Treaty of Versailles. To answer this, you need to know what the treaty said. Students who do well will have remembered the details of the treaty.

Activities

1. How did the Treaty of Versailles affect:
   - **a** Germany's land size
   - **b** Germany's armed forces?
2. Why did the German newspaper, quoted in the written source from June 1919, believe that 'German honour is being dragged to the grave'?

Make sure you know which 'land' you are talking about and what happened to it in post-First World War Germany. The 'Saar' land voted to go back into Germany, the 'Ruhr' land was occupied by the French in 1923 and the 'Rhine' land was remilitarised in 1936. None of them was taken from Germany at Versailles!

Hitler - a growing problem?

Learning objectives

In this chapter you will learn about:

- Hitler's advancement of German foreign policy
- British and French reactions to Hitler's actions.

Tear it up!

Even before Hitler became chancellor in January 1933, he had set out his ideas about future Germany foreign policy in his autobiography *Mein Kampf* (My Struggle). This book provided an opportunity for all to see what Hitler intended to do if he came to power.

1 **The Treaty of Versailles should be torn up**

Hitler saw Versailles as a symbol of the humiliation that Germans had been forced to suffer in 1919. It must be reversed.

2 **Germany must expand**

Hitler wanted back the land lost at Versailles, but he intended to go further. He wanted to create a *Grossdeutschland* (Greater Germany) by bringing together all Germans in one country. This meant joining Austria with Germany and taking over parts of Czechoslovakia and Poland where German-speaking people lived.

Hitler often discussed the expansion of Germany as Germany's need for *lebensraum* – living space. It was much better propaganda than talking about 'invasion' or 'empire'. It made it seem such a natural need. The Nazis said the obvious place to find this *lebensraum* was in the land to the east of Germany, because:

- these borders had always been more disputed and shifting. Some of the land to the east had been given to Germany by the Treaty of Brest Litovsk and unreasonably taken away by the Treaty of Versailles
- there were significant numbers of Germans, or people with German ancestry, living in Eastern Europe. The Nazis said these people, the *Volksdeutsche*, were being badly treated.

The Nazis did not feel it necessary to explain in any detail what would happen to the people already living in the land that would give Germany *lebensraum*. It was enough to say that these people would be 're-settled'.

3 **Communism must be destroyed**

Hitler hated communism and was determined to stop it spreading in Germany. One of the aims of his foreign policy, therefore, was to take over large parts of the Soviet Union.

Hitler's actions

1 **Rearmament**

When Hitler came to power in Germany in 1933, the League of Nations was holding the World Disarmament Conference. At that conference, Germany said it would be happy to accept disarmament if all the other powers gave up their weapons. The French would not agree to this as they feared further attack from Germany, and so Germany left the conference claiming that there was no real desire for disarmament among the major powers.

In 1935, Hitler announced that he had built an air force (the *Luftwaffe*) and that he was introducing **conscription** (compulsory military service). He wanted to create an army of 600,000 men. The Treaty of Versailles had banned conscription and limited Germany's army to 100,000 men but Britain, France and Italy did not take any action against Germany.

2 **The Saar rejoins Germany, 1935**

In 1919, the Saar, an important coal mining area, was placed under the control of the League of Nations for a period of 15 years. When that period ran out, a referendum (public vote) was held to see whether the local people wanted to return to German rule. As around 90% of the population voted to return to Germany, the area was returned to German rule. Hitler was delighted and claimed that the vote showed how popular his rule was.

3 **The re-occupation of the Rhineland, 1936**

At Versailles it had been agreed that the Germans would not station any troops or weapons in the Rhineland – the area bordering France. Hitler argued that this left Germany open to attack from the west.

So on 7 March 1936 he ordered his troops to march into the Rhineland. Hitler's troops were no match for the French army and he had instructed them to withdraw if the French showed any sign of resistance. But Hitler had judged things well. He thought the French would not act without British support, and many British people thought he was just 'marching into his own backyard'. Britain and France certainly didn't want to go to war to stop something which didn't really worry them. So although they condemned Hitler's remilitarisation of the Rhineland, Britain and France took no action.

4 **Making allies – links with Italy and Japan**

Hitler knew that Britain, France and Russia were suspicious of his policies. He knew he would need allies if he went to war, so looked for them in other **totalitarian** regimes.

- On 6 November 1936, Germany and Italy signed the **Rome-Berlin Axis**, an agreement to co-operate. Italy felt threatened by Anglo-French objections to their desire to expand. Later that year, they both supported the Nationalists in the Spanish Civil War, allowing them to test their new military prowess and continue the fight against communism.
- On 25 November 1936, Germany and Japan signed the **Anti-Comintern Pact**. This was supposedly aimed at opposing communism internationally; it did not specifically name the USSR. Japan broke the agreement signed at the Washington Conference with Britain, the USA and France in 1921 to join with Germany.
- On 6 November 1937, Italy joined the Anti-Comintern Pact. The growing solidarity with Germany encouraged Mussolini's invasion of Albania in April 1939. In May, the Rome-Berlin Axis became a military alliance, the Pact of Friendship and Alliance (**Pact of Steel**). Each agreed to help the other if at war.
- On 27 September 1940, Japan joined the Pact, making the **Tripartite Pact** and extending the war to the Pacific. They began to refer to themselves as the 'Axis Powers' – upon which the world revolved. Japan would threaten Britain's colonies and keep the USA at bay, and – Mussolini hoped – balance Hitler's dominance of the Pact.

The Saar was returned to Germany in 1935; Hitler reoccupied the Rhineland in 1936.

These alliances were clearly dangerous. Italy could hold France in check, Japan could threaten the USSR and Germany could hold off central Europe. Belgium, seeing trouble coming, had withdrawn from an alliance with France and declared itself neutral in October 1936. Germany agreed to respect this neutrality in October 1937

The three countries made natural allies: their militaristic rulers had much in common; they shared a desire for expansion through force; and they were united in their hatred of communism and democracy. Hitler knew he would need to fight as Britain moved away from appeasement and the Pact gave him the assurances that he would not do so alone; Mussolini hoped to gain some control over the timing, as he felt Italy's forces would not be ready before 1942; and the Japanese hoped to draw Hitler into war with the USSR - its major rival for dominance in the East.

Activities

1. How did Hitler use the World Disarmament Conference of 1932–33 to his advantage?
2. Explain whether you agree with the following statements:
   - **a** Britain should have stopped the Saar returning to Germany.
   - **b** Hitler knew that Britain and France would not stop him remilitarising the Rhineland.
   - **c** Hitler didn't do anything during the period 1933–36 that Britain and France needed to worry about.
3. Why do you think Hitler wanted to ally with Italy and Japan?

Appeasement in action: Anschluss

Learning objectives

In this chapter you will learn about:

- how appeasement affected Hitler's actions
- how Austria was absorbed into Germany.

Appeasement

In 1936 when Britain and France failed to stop Hitler marching into the Rhineland, it was because they were prepared to allow Germany to break the terms of the Treaty of Versailles, which they recognised as having been too harsh on Germany. There seemed little point risking war by resisting demands from Hitler which seemed perfectly reasonable. This policy of conceding to reasonable demands in order to avoid war became known as **'appeasement'**. It was a policy which Britain followed from the time Hitler came to power, but it is most associated with Neville Chamberlain, who became British prime minister in 1937.

Hitler believed that the policy of appeasement was one of weakness. He was convinced that appeasement meant that Britain and France would do nothing to stop him expanding his territories. He had built up his armed forces and remilitarised the Rhineland without Britain and France interfering. Now he wanted to unite with Austria. The union **(Anschluss)** of the two German-speaking countries, Germany and Austria, had been expressly forbidden in the Treaty of Versailles, but it was one of Hitler's major aims and an important step on the road to building a *Grossdeutschland*. How was Hitler to achieve his aim and at the same time persuade Britain and France that his actions were acceptable?

In 1934 Austrian Nazis had tried to seize power in Austria. Hitler was keen to help them, but the Italian leader, Mussolini, also wanted to have influence in Austria. Mussolini sent 100,000 troops to the Austrian border in case Hitler decided to invade. Hitler backed down. But by 1938 Hitler's armed forces were much stronger. Also, since 1936 Mussolini had been friendly to Germany, signing the Rome–Berlin Axis, so Hitler knew that the Italians would not stop him.

> More than once, even during the war, I heard Hitler say 'The forty eight hours after the march into the Rhineland were the most nerve-wracking of my life.' He always added, 'If the French had then marched into the Rhineland, we would have had to withdraw with our tails between our legs, as the military resources at our disposal would have been completely inadequate for even moderate resistance.'

Hitler's interpreter commenting in 1951 on his memories of the remilitarisation of the Rhineland.

Moves towards Anschluss

The Austrian chancellor, Schuschnigg, had appointed leading Nazis to positions in government, hoping that this would prevent further trouble and stop Germany interfering in Austrian politics. However, in 1938 Austrian police discovered that these Nazis were planning to overthrow the government. Schuschnigg met with Hitler in February 1938 to try to persuade him not to give support to any attempted takeover. To please Hitler, a leading Nazi, Seyss-Inquart, was appointed minister of the interior.

But Schuschnigg also announced that he would hold a **plebiscite** asking the Austrian people if they wished to join with Germany. Hitler was worried that the vote would go against Anschluss and demanded that Schuschnigg resign and Seyss-Inquart take his place. If this did not happen, Germany would invade. On the evening of 11 March, Schuschnigg stood down and was replaced by Seyss-Inquart. But the next morning German troops crossed into Austria to absorb the country into Germany.

Did you know?

Although Hitler is the most famous of all German leaders, he was not born a German. He was born in Austria in 1889 and lived there until 1913 when he moved to Munich. As a German speaker he considered himself German and enrolled in the German army in 1914.

Anschluss achieved

The Austrians did not resist the German invasion and many of them welcomed it. Mussolini offered no support to Austria, and Britain and France did not intervene. Although many people in Britain were concerned that the policy of appeasement had allowed Hitler to break the terms of the Treaty of Versailles once more, they were reassured when a the plebiscite was held on 10 April. In that plebiscite, 99.75% of Austrians who voted said they supported joining with Germany.

Britain and France

Neither Britain nor France took any military action against Hitler. The British believed that the Treaty of Versailles was too harsh when it said Germany and Austria could not unite. There was no way that Britain would go to war to enforce a clause in the treaty which it did not agree with. Hitler saw this as further proof that Britain and France were not prepared to take action to stop him.

German troops are welcomed into the Austrian city of Salzburg, in March 1938. People are waving the Nazi flag – a red background with a black swastika on a white circle.

> As the Austrian leader was leaving the room, Hitler could be heard shouting to his officials 'Tell General Keitel to come here at once' (Keitel was chief of the German armed forces). Keitel told us later that when he arrived and asked for orders, Hitler grinned and said 'There are no orders. I just wanted him [Schuschnigg] to hear me calling you.'

The German ambassador in Vienna describes the negotiations between Hitler and Schuschnigg in 1938.

ResultsPlus
Top Tip

A common exam question is to ask why something happened. For example, you could be asked to 'Explain why Hitler was able to unite Austria and Germany in 1938'. Remember when you get this type of question that it is not only about why Hitler was able to make it happen, it is also about why Britain and France did not stop him.

Activities

1. What was appeasement?
2. What were Hitler's views on appeasement?
3. Read the written source describing the negotiations between Hitler and Schuschnigg and the paragraphs on how Anschluss was achieved. You now have 30 seconds to report to one of your classmates on 'The tactics Hitler used to bring about Anschluss'.

The Sudeten Crisis 1938

Learning objectives

In this chapter you will learn about:

- how Hitler acquired the Sudetenland
- why Britain and France appeased Hitler at the Munich Conference

Next target

After the takeover of Austria, it was clear that Hitler's next target would be Czechoslovakia. Hitler saw Czechoslovakia as a symbol of Germany's humiliation in 1919. Although it had been created largely from territory in the Austro-Hungarian Empire, it contained 3 million German speakers in an area on the German border called the Sudetenland. It was these Sudeten Germans who gave Hitler the excuse to intervene in Czech politics.

The Czech problem

Although Hitler was keen to unite all the German-speaking people, he had other reasons for wanting to control Czechoslovakia. Its geographical position made it a threat to Germany, as its western border came deep into German territory. It was strong militarily and economically, with an army of 34 divisions, deposits of coal and lignite (a type of fuel), and the important Skoda armaments factory. Czechoslovakia could therefore prove a very difficult enemy if it chose to support any opponent of Germany in war. However, most of Czechoslovakia's military resources were in the Sudetenland, so if Hitler could gain those territories, he would extend *Grossdeutschland* and also weaken a potential threat.

Moving against Czechoslovakia

Hitler ordered the leaders of the Czech Nazi Party to begin making demands for a role in the Czech government. At first the Czech government made concessions but the Czech Nazis kept increasing their demands. President Benes of Czechoslovakia refused to make further concessions. Hitler told the Sudeten Germans he would support them if they caused further difficulties for Benes and, on 12 September 1938, they began rioting.

President Benes crushed the rioters, but knew German intervention was inevitable. It seemed that war between Czechoslovakia and Germany was only days away. Would he get support from the Western powers?

Chamberlain intervenes

Britain and France were not willing to go to war with Germany to help the Czechs. The British prime minister, Chamberlain, flew to meet Hitler at Berchtesgarden in Germany to discuss his demands. Chamberlain then visited Benes, the Czech leader. Benes realised that he would not get support from Britain and agreed to transfer to Germany those parts of the Sudetenland where the majority of the population was German. It looked as if a deal had been done. But when Chamberlain met Hitler on 22 September and told him about the agreement, Hitler said it was not enough. He had heard that the Sudeten Germans were being 'mistreated' and said that if he did not have all of the Sudetenland in his possession by 1 October, he would need to invade to 'rescue' the Sudeten Germans.

The Munich Conference

Chamberlain was dismayed by Hitler's reaction. He returned to Britain and began preparing for war. In London, trenches were dug to protect the people from air raids and gas masks were distributed. Chamberlain was determined to avoid war, but he could not see how this could be achieved.

Then Mussolini proposed a meeting between Britain, France, Italy and Germany to resolve the crisis. Chamberlain was delighted. The four powers met in Munich on 29 September. There they agreed that the Sudetenland should become part of Germany, but the new borders of Czechoslovakia were also guaranteed. The French and British were even able to congratulate themselves that they had 'saved' Czechoslovakia.

Czechoslovakia after the agreement at Munich.

German troops entered the Sudetenland on 1 October 1938. Within weeks, Hungary and Poland also took parts of Czechoslovakia where Hungarians and Poles were in the majority. No action was taken to stop this.

Neither the Soviet Union, nor Czechoslovakia, was invited to attend the Munich Conference. The two countries would have opposed the terms of the agreement but they were not consulted. The Czech leader, Benes, resigned in disgust. The Soviet leader, Stalin, saw the event as another example of the Great Powers ignoring the Soviet Union.

A cartoon from a British newspaper, 30 September 1938. In it Stalin is asking why he was not invited to the Munich Conference. Czechoslovakia was on his doorstep and Hitler was his enemy, so he was seriously offended by being left out.

On 30 September 1938, Chamberlain and Hitler signed the Anglo-German Declaration, in which Britain and Germany declared that they would settle all disputes between them by negotiation; they would never go to war again. As Chamberlain told the British people on his return from Munich, 'I believe it is peace for our time.'

ResultsPlus
Top Tip

In the exam, you might be asked a question like 'Describe the key features of the Sudetenland Crisis.' To answer this you should not just write everything you know. Students who do well will organise details under a number of headings (representing features) and then write to support those. For this exam question, the features might be:

- many German-speakers lived in the area
- Czechoslovakia was a powerful country
- Hitler encouraged Czech Nazis to begin causing trouble
- Britain and France would not support Benes if it meant war with Germany
- there was a conference and agreement at Munich.

ResultsPlus
Watch out!

Don't make the mistake of thinking that the Munich Agreement was just between Britain and Germany. Both Italy and France were at the conference too – but not Czechoslovakia or the Soviet Union!

Activities

1. Why did Hitler want the Sudetenland to become part of Germany?
2. How similar were Hitler's tactics in the Sudetenland to those he used in Austria?
3. Write a short paragraph explaining how each of the following might have felt about the Munich Agreement:
   - **a** Hitler
   - **b** Chamberlain
   - **c** Benes
   - **d** Stalin.

The road to war

Learning objectives

In this chapter you will learn about:

- the importance of the Nazi–Soviet Pact
- the events that resulted in Europe going to war in 1939.

Hopes shattered

Chamberlain's hope that he had achieved 'peace for our time' was soon shown to be misplaced. He had negotiated with Hitler in the belief that the German Chancellor was an honourable man who would keep his promises, but this was not the case. Six months after Munich, on 15 March 1939, Hitler ordered his troops into Bohemia and Moravia, two parts of Czechoslovakia that were protected by the Munich Agreement. Hitler could no longer claim that he was restoring German-speaking people to the rightful homeland or reversing injustices carried out at Versailles. Chamberlain now knew that Hitler could not be trusted. Appeasement was dead and Britain began building up its arms for a war which now seemed inevitable. Chamberlain introduced conscription – for the first time ever in peacetime Britain.

Memel

Then, on 20 March, Hitler demanded that the city of Memel, in Lithuania, be returned to Germany – Memel had been made a 'free city' under the Treaty of Versailles. Two days later, fearing a German invasion, Lithuania handed over control of Memel to Hitler. The League of Nations could do nothing to stop Hitler, and Britain and France were not prepared to go to war to protect the Treaty of Versailles. But they did realise that a stand now had to be made against Hitler's aggression.

Guaranteeing Poland

After the seizure of Czechoslovakia it was obvious that Hitler's next target would be Poland. The Germans had always resented the loss of the Polish Corridor at Versailles, and in 1938 Hitler had begun to talk of the need to bring this territory back into Germany. On 31 March, Britain and France promised Poland that if it were threatened, they would guarantee its independence. They offered similar guarantees to Romania and Greece. They also approached the Soviet Union to try to form an anti-Nazi alliance to stop Hitler. But Stalin did not trust Britain and France. They had not invited him to the Munich Conference and he was not keen to enter into an agreement just to protect Western Europe. So negotiations broke down in July 1939.

The Nazi–Soviet Pact

During 1939, Stalin had also received visits from the German foreign minister, Ribbentrop, and on 23 August 1939 the sensational announcement was made that the two bitter enemies, Hitler and Stalin, had signed the Nazi–Soviet Pact. They agreed not to fight each other, but secretly they also agreed to divide Poland between them. It seemed shocking that the Soviet Union had signed an agreement with a country whose leader wanted to wipe out communism. But Stalin wanted to stop an attack on his country. Britain and France had a deep suspicion of the Soviet Union and Stalin believed that what they really wanted was for Germany and the Soviet Union to go to war so that each would be weakened. This pact would give him time to strengthen his forces for the inevitable war with Germany.

Hitler did hate communism, but after signing the pact he knew that if he invaded Poland he would not have to fight the Soviet Union. He did not believe that Britain and France would go to war to support Poland, so he believed that the pact would allow him to take a large part of the country without war. Even if Britain and France did declare war, Germany's eastern border was now secured by an alliance with the Soviet Union and he did not have to face the prospect of a war on two 'fronts'.

Watch out!

Students sometimes confuse the Nazi–Soviet Pact, with the Rome–Berlin Axis. It's easy to remember which is which: the 'M' in Mussolini (who signed the Axis) comes before the 'S' in Stalin (who signed the Pact). Axis also comes before Pact, so you should be able to work out which agreement is which and which came first.

To Hitler's surprise, Chamberlain reacted to the Nazi–Soviet Pact by offering support to Poland in the Anglo-Polish Mutual Assistance Pact on 25 August. But Hitler was not put off by Chamberlain's action. His experience over the Sudetenland had convinced him that Britain and France would not go to war. He also knew that the Soviet Union would be happy to see him invade Poland.

So, on 1 September, Germany invaded Poland. Britain and France demanded Hitler withdraw his forces and when he did not, they declared war on Germany on 3 September. The Soviet Union invaded Poland on 17 September. Within weeks Polish forces had been defeated and Poland was divided between Germany and the Soviet Union.

Why did Germany and the Soviet Union sign the Nazi–Soviet Pact?

 Germany can invade Poland without having to fight the Soviet Union. I can continue my policy of building Grossdeutschland, reversing Versailles and gaining new lands for Germans to settle in. The agreement will stop the Soviet Union allying with Britain and France.	 The Soviet Union will regain parts of Poland which have historically been part of Russia. There will be no war with Germany. I do not trust Britain and France. In 1939 our military forces are weak. I am sure war with Germany will come eventually. This pact will give me time to strengthen our forces.

Someone is taking someone for a walk. A British cartoon published shortly after the signing of the Nazi–Soviet Pact. It suggests that Hitler and Stalin were each trying to fool the other by signing the pact.

ResultsPlus

Build Better Answers

Exam question: Describe the key features of the Nazi–Soviet Pact. (6 marks)

You need to identify important points, not simply write all you know. Here, for example, you could choose to describe a cause of the crisis, an event within it and an effect of it.

■ **A basic answer (level 1)** gives simple statements that are accurate, but contain no supporting detail.

● **A good answer (level 2)** gives a statement that is accurate and is developed with specific information.

▲ **An excellent answer (full marks)** contains two or three statements. Each statement describes a relevant key feature and is backed up with specific information.

For the question above, the following would be good features to develop:

- Soviet fears
- German plans
- the policies of Britain and France.

Activities

1. What events took place in March 1939 which showed that appeasement was dead?
2. What steps did Britain and France take to protect Poland?
3. Why was the Nazi–Soviet Pact such a surprise to people in Britain and France?

Flashpoint Europe!

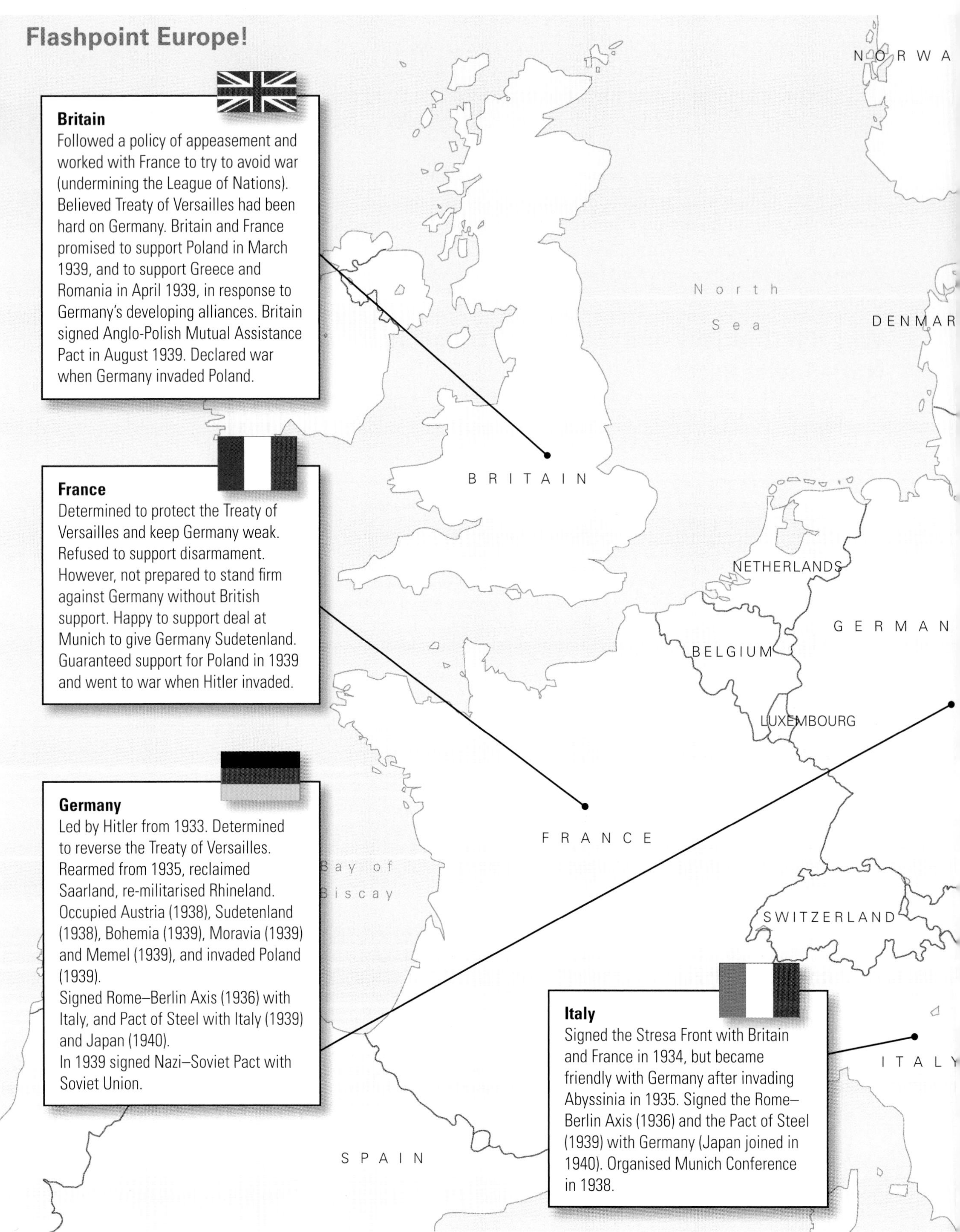

Britain

Followed a policy of appeasement and worked with France to try to avoid war (undermining the League of Nations). Believed Treaty of Versailles had been hard on Germany. Britain and France promised to support Poland in March 1939, and to support Greece and Romania in April 1939, in response to Germany's developing alliances. Britain signed Anglo-Polish Mutual Assistance Pact in August 1939. Declared war when Germany invaded Poland.

France

Determined to protect the Treaty of Versailles and keep Germany weak. Refused to support disarmament. However, not prepared to stand firm against Germany without British support. Happy to support deal at Munich to give Germany Sudetenland. Guaranteed support for Poland in 1939 and went to war when Hitler invaded.

Germany

Led by Hitler from 1933. Determined to reverse the Treaty of Versailles. Rearmed from 1935, reclaimed Saarland, re-militarised Rhineland. Occupied Austria (1938), Sudetenland (1938), Bohemia (1939), Moravia (1939) and Memel (1939), and invaded Poland (1939).
Signed Rome–Berlin Axis (1936) with Italy, and Pact of Steel with Italy (1939) and Japan (1940).
In 1939 signed Nazi–Soviet Pact with Soviet Union.

Italy

Signed the Stresa Front with Britain and France in 1934, but became friendly with Germany after invading Abyssinia in 1935. Signed the Rome–Berlin Axis (1936) and the Pact of Steel (1939) with Germany (Japan joined in 1940). Organised Munich Conference in 1938.

Poland
A target for both Germany and the Soviet Union. Despite promises from Britain and France, its fate was sealed when Germany and the Soviet Union signed the Nazi–Soviet Pact (1939).

Soviet Union
Communist country with very poor relations with Britain and France. Not invited to Munich Conference (1938) even though Czechoslovakia was on Soviet border.
Shocked Britain and France by signing Nazi–Soviet Pact in 1939 and seizing eastern Poland (1940) after Germans invaded.

Czechoslovakia
Strong military force and solid economy. However, no match for Germany and forced to give up Sudetenland to Germany when Britain and France agreed to this at Munich Conference (1938). Hitler then invaded Bohemia and Moravia in 1939.

Austria
Only a minor European power after the First World War. Unable to stop Hitler taking control in 1936.

Appeasement: right or wrong?

Learning objectives

In this chapter you will learn about:

- how to take an overview of Britain's reaction to German foreign policy, 1933–39
- how to make a historical judgment based on a series of events.

By September 1939 it was clear that Britain's policy of appeasement had failed. Chamberlain had tried to avoid war by making concessions to Hitler in the hope that each demand Hitler made was his last one. But eventually Britain and France had been forced to take a stand and had declared war when Germany invaded Poland.

At the time there were many opponents of appeasement. Politicians such as Winston Churchill saw it as a policy of weakness and believed that Hitler could not be trusted. The vast majority of the British people did not trust Hitler either.

Looking back after the horrors of the Second World War, it is easy to criticise Britain for not acting more decisively. Appeasement was based on avoiding war by making concessions and trusting Hitler. But Hitler showed that he could not be trusted and drove Europe to war. So does this mean that appeasement was the wrong policy? Here are the arguments for and against appeasement. Read them and decide what you think.

Arguments in favour of appeasement

- In 1938 it was just 20 years since the end of the most devastating war in the history of mankind. Some 20 million people died in the First World War and the economies of the major powers were destroyed. No one wanted to see more killing, and with Europe still in the grips of the Great Depression, there was little money to spare to bear the costs of another war.
- There was great sympathy for Germany in Britain as many people felt that it had been badly treated at Versailles. Thus, reaching a naval agreement with Britain, remilitarising the Rhineland and uniting with Austria all seemed acceptable moves for Germany to take – even the Nazi occupation of the Sudetenland could be seen as reasonable. Chamberlain himself had talked about 'how horrible, fantastic, incredible' it was that Britain was thinking of going to war 'because of a quarrel between people of whom we know nothing', and many Britons agreed with him.
- In the years leading up to the Second World War, Stalin had carried out reforms in the Soviet Union which made his country stronger. Western politicians had genuine fears that Stalin would try to spread communism into their countries. Hitler was strongly anti-communist and so remaining on good terms with him made sense.
- Perhaps the most convincing argument for appeasement was that in 1936, Britain was not ready for war. It simply did not have the military resources to fight Hitler. The policy of appeasement gave Britain time to rearm and be better placed to fight.

The arguments against appeasement

- Appeasement was based on trust and people acting in an honourable way. Chamberlain was an honourable man who believed what Hitler told him. So, at every step, Chamberlain believed that Hitler was happy with what they had agreed and would make no further demands, but Hitler was unscrupulous and just saw each concession as weakness.
- Hitler exploited each concession by making more demands. When Britain and France took no action, his belief that they would not stop him became stronger.
- A major issue in considering whether appeasement was justified is to look at it from a moral point of view. Britain and France did not want war, but does that mean it is justifiable to allow Hitler to break international agreements designed to keep peace? Was it acceptable to betray the Czechs by giving their land away at Munich, a conference to which they had not been invited?
- Appeasement was too one-sided. It is one thing to make concessions to avoid war, but Britain and France could have stopped Hitler without war – or at least made him realise that he could not always get what he wanted. Even a moderate show of force in 1936 would have stopped Hitler remilitarising the Rhineland, for example.

So was appeasement a wise policy or just a weak reaction to the threat from Hitler?

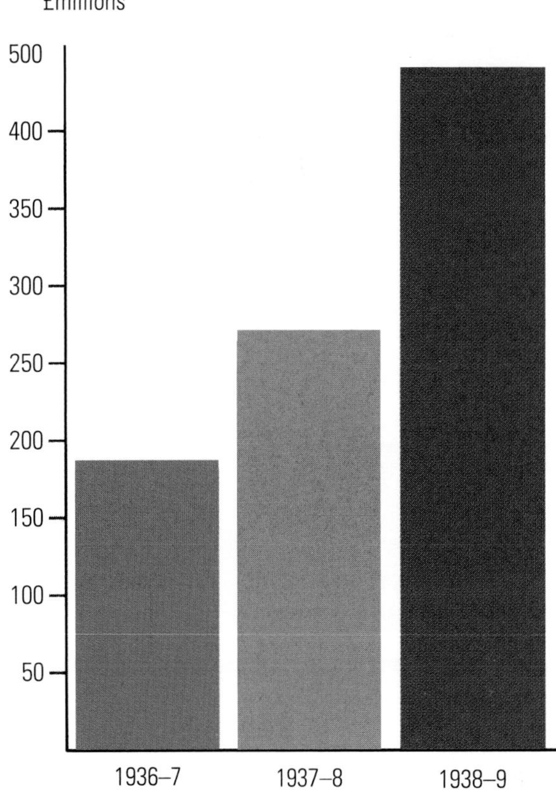

British spending on its armed forces (in £ millions).

Activities

You are taking part in a debate on appeasement. The problem is that you don't know whether you are speaking for or against appeasement. The debate will be about Britain's reaction to the following events:

a German rearmament

b the remilitarisation of the Rhineland

c Anschluss

d the Sudetenland crisis.

For each event, you need to prepare an argument as if you were a supporter of appeasement and an argument as if you were an opponent of appeasement.

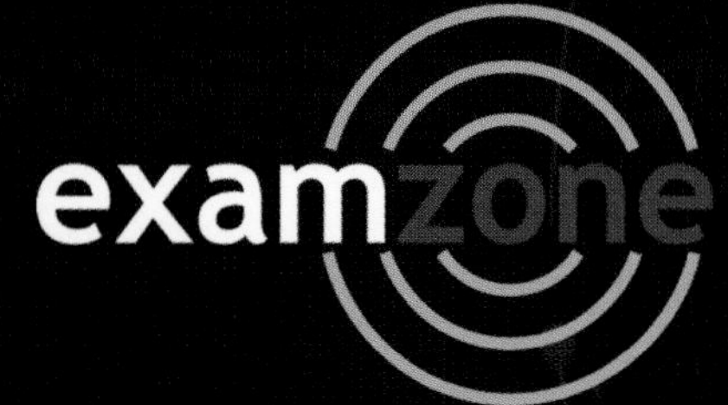

Know Zone
Unit 1 - section 3

In the Unit 1 exam, you will be required to answer questions from three sections. In each of those sections you will have to answer three questions: Part (a), Part (b) – where you have to do one of two questions set – and Part (c).

You have about 25 minutes to answer the three questions on each section. Use the number of marks available for each question to help you judge how long to spend on it and how much to write.

Here we are going to look at questions for Parts (a) and (c) of Section 3.

ResultsPlus
Build Better Answers

Question (a)

Tip: Part (a) questions will ask you to identify an action, decision, cause, factor or way something changed and then give some supporting detail to get the second mark.
Let's look at an example:

Describe one reason why the Germans hated the Treaty of Versailles. (2 marks)

Student answer	Examiner comment
The Germans hated the Treaty of Versailles because they lost strength.	The answer is certainly brief and it does give a reason, but we need to do a little more to get the second mark. We need to provide a bit more support for our statement.

Let's rewrite the answer with supporting detail.

The Germans hated the Treaty of Versailles because they lost strength. They had to agree to a reduction in armed forces.	A reason identified and supported with knowledge. That's all you have to do for 2 marks.

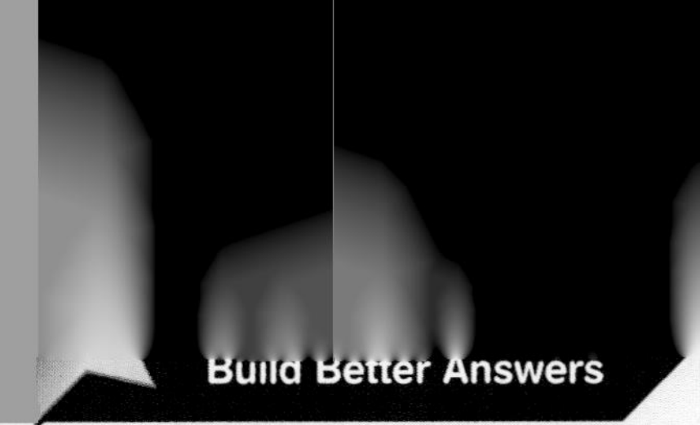

Question (c)

Tip: Part (c) questions require extended writing. They will ask you to use your knowledge to explain why something happened. You should try to find three reasons and explain them. Remember that you will have only about 15 minutes to answer this question and so you need to get straight to the point. Let us look at an example.

Explain why relations between Britain and Germany changed in 1939. (12 marks)

Student answer	**Examiner comment**
At the beginning of 1939 Britain and Germany were on quite good terms. It was only a few months since they had signed the Munich Agreement and the Anglo-German Declaration. But during 1939 a number of things happened which caused the relations to get worse. First of all Hitler invaded Czechoslovakia, then he signed the Nazi-Soviet Pact and finally he invaded Poland. So relations changed.	This isn't really a very good answer. It tells the story of 1939 briefly and does say relations got worse because of events. *But*, remember that you need to identify the causes, give some historical detail and make a link between the causes and the question. In the above example we aren't told why the Nazi–Soviet Pact caused a change of relations – just that it did!

Let's rewrite this so that it explains the causes.

At the beginning of 1939 Britain and Germany were on quite good terms. It was only a few months since they had signed the Munich Agreement and the Anglo-German Declaration. But during 1939 a number of things happened which caused the relations to get worse. First of all it became apparent to Britain that they could not trust Hitler. British foreign policy was based on appeasement. This involved negotiating with Hitler to reach agreement. Hitler had said that after Munich he had no more territorial demands. So when he invaded Czechoslovakia he showed he was a liar and British policy had to change. The policy also had to change when he signed the Nazi-Soviet Pact. This was an agreement between Hitler and Stalin not to go to war. Britain had been presuming that Hitler could not invade Poland because Stalin would stop him. Now Chamberlain knew this was not the case relations had to change. So Chamberlain made an agreement with Poland.	Now we have two distinct reasons: the invasion of Czechoslovakia and the Nazi–Soviet Pact fully explained to show why relations changed. But if you want full marks you have to give three reasons and prioritise them by making links between them. Something like this would do the job nicely. …I suppose, in the end, the invasion of Czechoslovakia and the signing of the Nazi–Soviet Pact amount to the same thing. In 1939 Hitler showed that he could not be trusted. When Chamberlain realised this, he knew it was rearmament, not appeasement, that was needed.

Section 4: How did the Cold War develop? 1943–56

How many world wars have there been? This seems like an easy question. There were two – the first between 1914 and 1918, and the second between 1939 and 1945. However, some American writers have suggested that there was a Third World War, between Russia and America, which started in 1945 and ended in 1991 with the fall of the Soviet Union. This war is better known as the Cold War.

In this section you will study:

- why the Cold War began: the end of the Grand Alliance – how allies became enemies
- the development of the Cold War: dividing Germany and Europe, 1947–49
- Hungary under Soviet rule, 1949–56.

You will consider the breakdown in trust between the USSR (the Union of Soviet Socialist Republics, also known as the Soviet Union or by its old name, Russia) and America following their victory in the Second World War, and how this led to a division of Europe. Additionally, you will see how ideology, the personalities of powerful men, and the development of the atom bomb intensified conflict in the late 1940s. Finally, you will consider the first two flashpoints of the Cold War: Berlin and Hungary.

What was the Cold War?

Can we really call the Cold War the Third World War? There were important differences between the First World War and the Second World War on the one hand, and the Cold War on the other. The Cold War was a new kind of conflict in which America and the USSR never declared war on each other, nor did American and Soviet soldiers face each other in battle. In fact, during much of the time there was a 'Cold Peace' – a stand-off between the USSR and America – because both sides knew that a real Third World War, a nuclear war, would be unwinnable.

However, although the USSR and America never fought each other, the Cold War had many of the characteristics of an actual war. For example, both sides were involved in an **arms race**, a military build-up of nuclear weapons as well as armies, navies and air forces. Both sides formed military **alliances** and were involved in spying on each other. Each side was committed to a different set of ideas or ideology. Finally, **propaganda** was an essential aspect of the Cold War. Governments used propaganda to persuade their own citizens that they were under threat and therefore that the military build-up was necessary. Propaganda was also essential to show why enemies were evil and why they needed to be fought.

A thermonuclear test explosion in 1954. The USSR and America never used atomic weapons against each other, however, the development of arms and fear of a nuclear holocaust characterised the Cold War period.

Why did the Cold War begin? The breakdown of the Grand Alliance

Learning objectives

In this chapter you will learn about:

- the difference between communism and capitalism
- the three key meetings of the Grand Alliance
- the difficult relationship between Russia and America.

The Grand Alliance (1941)

Prior to the Cold War, America and the USSR worked together as members of the **Grand Alliance**: an alliance created in 1941 to defeat the **Nazis**. However, the Grand Alliance was a marriage of convenience between communists and capitalists united only in their opposition to Hitler. Once Hitler had been defeated, the Alliance became increasingly uneasy. Between 1943 and 1945, the leaders of the Grand Alliance met at three international conferences: Teheran, Yalta and Potsdam.

	Capitalism	Communism
Focus	Individual rights	The rights of the working class
Values	Individual freedom	Equality
Economy:	Free trade	Government planned
Politics	Democratic elections	Communist Party controls government

The leaders each wanted the others to recognise that there were countries that fell within their 'sphere of influence' and countries that did not. None of the official documents that were signed laid out these spheres. Nevertheless, by the end of the three conferences, it was clear that there was broad agreement over what these were.

- The USSR would 'influence' Poland, Czechoslovakia, the Baltic States, Hungary and Romania. This would build a line of 'buffer states' between the USSR and the West. Stalin agreed this could be 'influence' only, with these states having free elections and a level of democracy (this was built into the signed document at Yalta).
- The USSR also wanted its influence in Yugoslavia (which had its own communist government) accepted. Yugoslavia was officially accepted as a communist country at Yalta.
- Britain and the USA were keen to get the USSR to accept their influence in Western Europe, Greece and Italy.

The Teheran Conference (1943)

When Churchill, Stalin and Roosevelt met at Teheran (28 November-1 December 1943), they reached some definite agreements and some agreements in principle (without outlining the detail). Stalin was annoyed that Britain and the USA had delayed opening a second front in the war. He was convinced they were waiting for the communist USSR to damage itself fatally in the battle against Nazi Germany before they would intervene.

- The USA and Britain would open a second front to split the German defences and take some of the pressure off the USSR. Stalin had been urging them to do this for some time, while Britain and the USA had wanted to focus on a single front. However, Roosevelt supported the second front idea and it was agreed to start in June 1944.
- The USSR would declare war on Japan once Germany was defeated.
- Poland should be given more land from Germany, but lose some to the USSR.

But there were points of disagreement, over which Roosevelt often sided with Stalin, not Churchill. For example, Churchill wanted to begin an invasion of the Balkans. While this would help the war effort, he mainly wanted it to stop the Soviet advance in Eastern Europe (and via this the spread of communism).

Not surprisingly, Stalin opposed this and Roosevelt supported Stalin. He favoured the second front in the west proposed by Stalin and an invasion of the Balkans as well would have weakened the Allied forces by splitting them up too much.

The Yalta Conference (1945)

When Churchill, Stalin and Roosevelt met at Yalta (4-11 February 1945), they agreed on some of the same things they had agreed at Teheran, but with some changes.

- Germany, when defeated, would be reduced in size, would be demilitarised and would have to pay reparations (these would be taken in materials, goods and labour).
- Plans were begun for how Germany would be divided after the war. The rebuilding of Europe was to be done along the lines of the Atlantic Charter agreed between the USA and Britain in 1941, the most important policy of which was the right of countries to choose their own governments.
- The Nazi Party would be banned and war criminals tried in front of an international court.
- A United Nations Organisation (UN) would be set up to replace the League of Nations. It would meet for the first time on 25 April 1945. It was decided who would be members: all the Allies and those who had agreed to join the UN on 8 February 1945. The Soviet Republics of Ukraine and Belorussia were to be seen as separate countries from the USSR and to have their own voting rights. The USA would draw up the Charter.
- The USSR would declare war on Japan three months after the defeat of Germany. There was an outline of how lands held by Japan would be divided after the war (the USSR would have land Japan had captured returned).
- Poland (at present communist, under Soviet control) should be in the Soviet 'sphere of influence' but be run on 'a broader democratic basis'.

The conference was a success largely because of the understanding between Stalin and Roosevelt, established at Teheran in 1943. Roosevelt also worked well with Churchill. However, splits were growing. Britain and the USA had been reluctant to agree to Poland becoming communist. Britain had entered the Second World War to defend Poland, while America wished to avoid communism spreading further west and antagonising the many Americans who had Polish roots. Stalin, on the other hand, desperately wanted Poland as a buffer between the USSR and the West. The USSR had been invaded from the West no less than three times already that century.

Signs of tension

In spite of the apparent unity, there were important issues that divided the 'Big Three' – Stalin, Roosevelt and Churchill. For example, although they all agreed to work for democracy, there were significant disagreements over what democracy meant.

Stalin believed that a democratic government had to be a communist government because only the communists truly represented the working people. Roosevelt, on the other hand, believed that democracy involved a number of different political parties competing to win the people's support in free elections.

The success of the conference was based largely on Stalin's relationship with Roosevelt. However, within two months Roosevelt had died and the new American President, Harry S. Truman, was less willing to compromise with Stalin. This led to further tensions at the Alliance's final conference.

The 'Big Three' at the Yalta Conference, February 1945. From left to right: Churchill, Roosevelt, Stalin.

The Potsdam Conference (1945)

When Churchill, Stalin and Truman met at Potsdam (July and August 1945), there was far more tension. President Truman had been briefed about the earlier conferences. But he had no relationship with Stalin. To add to the disruption, the result of the British election came during the conference, and the new Labour Prime Minster, Attlee, replaced Churchill.

So the personal trust and understanding built up in earlier conferences was lost. Truman had delayed the first meeting of the conference until after the new **atomic bomb** had been tested. The fact that Stalin had been told nothing of the bomb until this point increased his suspicion of his allies. Also, Germany was defeated, so the Big Three were no longer united by a common enemy.

Despite this, they reached agreement on many points concerning the reconstruction of Europe. It went into great detail about the terms as they applied to Germany – from how reparations were to be paid to how the military equipment was to be broken up. They agreed to:

- set up a Council of Foreign Ministers to organise the re-building of Europe.
- ban the Nazi Party and prosecute surviving Nazis as war criminals in a special court run by the Allies at Nuremberg
- reduce the size of Germany
- divide Germany into four zones, to be administered by the USA, the USSR, Britain and France, with the aim of re-uniting it under one government as soon as possible
- divide Berlin, Germany's capital, into four as well, despite it being deep in the USSR's zone
- the USSR could have a quarter of the industrial equipment from the other three zones, because its zone was the least developed industrially, but had to provide the other zones with raw materials such as coal.

Once again, however, there was disagreement on bigger issues.

Examination question

Describe one issue that caused tension at the Potsdam Conference (1945). (2 marks)

Reparations

The USSR wanted to impose heavy reparations on Germany, whereas America wanted Germany to be rebuilt. The Conference agreed a compromise whereby each ally would take reparations from the zone they occupied. This was far less than Stalin wanted, as the part of Germany that he controlled was poorer than the rest and had much less industry. As a result, the Western Allies agreed that the USSR could have a quarter of the industrial equipment from the Western zones, but stated that they would have to pay for much of this with East German raw materials such as coal.

The atomic bomb

Truman attempted to assert his authority during the Potsdam Conference. He believed that America possessed the ultimate weapon in the atomic bomb and therefore, in Churchill's words, 'generally bossed the whole meeting'. Truman believed that the atomic bomb was 'the master card' in the Potsdam discussions. It gave America the power to destroy entire enemy cities without risking a single American life. Stalin refused to be pushed around. Truman later remarked that when Stalin was informed about the bomb he 'showed no special interest'. However, Stalin was well aware of the significance of the atomic bomb and had, as early as 1940, instructed Soviet scientists to develop their own. News of the American bomb made Stalin more determined than ever to protect the interests of the USSR. Stalin's plan was to protect the USSR by creating a 'buffer zone' – a communist area in Eastern Europe between the USSR and the capitalist west.

Poland

Truman's arrogance and Stalin's determination soured the relationship at the centre of the Grand Alliance. Their relationship was further strained by the USSR's actions in Poland. Stalin had agreed to set up a government in Poland that included both communists and capitalists. However, by the time of the Potsdam Conference it was evident that he had broken his word.

Although the Potsdam Conference finished with a show of unity, insiders at the conference were aware that there were bitter divisions between America and the USSR, which some thought would lead to a new war.

Greece

An early battleground for these tensions was found in Greece. The German retreat in 1944 left two groups fighting to rule the country: monarchists and communists. In 1945 British troops were sent in to support the monarchists under the claim of restoring order and supervising free elections. The USSR complained to the United Nations and a civil war erupted. When the British decided to pull out, in 1947, the US stepped in to prop up the king's government.

Exam question: Describe one decision that was made about the division of Europe at the Yalta Conference in 1945. (2 marks)

You need to make a developed statement, a statement that both answers the question and provides some detailed support.

■ **A basic answer (level 1):**
At the Yalta Conference it was agreed that the USA and USSR would have influence in Europe.

● **A good answer (level 2):**
At the Yalta Conference it was agreed that both the USA and USSR should have a 'sphere of influence' in Europe within which their interests would be respected. The USSR's sphere of influence would be Eastern Europe.

Activities

1 Divide the following conference aims into those belonging to the USA, those belonging to the USSR, and those shared by both:

- a 'sphere of influence' in Eastern Europe
- reparations from Germany
- governments representing working people
- a peaceful and prosperous Germany
- governments elected by the people
- prosecution of Nazi war criminals
- a communist government in Poland
- democratic governments across Europe.

2 The three conferences – Teheran, Yalta and Potsdam – form the background to the Cold War. During this period it became clear that relations between the USSR and America were uneasy. This activity will help you to understand how these relationships developed.

- On a large piece of paper, draw the following axes:

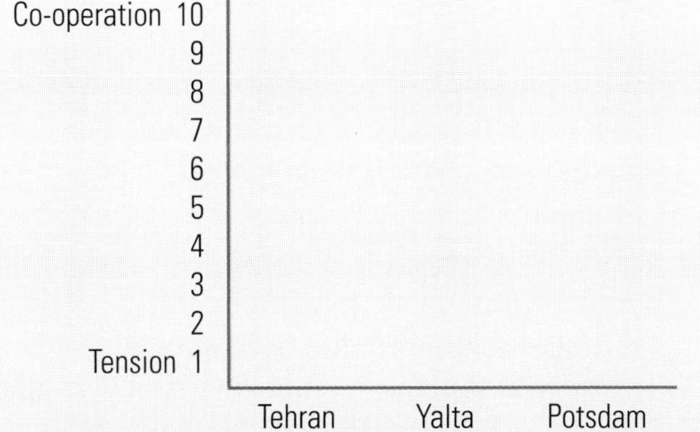

- For each conference, make two lists: a) evidence that the 'Big Three' were co-operating, and b) evidence that there was tension in their relationship.
- Use the information on your lists to reach a judgment about the extent to which the 'Big Three' were co-operating at each conference. Give the 'Big Three' a mark out of 10, where 10 represents complete co-operation and 1 represents great tension.
- Plot the scores for each conference on your graph.
- In what ways did the relationship between the 'Big Three' change during this period?
- Make a list of reasons why the relationship between the 'Big Three' changed between the Teheran Conference in 1943 and the Potsdam Conference in 1945.

Why did the Cold War begin? Fear of war

Learning objectives

In this chapter you will learn about:

- the breakdown of trust between Russia and America
- how Russia and America viewed each other in 1946.

The war of words

During 1946 it became increasingly clear that Europe had been divided between capitalism in the west and communism in the east. Stalin, representing the East, and Churchill, representing the West (despite no longer being Britain's leader), responded with a 'war of words', showing that the former allies now viewed each other with tremendous suspicion. This suspicion became an important part of the Cold War.

> From Stettin in the Baltic to Trieste in the Adriatic, an iron curtain has descended across the continent. Behind the line lie all the capitals of the ancient states of Central and Eastern Europe... all these famous cities and the populations around them lie in the Soviet sphere and all are subject, in one form or another, not only to Soviet influence but to a very high and increasing measure of control from Moscow.

Churchill's 'Iron Curtain' speech, March 1946.

> Essentially, Mr Churchill now adopts the position of the warmonger, and in this Mr Churchill is not alone. He has friends not only in Britain but in the United States of America as well. A point to be noted in this respect is that Mr Churchill and his friends bear a striking resemblance to Hitler and his friends.

Stalin's response to Churchill's speech, March 1946.

Churchill gave his speech during a trip to America, and everyone understood that President Truman supported what he had said. Clearly, both sides had started to view each other as opponents rather than allies.

Secret telegrams

Truman and Stalin were concerned about the breakdown of the Grand Alliance and the threat of a new war. Both men asked for secret reports from their embassies to help them to understand how their opponents were thinking. Both reports were sent as telegrams.

The Long Telegram (1946)

Truman received worrying news in the 'Long Telegram', a secret report from Kennan, America's ambassador in Moscow. The telegram reported that:

- Stalin had given a speech calling for the destruction of capitalism
- there could be no peace with the USSR while it was opposed to capitalism
- the USSR was building up its military power.

Novikov's Telegram (1946)

Novikov, the Soviet ambassador to America, sent a telegram to Stalin which was equally concerning. It reported:

- America desired to dominate the world
- following Roosevelt's death, the American government was no longer interested in co-operation with the USSR
- the American public was being prepared for war with the USSR.

Following these secret telegrams, both governments believed that they were facing the possibility of war. Indeed, the government of the USSR came to believe that war with America was inevitable. In America, some soldiers who had fought in the Second World War and entered politics when they returned home called Stalin 'the new Hitler'. Their point was simple: Stalin, like Hitler, was preparing for war and must be stopped.

On the verge of the Cold War

By the end of 1946, the Grand Alliance was all but over. America had come to believe that the USSR was planning world domination and many in the USSR feared that America was planning the same. At the beginning of 1947, Truman addressed the American government, setting out his belief that America must stand against communism. This speech, setting out the 'Truman **Doctrine**', can be seen as the unofficial declaration of the Cold War. You will read more about the Truman Doctrine on page 90.

President Truman making the Truman Doctrine speech in March 1947.

ResultsPlus

Watch out!

Do not confuse Churchill's 'Iron Curtain' with the Berlin Wall! The 'Iron Curtain' is a metaphor for the division of Europe, whereas the Berlin Wall was an actual barrier, put up in 1961 that divided Berlin (see pages 110–111).

ResultsPlus

Top Tip

The sources in this book contain evidence of how people thought about the Cold War at the time. You do not have to memorise these sources. However, if you can summarise their information in one sentence you may be able to use this in the exam.

ResultsPlus

Build Better Answers

Exam question: Describe one factor that led to a breakdown in the Grand Alliance in 1946. (2 marks)

■ **A basic answer (level 1)** is accurate, but lacks detail.

● **A good answer (level 2)** is accurate and includes supporting information.

Look at the question above. Take one of the following factors:

- Churchill's 'Iron Curtain' speech
- the Long Telegram
- Novikov's Telegram.

What supporting information would you use to develop your point?

Activities

1. Divide your class into three teams. Each team must prepare a short speech explaining who they believe was responsible for the breakdown of the Grand Alliance.
   Team 1 will argue that the USA was to blame.
   Team 2 will argue that the USSR was to blame.
   Team 3 will argue that both sides share the blame.
2. Present your speeches in turn. Your teacher will award marks in the following way:
   - relevant and accurate statement – 1 point
   - specific supporting detail – 2 points
   - clear explanation of why the opposing side is to blame – 3 points.

   The team with the most points wins!

The development of the Cold War: the Truman Doctrine and Marshall Aid

Learning objectives

In this chapter you will learn about:

- the key features of the Truman Doctrine and Marshall Aid
- America's reasons for offering Marshall Aid.

The Truman Doctrine (1947)

Following the 'Long Telegram' (see page 88), Truman asked the American military to assess the strength of the USSR's army. He learned that the USSR was in no position to wage a war. Nonetheless, Truman believed that the USSR had a second strategy that would allow it to conquer more and more territory without having to declare war: Stalin would encourage communist revolutions across Europe. After the Second World War, much of Europe was devastated and citizens in countries such as Italy, France, Greece, Turkey and the United Kingdom were suffering great hardships. In these conditions communism was highly appealing because communists believed that the wealth of the richest people should be shared out among the poor. To address this threat, in 1947 Truman set out a new policy that soon became known as the 'Truman Doctrine'.

The Truman Doctrine stated that:

- the world had a choice between communist tyranny and democratic freedom
- America had a responsibility to fight for liberty wherever it was threatened
- America would send troops and economic resources to help governments that were threatened by communists
- communism should not be allowed to grow and gain territory.

The significance of the Truman Doctrine

The Truman Doctrine was important because it suggested that America, rather than the United Nations, had a responsibility to protect the world. This marked a reversal of the USA's traditional policy of '**isolationism**' by which America had stayed out of international affairs. It was also significant because it divided the world according to ideology: it stated clearly that capitalism and communism were in opposition.

This suggested that there could be no further co-operation between East and West due to their ideological differences, and in this sense it marked the unofficial end of the Grand Alliance and the beginning of the Cold War. Finally, it set a realistic goal for American foreign policy: Truman was committed to 'containment'. This implied that although America would not invade the USSR, it would make every effort to stop the spread of communism.

The Marshall Plan (1947)

Truman described containment and the Marshall Plan as 'two halves of the same walnut'. By this he meant that America had a dual strategy for dealing with communism. First, containment aimed to beat communism through military force. Secondly, the Marshall Plan of 1947 committed $13 billion of American money to rebuild the shattered economies of Europe. By encouraging prosperity, the Marshall Plan would weaken the attraction of communism. To those suffering economic hardship following the Second World War, the promise of sharing resources equally under communism had great appeal. If people were wealthy, however, the idea of sharing resources would have less appeal. In order to qualify for American money, European countries had to agree to trade freely with America. In this way, the Marshall Plan also helped the American economy.

Did you know?

The United Nations (UN) is an organisation created in 1945 to maintain international peace. The first meeting of the UN, in 1946, was attended by 51 nations. Today, the UN is made up of 192 nations.

Initial reaction to the Marshall Plan

European leaders met at the Paris Conference of 1948 to discuss the American offer. Many European countries were keen to receive Marshall Aid. However, representatives from the USSR walked out of the conference claiming that the Americans were attempting to split Europe into 'two camps'. They argued that Marshall Aid was the first step in creating a military alliance that would wage war on the Soviet Union. Stalin also insisted that Eastern European countries in the Soviet 'sphere of influence' refuse the help offered by America. By contrast, 16 countries including Britain and France welcomed the offer, seeing it as a way of rebuilding their economies and defeating communism in their own countries.

A British newspaper cartoon from June 1948 showing the 'Iron Curtain' and Marshall Aid. The figure on the right is Stalin. The figure looking over the 'Iron Curtain' is Tito, the communist leader of Yugoslavia. Although Tito was a communist, he did not see eye-to-eye with Stalin and found some aspects of Western Europe very attractive.

Activity

You are one of Truman's advisors. Prepare a letter to be sent to the leaders of all European governments inviting them to the Paris Conference of 1948. The letter should:

- describe America's offer of assistance (the Marshall Plan)
- explain why America is offering this assistance
- set out what governments must do in order to qualify for this offer.

Remember to be persuasive!

ResultsPlus
Build Better Answers

Exam question: Describe the key features of the Truman Doctrine. (6 marks)

You need to identify important points, not simply write all you know. Here, for example, you could choose to describe an aim and an effect of the Truman Doctrine and a key point from what Truman said.

■ **A basic answer (level 1)** gives simple statements that are accurate but contain no supporting details.

● **A good answer (level 2)** gives a statement that is accurate and is developed with specific information.

▲ **An excellent answer (full marks)** contains two or three statements. Each statement explains a relevant key feature and is backed up with specific information.

For the exam question above, develop the following key features of the Truman Doctrine:

- containment
- the division of the world into two rival ideologies
- America has a responsibility to protect the world.

The development of the Cold War: satellite states

Learning objectives

In this chapter you will learn about:

- the setting up of satellite states
- why Stalin established Cominform and Comecon
- how the 'spheres of influence' became 'two camps'.

What is a satellite state?

A satellite state is a country that is officially independent, but is in reality controlled by another country. Between 1947 and 1949, the USSR extended its influence over Eastern Europe, turning countries such as Czechoslovakia, Hungary and Poland into satellite states.

Why did Stalin set up satellite states?

Stalin described the Marshall Plan as 'dollar imperialism': he believed that the Americans were trying to buy influence over Europe, as any country that accepted Marshall Aid would effectively become an American ally. To prevent this, Stalin extended his control over Eastern Europe, creating a series of satellite states.

How did Stalin take control of them?

This emerged from the 'spheres of influence' discussed at the Teheran, Yalta and Potsdam conferences. At Yalta and Potsdam, the USSR agreed to free elections in these countries. It hoped at first that people would naturally choose communism in the free elections that the West wanted them to have. Some did, but most did not. So the USSR pushed for new 'free' elections that they fixed as much as they could. Once in power, they got rid of opposition parties and made each country a single-party state.

The USSR kept control by:

- making sure the Communist Party in each state had leaders that would obey Moscow
- creating an atmosphere of fear and mistrust so that it was difficult for people who wanted to oppose Soviet rule to trust each other enough to work together
- ruthlessly using the police and army in these states to stamp on any kind of opposition
- arranging the economies of these countries so that they were dependent on the USSR by 'rationalising' industries to stop the satellites being self-sufficient (e.g. Poland did all the shipbuilding, Hungary produced all the trucks).

Soviet expansion, 1945-48.

Yugoslavia

Communists, led by Marshall Tito, took over Yugoslavia in 1945, while the war was still going on. At first, Tito worked well with the USSR, but he wanted to run Yugoslavia himself, not follow orders as a satellite state. Relations worsened and Tito split from the USSR in 1948. He even took aid under the Marshall Plan.

Albania

Communists took over in Albania in 1945, while the war was still going on. It had the least opposition to becoming a satellite state.

The Baltic States

Estonia, Latvia and Lithuania became part of the Soviet Union after the war, as did what had been eastern Poland and part of Romania. There was no pretence of them being separate from the USSR, as there was with the satellite states. They were treated as part of the USSR.

East Germany

East Germany was the part of Germany that the USSR was given to administer when Germany was divided into zones at the end of the war. In 1949, after supposedly 'free' elections, it announced it was a separate country from the other three, Western controlled, zones. It became the communist German Democratic Republic. In June 1953, demonstrations broke out across East Germany against communist policies, but the protests were crushed by Soviet tanks. Thousands were arrested and hundreds wounded.

Bulgaria

Late in 1944, while the war was still going on, a coalition of left-wing parties, including communists, took over in Bulgaria. In November 1945, they held 'free' elections which the communists won by intimidation. They then abolished all other political parties and executed anyone who looked able to oppose them, including many non-communists who had managed to get elected despite communist pressure.

Hungary

In 1945, free elections were held. The communists won some seats, but not enough to come to power. In 1947, after supposedly 'free' elections that they managed by intimidation, the communists were elected (for more on this see pages 100-103).

Poland

In free elections in 1945, a coalition of left-wing parties, including communists, came to power. Britain and the USA urged Stalin to take some Poles who had been in exile in London during the war into the government. He did so but, in 1947, after supposedly 'free' elections that they managed by intimidation, the communists took over entirely. The London Poles were either executed, imprisoned or fled.

Romania

In 1945, as soon as the war ended, a coalition of left-wing parties, including many communists, took over in Romania. In February 1945, the king was forced to take a communist prime minister. By June, the communists were in control of the government. 'Free' elections in 1947 gave the communists complete control.

Czechoslovakia

In free elections in 1945, a coalition of left-wing parties, including communists, came to power. In 1946, the government was dominated by communists. But they could not win complete control in fair elections and began to lose, not gain, support. So, in 1948, they used the army to take over, having removed any officers who might object to doing so. Many non-communists were arrested, some were imprisoned, some executed.

Cominform: The Communist Information Bureau (1947)

In order to extend his control, Stalin established Cominform in 1947. Cominform was an international organisation that represented Communist Parties across Europe and brought them under the direction of the USSR.

The first Cominform Conference rejected the Marshall Plan. Consequently, Eastern European governments refused to accept Marshall Aid and Communist Parties in Western Europe were encouraged to organise strikes and demonstrations against the American plan. In France, for example, 2 million workers, sympathetic to the communists, went on strike in the winter of 1947, demanding that the French government reject Marshall Aid.

Cominform was also used to ensure the loyalty of Eastern European governments. It did this by investigating government ministers and employees, and removing those who were not loyal to Stalin.

This process was often violent. In Hungary, for example, 5% of the population was in prison by 1953. In this way, Cominform **consolidated** the power of the USSR through Eastern Europe by stamping out opposition and ensuring the loyalty of Eastern European governments.

Comecon: The Council for Mutual Economic Assistance (1949)

Comecon was Stalin's answer to the Marshall Plan. Stalin was aware that the Marshall Plan was very attractive to some Eastern European governments. Having ordered his satellite states to **boycott** Marshall Aid, he needed to set up a communist alternative. Therefore, in 1949 he established Comecon. In the first year, Comecon comprised the USSR, Bulgaria, Czechoslovakia, Hungary, Poland and Romania. Albania and Eastern Germany joined in 1950. Comecon aimed to encourage the economic development of Eastern Europe. It also attempted to prevent trade with Western Europe and America. This had political and economic implications.

- Politically, it would minimise American influence in Eastern Europe and the USSR.
- Economically, it ensured that the benefits of economic recovery in Eastern Europe remained within the Soviet 'sphere of influence'.
- It also meant that Eastern Europe did not have access to the prosperity of Western Europe.

'Two camps'

The USSR and America both recognised that, following the Potsdam Conference, Europe had divided into 'two camps'. This division had hardened as a result of Marshall Aid, which brought Western Europe into America's camp, and Cominform and Comecon, which established a Soviet camp in the East. In 1945, there had been two unofficial 'spheres of influence' in Europe. Marshall Aid and Comecon turned these 'spheres of influence' into two official economic alliances.

ResultsPlus
Watch out!

Do not confuse Cominform with Comecon. Remember Com<u>econ</u> is <u>econ</u>omic, and Cominform is political.

ResultsPlus
Build Better Answers

Exam question: Describe the key features of Cominform. (6 marks)

You need to make developed statements that answer the question and describe why the features mentioned in the answer are important.

■ **A basic answer (level 1):**
One key feature of Cominform was that it allowed Stalin to control Eastern Europe.

● **A good answer (level 2):**
One key feature of Cominform was that it allowed Stalin to control Eastern Europe. At Cominform's first conference, leaders of Eastern European countries agreed with Stalin to boycott Marshall Aid.

 **An excellent answer (full marks)** fully describes two or three key features.

Activity

Complete the following table, summarising the key features of Cominform and Comecon.

	Cominform	Comecon
Full name		
Date established		
Aims		
Effects		

The development of the Cold War: first confrontation

> **Learning objectives**
>
> In this chapter you will learn about:
> - the division of Germany into East and West
> - the impact of the Berlin Blockade
> - the formation of NATO and the arms race.

Germany: Unfinished business

Following the Second World War, Russia and America were unable to agree about the future of Germany. There were four key issues.

- Should a reunited Germany be part of the Soviet 'sphere of influence', the American 'sphere of influence', or should it be neutral?
- Should a reunited Germany have a communist or a capitalist government?
- Should a reunited Germany receive Marshall Aid?
- Should troops from America and the USSR be allowed to remain in a united Germany?

Bizonia

By 1947, the British and American zones were essentially operating as one, and therefore became known as 'Bizonia' (meaning two zones). The relationship between Bizonia and the French zone was also very good, and therefore the three western zones were referred to as 'Trizonia'.

Although Germany's capital, Berlin, was deep within the Soviet zone, it too was divided into four regions, with the western section under American, French and British control.

The division of Germany after the Second World War.

East and West Germany

The future of Germany was still the subject of intense negotiations between East and West. However, in 1948 the Western Allies started to develop a policy for western Germany that was at odds with Russia's plans. First, Britain, France and the USA agreed to set up a German assembly to create a German constitution. Secondly, they introduced a new currency – the Deutschmark – which would become the official currency for Trizonia.

Stalin had not been consulted about these developments and believed they were the first steps to creating a permanently divided Germany. He opposed the division of Germany for the following reasons.

- He was reluctant to allow America to have further influence over Germany.
- He did not want American troops to remain stationed in Germany.
- He realised that Germany's most valuable economic resources were in the west and feared that they would be used to wage war on the USSR.

The Berlin Blockade (1948–49)

In order to prevent the establishment of a separate state in western Germany, Stalin set up a military **blockade** around West Berlin in June 1948. His plan was to cut western Germany off from its capital (Berlin) so that the new government, based in Berlin, could not control its territory in western Germany. Stalin hoped that this would prove that a divided Germany could not work in practice.

President Truman responded with the 'Berlin Airlift'. Allied planes transported supplies to West Berlin around the clock. Initially, America committed 70 large cargo planes and airlifted between 600 and 700 tonnes of food and supplies every day. This had increased to 1000 tonnes a day within a couple of weeks. The British authorities maintained a similar system and, at its height, the airlift provided over 170,000 tonnes of supplies during January 1949.

The airlift prevented the blockade from succeeding. What is more, Truman's response was peaceful and made Stalin's military blockade appear highly aggressive.

The Berlin Blockade was a propaganda success for the Americans, and an utter failure for the USSR. In May 1949, Stalin ended the blockade, and in September 1949, West Germany (officially called the Federal Republic of Germany, or FDR) was officially created as an independent state. One month later, the USSR established a second independent state – East Germany (officially known as the German Democratic Republic, or GDR).

An aircraft participating in the Berlin airlift in 1949.

The Formation of NATO (1949)

The Berlin Blockade was the first military confrontation of the Cold War. It raised the possibility of a war in Europe. As a result, Western European nations tried to establish an alliance in order to 'keep the USA in, and the USSR out'. In April 1949, NATO (the North Atlantic Treaty Organisation) was established as an alliance between America and many of the countries in Western Europe. NATO members agreed that if any NATO country came under attack, all members of NATO would come to their defence.

The creation of NATO marked a significant development in the Cold War. The Marshall Plan had created a trading alliance but NATO went further. It was a military alliance with the specific aim of defending the West against communism. In 1955, the USSR responded by creating the Warsaw **Pact**, a military alliance of Eastern European countries which mirrored NATO. The USSR already had Cominform but, when West Germany joined NATO, it was too provocative to ignore.

NATO members USA: Britain, Belgium, Canada, Denmark, France, Iceland, Italy, Luxembourg, Netherlands, Norway, Portugal (Greece 1952, West Germany 1955)

Warsaw Pact: Soviet Union, Albania (until 1968), Bulgaria, Czechoslovakia, East Germany, Hungary, Poland, Romania

The arms race

The arms race was an important feature of the Cold War. It included both a continuing commitment to maintaining a large army, navy and air force, and the development of ever-more-deadly nuclear weapons. In 1945, the USA became the first country to develop and use a nuclear bomb. By 1949, the USSR had caught up – it had developed and tested its own nuclear bomb. This prompted the Americans to develop hydrogen bombs – a second generation of more powerful nuclear weapons. By 1953, both countries had hydrogen bombs, and during the 1950s and 1960s both countries competed to create large numbers of nuclear weapons.

Did you know?

America and Russia named their nuclear bombs. Two of America's first nuclear bombs were named 'Fat Man' and 'Little Boy'. Russia named a bomb 'Layercake'.

Why was the arms race significant?

The arms race was significant because it prevented a war in Europe. The USSR had 3 million troops and could easily capture Western Germany. However, the Soviet leaders would never order an invasion because they feared an American nuclear **retaliation**. One atomic bomb could turn an entire city into ashes and kill hundreds of thousands of people in a few seconds. Soviet leaders had paid close attention to the American bombings of Hiroshima and Nagasaki at the end of the Second World War and understood the awesome power of the new weapons.

Castle Romeo detonation, March 27 1954. Romeo was the third largest nuclear test carried out by the United States.

Cartoon A

Cartoon B

Activities

Cartoons A and B are from British newspapers published during the time of the Berlin Blockade.

1. Study each of these cartoons carefully. The message in Cartoon A is that the West is helping West Berlin with an airlift and increased supplies, whereas Stalin is sending nothing but 'lies', 'scares' and 'rumours' to threaten the West. Cartoon B likens the Berlin Blockade to a game of chess between Stalin and President Truman. Stalin's chess pieces are labelled **'Eastern Bloc'** and 'Berlin Blockade'. Truman's chess pieces are labelled 'Berlin Airlift' and 'Atlantic Pact'.
2. These cartoons offer a Western point of view. Now try to produce your own cartoon about the Berlin Airlift from a Soviet point of view.

Hungary under Soviet rule: liberation and oppression

Learning objectives

In this chapter you will learn about:

- the effect of Soviet rule on Hungary
- the causes and consequences of 'de-Stalinisation'
- the impact of the Hungarian revolt of 1956.

Hungary under Stalin

Stalin claimed that Soviet troops had **liberated** Hungary from the Nazis. However, in 1949, Cominform imposed an **oppressive** regime on Hungary.

- Hungarian land was redistributed to other Eastern European countries.
- Hungarian coal, oil and wheat were shipped to Russia while Hungarian citizens were deprived of food.
- Non-communist political parties were abolished.
- Russian officials controlled the government, the police and the army.
- Cominform began a reign of terror, executing popular political leaders and their supporters.
- Matyas Rakosi was appointed as Hungary's **dictator**.

Matyas Rakosi

Rakosi was Hungary's dictator from 1949 to 1956. He described himself as 'Stalin's best pupil' but the people of Hungary nicknamed him 'the bald butcher'. He developed what were known as 'salami tactics' for dealing with his opponents 'slice by slice', meaning he got rid of opposition by dividing it bit by bit. His oppressive regime imprisoned 387,000 and was responsible for more than 2,000 deaths.

'De-Stalinisation'

Stalin's death in 1953 was a turning point in the Cold War. Stalin's style of government, which is known as 'Stalinism', was extraordinarily oppressive. For example, it is believed that Stalin was responsible for the deaths of around 20 million people during his time in power. Russia's new leader, Nikita Khrushchev, opened the way for a more liberal approach to governing the USSR and Eastern Europe. In 1956, he gave the 'Secret Speech'. This speech, which did not remain secret for very long, promised an end to Stalinism throughout the entire Soviet sphere of influence.

Matyas Rakosi.

Top Tip

In this section you have learned about three American presidents and two Russian leaders. The examiners will know which leaders are relevant to each question – you cannot get away with guessing. Make sure that you know who was in charge and when.

Activities

Use the information on pages 100-103 to create a timeline of the events in Hungary 1949-56.

Imre Nagy

Nagy had fought in the First World War and was captured and imprisoned by the Russians. He escaped from prison and fought for the Bolsheviks in the Russian Revolution. This was when he became a communist.

In 1919, Nagy joined the communist uprising in Hungary led by Bela Kun and funded by the USSR. Their takeover was quickly defeated and the new government was anti-communist. Nagy moved from place to place to avoid arrest, in Hungary and neighbouring countries. He returned to the USSR in 1929 and studied agriculture in Moscow.

Nagy returned to Hungary in 1944 and became involved in politics as a supporter of the USSR. In 1945, he was made Minister of Agriculture and set up land reforms to move the country towards collectivisation (state ownership of all the land). However, his concern for the welfare of the peasants (rather than the state) led to him being excluded from the Communist Party in 1949. After he made a public announcement of his support for the USSR, Nagy was allowed back into government.

He replaced Rakosi as Prime Minister between 1953 and 1955 (although Rakosi kept much of the real power, as Secretary of the Communist Party). In 1955, Nagy was again thrown out of the Communist Party for his opposition to Rakosi's tactics. Rakosi became Prime Minister, as well as Party Secretary, again

Nagy's programme of reform

Hungary's people were clearly dissatisfied with Soviet rule.

- Khrushchev's 'Secret Speech' created hopes of reform in Hungary. But nothing happened. Rakosi was forced out of power in July 1956, but still nothing happened.
- Bad harvests, and fuel and bread shortages, led to riots in Budapest on 23 October 1956. Students demonstrated in Parliament Square against the government and called for a 16-point list of reforms. Fighting broke out between students and police. This rapidly developed into a conflict that pulled in workers and even some members of the army, spreading from Budapest across the country.

To calm the situation, Khrushchev agreed to make Nagy Prime Minister and to withdraw the Red Army from Hungary. On 31 October 1956, Nagy announced his proposed reforms, which included Hungary's leaving the Warsaw Pact and holding free elections. They made these bold moves because they hoped for support from the West.

- They asked the UN to recognise them as a neutral country. This would mean that any Soviet army entering Hungary would be breaking the rules of the UN, and so the UN could send in troops to remove them. The UN tried to intervene, but the USSR took no notice.
- The USA spent a lot of time encouraging Eastern European countries to get rid of their communist governments. US promises of aid were seen as promises of military help. The US-sponsored Radio Free Europe urged people to take a stand against their 'communist oppressors'. However, the aid the USA promised stopped short of military help because its highest priority was preventing a nuclear war with the USSR that would cause world-wide destruction.

The government split. Janos Kadar, a supporter of the USSR, set up a rival government in eastern Hungary.

Khrushchev responds to Nagy

Nagy's reforms ended Hungary's alliance with the USSR. Khrushchev believed that the reforms were unacceptable and that if Hungary was allowed to leave the Warsaw Pact, other Eastern European countries would soon follow. Indeed, Khrushchev had access to secret intelligence reports which indicated that discontent with communism was widespread across Eastern Europe. These reports reinforced his view that allowing greater freedom for these discontented countries could mean the end of Soviet dominance in Eastern Europe.

Khrushchev responded with a decisive show of force. On 4 November 1956, 200,000 Soviet troops and 1,000 tanks entered Hungary in support of Kadar's government. They marched on Budapest, where they fought with supporters of Nagy's government, through two weeks of bitter fighting.

- About 2,500 people were killed by the Soviet troops and about 20,000 were wounded.
- Almost 200,000 fled to the West.

- About 650 Soviet troops were killed and about 1,250 were wounded.

The trouble rumbled on into 1957, with strikes in various parts of the country and outbreaks of fighting. But the revolution was really over in November.

Nagy's trial and execution

Nagy sought protection in the Yugoslavian embassy. The Yugoslavian ambassador agreed with Khrushchev that Nagy was free to leave Hungary. However, as soon as Nagy left the embassy, he was arrested by Soviet troops. Nagy was accused of treason and, in a trial overseen by Khrushchev, was found guilty. He was hanged in June 1958. Following his execution, Khrushchev stated that Nagy's fate was 'a lesson to the leaders of all socialist countries'.

The international reaction

Following Nagy's arrest, America offered food and medical aid worth $20 million to Hungary and allowed 80,000 Hungarian refugees to move to the USA. President Dwight D. Eisenhower (1953-61) praised the bravery of the Hungarian people and encouraged them to fight on.

The UN officially condemned the Soviet invasion and conducted a thorough enquiry into it, but did nothing more. Spain, the Netherlands and Sweden boycotted the 1956 Olympics in protest at Soviet action in Hungary and thousands of people left the communist parties of many European countries. The USA's failure to support the Hungarians showed its commitment to liberating Europe from communism did not include military support. Consequently, radicals in Eastern Europe were discouraged from following Hungary's example.

ResultsPlus

Top Tip

Detailed answers tend to gain higher marks than answers that are vague. One good way of making answers more detailed is to include names. For example, rather than saying 'the American president' in a question relating to the Soviet invasion of Hungary, you could say 'President Eisenhower'.

Activity

It is November 1956. Kadar has been in power for one month. The people below are reflecting on how the events in Hungary have affected them and changed the balance of power in the Cold War. Complete their thought bubbles to show what they are thinking.

Eisenhower *Khrushchev* *Kadar* *a Hungarian revolutionary*

Reasserting Soviet control

Following the Soviet invasion, Khrushchev appointed Janos Kadar as the new Hungarian leader. Initially, Kadar had no real power as Hungary was under the control of the Soviet army. Nonetheless, Kadar published his Fifteen-Point Programme setting out the new government's direction. Kadar's programme included:

- re-establishing communist control of Hungary
- using Hungarian troops to stop attacks on Soviet forces
- remaining in the Warsaw Pact
- negotiating the withdrawal of Soviet troops once the crisis was over.

The Hungarian people soon accepted Kadar's new government. America's failure to support Nagy's government left them with no choice.

Activities

1 Use the information in Section 4 of this book to produce a timeline of the changing relationship between Russia and America in the period 1943–56.

2 Using the information on your timeline, select the three events that you feel led to the greatest change in the relationship between Russia and America.

3 In each case, highlight the event and write a short paragraph explaining how this event changed the relationship and why it was so important.

ResultsPlus

Build Better Answers

Exam question: Explain why relations between the Soviet Union and the USA changed in the years 1943–56. (12 marks)

You need to make relevant points, supported by specific examples, with a clear focus on how each factor led to the situation described.

In each level, the number of statements you make will affect your mark. For example, in level 2, a single developed argument is unlikely to get more than 5 marks, whereas three developed arguments will achieve 8 or 9 marks.

■ **A basic answer (level 1)** is correct, but does not have details to support it (for example, *One reason why the relationship between the Soviet Union and the USA changed is because of Roosevelt's death*).

● **A good answer (level 2)** provides the details as well (for example, *One reason why the relationship between the Soviet Union and the USA changed is because of Roosevelt's death. Roosevelt had been prepared to work with Stalin at the Teheran and Yalta Conferences*).

▲ **A better answer (level 3)** shows the links between reasons or shows why one is more important (for example, *One reason why the relationship between the Soviet Union and the USA changed is because of Roosevelt's death. Roosevelt had been prepared to work with Stalin at the Teheran and Yalta Conferences. Following his death, the new president – Truman – was very suspicious of Stalin and was less willing to work with him. This was the most important reason for the change in the relationship because, had Roosevelt survived, he may have been willing to work with Stalin and preserve the Grand Alliance*).

▲ **An excellent answer (full marks)** shows how three reasons are linked and reaches a judgment about their relative importance.

Now write another paragraph in answer to this question. Choose one of the following points, add examples and explain how important this factor was:

- disagreement over the future of Germany
- the effects of the Truman Doctrine
- the creation of NATO and the Warsaw Pact.

Know Zone Unit 1 - section 4

In the Unit 1 exam, you will be required to answer questions from three sections. In each of those sections you will have to answer three questions: Part (a), Part (b) – where you have to do one of the two questions set – and Part (c).

You have about 25 minutes to answer the three questions on each section. Use the number of marks available for each question to help you judge how long to spend on it and how much to write.

Here we are going to look at questions for Parts (b) and (c) of Section 4.

Question (b)

Tip: Part (b) questions will usually ask you to describe the 'key features' of a major policy or an event. This question is worth 6 marks. Make sure that when you describe you don't just tell the story: think about the information and organise it as if you were putting it under headings. Let's look at an example.

Describe the key features of the arms race. (6 marks)

Student answer	Examiner comment
One key feature of the arms race was the competition between the superpowers to create more and more powerful nuclear weapons. At first, the United States was ahead in the race as it was the first country to make atomic bombs. These were 'Fat Man' and 'Little Boy', which were dropped on Japan at the end of the Second World War. By 1949, the USSR had caught up and had tested its own atomic bomb. Next were hydrogen bombs, which were even more powerful. Once again, America was first, but the USSR soon caught up with its first hydrogen bomb, which it called 'Layer Cake'.	This is a very detailed account of one key feature of the arms race. However, in order to get maximum marks, you need to make two or three developed points about key features.

Let's rewrite the answer to mention the competition between the superpowers but also explain two more key features. So that you can spot them easily we will put the key features in bold.

One key feature of the arms race was the competition between the superpowers to create more nuclear weapons. The USA was the first country to use atomic bombs in 1945. By 1949, the USSR had caught up and tested its own atomic bomb. **Another key feature of the arms race was that it preserved peace in Europe.** The USSR had three million troops in Eastern Germany and could have easily defeated Western Germany. However, America put nuclear missiles in Western Europe and this prevented a Soviet invasion. **A third key feature of the arms race was that it led to better military technology.** The first nuclear bombs were very powerful, but the second generation of nuclear bombs were hydrogen bombs, such as the Russian 'Layer Cake', which were even more deadly.	This answer makes three points and backs them up with examples. It would therefore receive full marks.

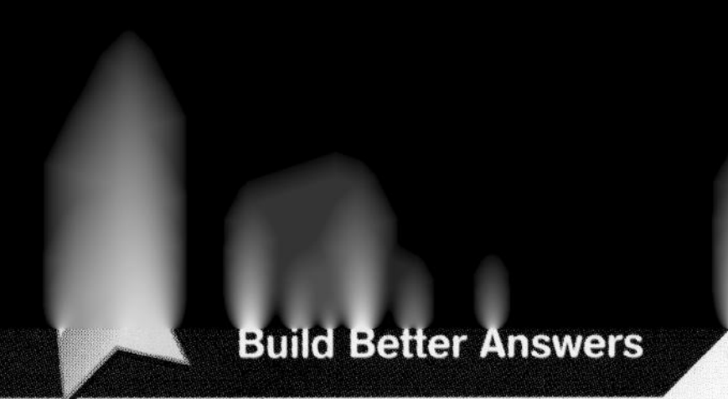

Question (c)

Tip: Part (c) questions require extended writing. They will ask you to use your knowledge to explain why something happened. You should try to find three reasons and explain them. Remember that you will have only about 15 minutes to answer this question and so you need to get straight to the point.

Explain why relations between the Soviet Union and the USA changed in the years 1943–49. (12 marks)

Student answer	Examiner comment
In 1943, the Soviet Union and the USA were allies. They were part of the Grand Alliance with Britain and they fought together against Nazi Germany. After 1946, the Grand Alliance was over. Things got worse after telegrams were sent from the USSR to America, and from America to the USSR. Economic policies also affected the relationship. By 1949, the Grand Alliance had ended, and the USA and the Soviet Union were enemies.	This is not a good answer. All it does is tell the story of superpower relations between 1943 and 1949. What is more, the story is not very detailed. To improve this answer, the candidate would have to: • identify three clear causes of change • provide examples • show how the causes are linked.

Let's rewrite the answer to mention three clear causes of change with examples and explanation. The causes are in bold to make them easy to spot.

Between 1943 and 1949 the relationship between the Soviet Union and the USA got worse for three reasons. **First, the two great powers could not agree on how Germany should be divided following the Second World War.** The USSR wanted Germany to be very weak so that it would never threaten to invade again. The USA, on the other hand, believed that Germany needed to be strong otherwise Germany might collapse and another dictator might come to power. **Secondly, both countries were suspicious of each other because of the reports they received.** The Long Telegram told the American president that Stalin was preparing for a war on capitalism. The Novikov Telegram told Stalin that the new American president did not want to work with the USSR. **Thirdly, trade agreements divided Europe between the superpowers.** Marshall Aid and Comecon turned the two spheres of influence into economic alliances. In this way, the relationship between the Soviet Union and the USA got worse in the period 1943–49 as disagreement turned into suspicion, and this suspicion led President Truman to offer economic aid to win allies against communism in case Russia declared war.	This answer is much better because it answers the question in a detailed way and because it explains why the relationship between the superpowers changed. It also links the factors together, showing how suspicion led to the formation of economic alliances. To get full marks this answer would have to give three reasons and prioritise them by making links between them.

Section 5: Three Cold War crises: Berlin, Cuba and Czechoslovakia c.1957–69

Between 1958 and 1962, the world faced what President John F. Kennedy called a period of 'maximum danger'. Indeed, the world faced annihilation in a nuclear war twice in these years. After 1963, tensions began to ease but the Cold War was still far from over.

In this section you will study three Cold War flashpoints:

- the Berlin Crisis of 1958–63
- the Cuban Missile Crisis of 1962
- Czechoslovakia and the Prague Spring, 1968–69.

You will see how the disputed status of Berlin and the development of the arms race took the world to the brink of **nuclear holocaust**. Additionally, you will consider how tensions in Eastern Europe led to the most significant challenge to Soviet authority since the Hungarian crisis of 1956.

The Berlin Crisis: a divided city

Learning objectives

In this chapter you will learn about:

- the refugee problem facing the East German government
- Khrushchev's response to this crisis.

Following the Second World War, the USSR and America had been unable to agree on how Germany should be governed. Consequently, Germany had been divided but the USSR refused to recognise West Germany and America refused to acknowledge East Germany.
The city of Berlin caused problems as it was partly controlled by the Americans although it was located inside the **Eastern Bloc** – those countries belonging to the Warsaw **Pact**. See the map on page 109, showing the division of Berlin.

Refugee problems

The East German government was extremely unpopular and therefore many East Germans fled to West Germany. West Germany was highly attractive as its citizens enjoyed greater freedom and wealth than those of East Germany. Indeed, between 1949 and 1961, 2.7 million East German **refugees**, many of whom were highly skilled, escaped to West Germany. Berlin was the centre of East Germany's refugee problem because it was easy for East Germans to get from East Berlin to West Berlin, and from there to West Germany.

Khrushchev's challenge

The refugee problem was a **propaganda** disaster for Khrushchev because it proved that many people preferred the capitalist West to the communist East. For this reason, in November 1958, Khrushchev declared that the whole of the city of Berlin officially belonged to East Germany and gave American troops six months to withdraw. Khrushchev's plan was to prevent East Germans fleeing to the West and to humiliate America.

ResultsPlus

Build Better Answers

Exam question: Describe one reason why Khrushchev demanded the withdrawal of American troops from Berlin in 1958. (2 marks)

You need to make a developed statement, a statement that both answers the question and provides some detailed support.

■ **A basic answer (level 1):**
Khrushchev wanted to control all of Berlin to stop so many East Germans leaving.

● **A good answer (level 2):**
Khrushchev wanted to control all of Berlin to stop so many East Germans leaving via West Berlin. Almost 3 million Germans had chosen to leave communist Eastern Europe for the capitalist West.

Activity

It is November 1958. You are one of President Eisenhower's top advisors. You are helping Eisenhower to decide how to respond to Khrushchev's challenge. From the list on the right, choose two options: the one you believe to be most appropriate, and the one you feel would be least effective. Write a paragraph for each, explaining why you believe Eisenhower should or shouldn't take this course of action.

Possible courses of action:

- hold a summit meeting to try to persuade Khrushchev to change his mind
- withdraw American troops from Berlin
- invade Eastern Germany
- agree to withdraw troops only if Khrushchev withdraws his troops from East Germany
- do nothing.

The Berlin Crisis: negotiation and stalemate

Learning objectives

In this chapter you will learn about:

- the failure of negotiations with Khrushchev over the future of Berlin
- Khrushchev's ultimatum and Kennedy's preparation for war.

Eisenhower's response

In November 1958, Khrushchev demanded that the Western powers remove their troops from West Berlin within six months. The Americans were uncertain about how to respond to this. Eisenhower did not want to lose West Berlin, but neither did he want to start a war. Consequently it was agreed to hold an international meeting in order to discuss Berlin's future.

Four summits

That meeting took place in May 1959. Talks were held in a '**summit**' meeting in Geneva between foreign representatives from the USA and the USSR. No solution to the problem was agreed at this meeting. However it did lay the ground work for Khrushchev to visit the USA and hold face-to-face talks with Eisenhower. In September 1959 Khrushchev and Eisenhower met at a second summit meeting in Camp David, the US presidential retreat. The two leaders spoke frankly. Despite not agreeing a solution to the problems, it was decided that a further summit meeting would be held the following year between the two leaders. Additionally Khrushchev agreed to withdraw his six-month **ultimatum**.

This meeting took place in Paris in May 1960, but was a disaster. Just before the conference the USSR had shot down an American spy plane over Russia and captured its pilot. Khrushchev walked out of the conference in protest when Eisenhower refused to apologise for the incident.

When John F. Kennedy became the new president of the USA, a further summit was arranged to discuss Berlin. At the Vienna Conference of June 1961, neither side seemed willing to back down over the US presence in Berlin. However, Khrushchev saw Kennedy's inexperience as a weakness to be exploited. Confident that Kennedy would back down if pushed, Khrushchev once again gave the USA a six-month ultimatum to remove its troops from Berlin.

Khrushchev and Kennedy at the Vienna Conference in June 1961.

Watch out!

The Berlin Crisis can be very confusing if you forget Germany's geography. During the Cold War, West Berlin was in East Germany.

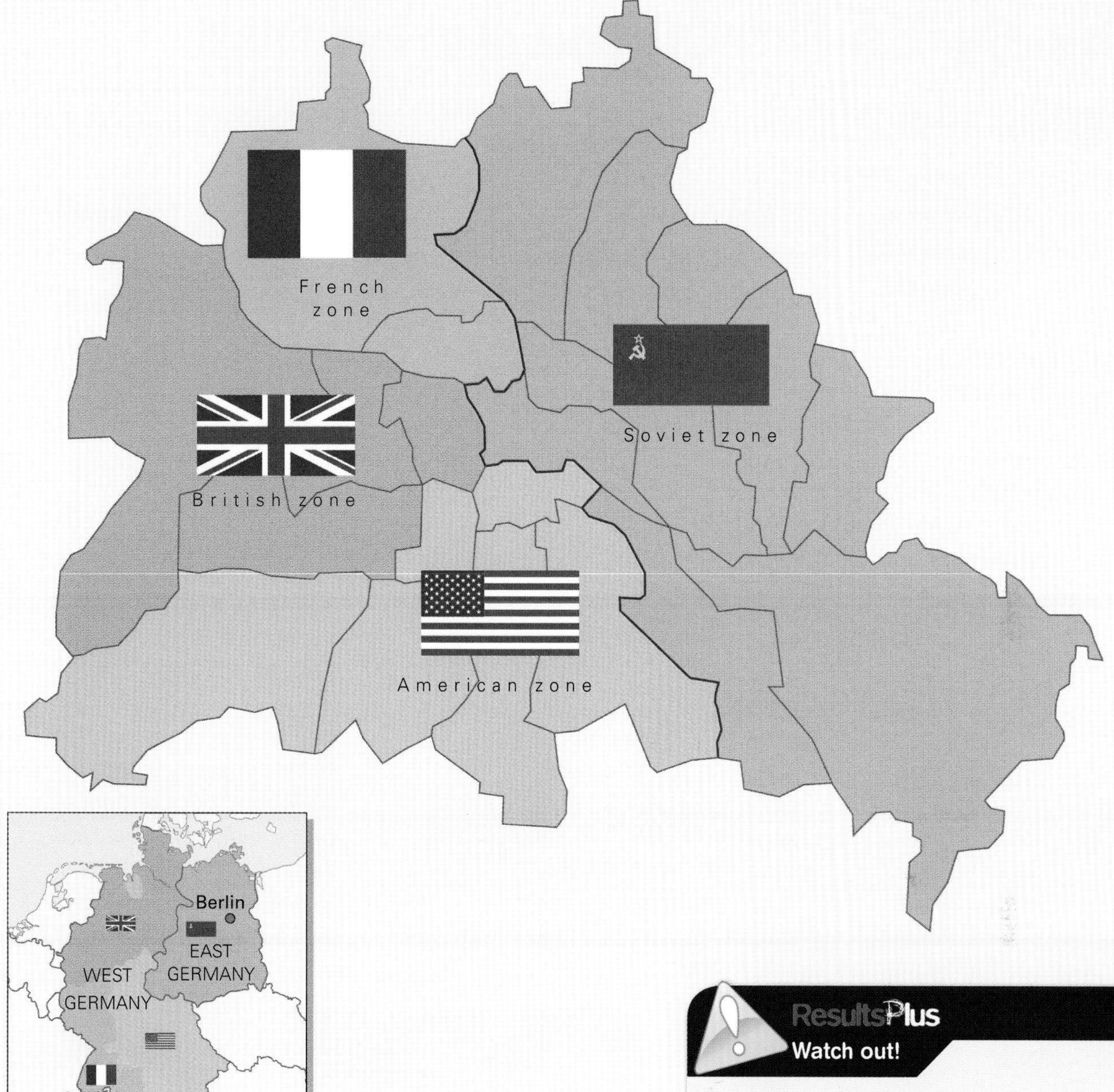

Map showing the division of Berlin into American, British, French and Soviet zones and, inset, the location of Berlin within Soviet-controlled East Germany.

Kennedy prepares for war

Despite Khrushchev's ultimatum, Kennedy refused to back down. He declared that he would not remove American troops from Berlin. He also started preparing America for war, committing the US government to an additional $3.2 billion of defence spending. More worrying still was Kennedy's decision to spend an extra $207 million on building nuclear **fallout shelters**. A point of stalemate had been reached.

ResultsPlus
Watch out!

Students often confuse the different summits and forget which American president attended which summit. You could draw a timeline to help you to remember this information.

Activity

Design a propaganda poster on behalf of the American government justifying the increased spending on defence and fallout shelters. Ensure that you explain why this money needs to be spent, how it will benefit the American population, and how it will help to promote world peace.

The Berlin Crisis: the Berlin Wall

Learning objectives

In this chapter you will learn about:

- the reasons for the creation of the Berlin Wall
- Kennedy's response to the building of the Berlin Wall.

Building the wall

Khrushchev knew that the USSR could not win a nuclear war. In 1961, America had almost 20 times more nuclear weapons than the USSR. What is more, American nuclear weapons were able to reach the USSR, whereas Soviet weapons could not reach America. Kennedy's refusal to retreat called Khrushchev's bluff, forcing the Russian leader to back down.

Khrushchev could not force the Americans to leave West Berlin but he still had to solve the refugee problem. His solution was to build a wall separating East and West Berlin, making it impossible for East Germans to escape to the West.

On the night of 12 August 1961, East German troops secretly erected a barbed wire fence around the whole of West Berlin. The next morning, Berliners awoke to a divided city. In the coming months the fence was reinforced and eventually became a heavily guarded wall. Soviet tanks were deployed to block further Western access to the East, causing a day-long stand-off with US tanks on 27 October. Finally, after 18 hours, the tanks began to pull back – one by one. The crisis had passed. Kennedy commented 'it's not a very nice solution, but a wall is a hell of a lot better than a war'.

Did you know?

There were numerous attempts to cross the Berlin Wall, many of which ended in tragedy. Peter Fechter, for example, planned to cross the wall to West Germany in 1962. He jumped from a window into the 'death strip' between the East and West sides of the wall. However, during his attempt to climb into West Berlin, he was shot. He fell back into the 'death strip', where he lay screaming for help for almost an hour while he bled to death. Guards on the Western side of the wall were unable to help him as they knew this would trigger further violence from guards on the East.

The impact of the Berlin Wall

The Berlin Wall was significant for the following reasons:

- it stopped East Germans escaping to the West and therefore ended the refugee crisis
- it allowed Khrushchev to avoid war with America while still appearing strong
- it became a powerful symbol of the division of Germany and the division of Europe.

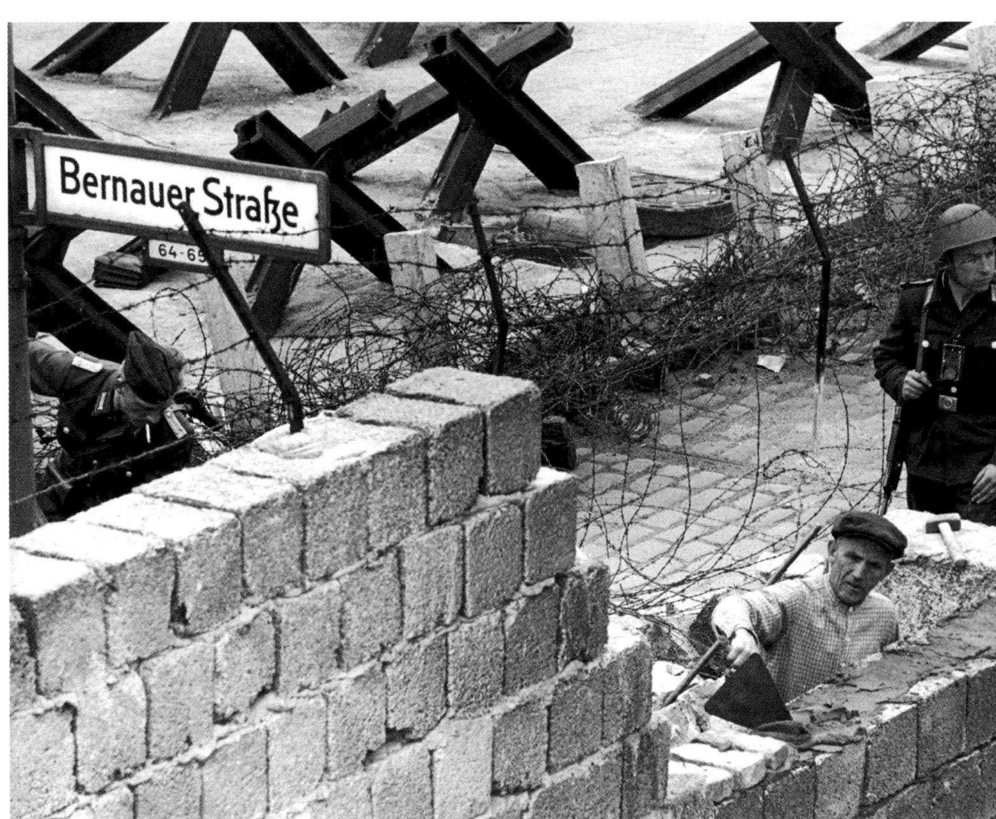

The building of the Berlin Wall.

Kennedy making a speech during his visit to Berlin, 1963.

Kennedy's visit to Berlin

Kennedy was unable to prevent the wall's construction. However, in 1963 he toured West Berlin expressing his feelings of solidarity with its people. Crowds of West Germans lined the streets shouting 'Kenne-dy – Kenne-dy!' In a famous speech, Kennedy said 'All free men, wherever they live, are citizens of Berlin and therefore as a free man, I take pride in the words *Ich bin ein Berliner*'. West Berlin had become a symbol of freedom.

Examination question

Describe one reason why the Berlin Wall was built in 1961. (2 marks)

Activities

1. Copy and cut out the cards on the right.
2. Group the cards into those that describe causes of the building of the Berlin Wall, and those that describe consequences of the building of the Berlin Wall.
3. For each group, decide which cause/consequence was the most important and write a sentence explaining why.

The USSR realised it could not win a nuclear war.	The East German economy lost skilled labourers.	The problem of the division of Berlin was solved.
Refugees were unable to leave East Germany.	Many people from East Germany escaped to West Germany.	Khrushchev avoided war with America.
The East German government was unpopular.	Kennedy refused to back down.	Peter Fechter was killed.
An important symbol of the Cold War was created.	Kennedy showed solidarity with the people of West Berlin.	Kennedy increased the USA's defence budget.

The Cuban Missile Crisis: origins

Learning objectives

In this chapter you will learn about:

- the development of the arms race between 1945 and 1961
- the effects of Cuba's revolution
- Khrushchev's decision to build missile bases on Cuba.

The arms race

America was the clear winner of the **arms race** in the 1940s and 1950s. America had an early lead and dropped the first nuclear bombs on Hiroshima and Nagasaki in August 1945. By 1949, the USSR was producing atomic bombs too. The arms race to develop and stockpile nuclear weapons was a big part of the Cold War. If the Cold War became actual war, then both governments expected that nuclear weapons would be used. In the USA, schools held regular 'duck and cover' rehearsals of what to do in case of nuclear attack. By 1960, Britain, France and China had nuclear weapons too.

In theory, it would soon be far too destructive for either side to use their nuclear weapons. But neither side trusted the other enough to stop the race; and each mistrusted the other side enough to fear they just might attack.

Both sides produced 'statistics' about their nuclear capacity, much of which was designed to frighten the other side, rather than reflect the real situation. Also, statistics could be confused – the number of weapons was not the only consideration, there was also the size of their warheads and the accuracy with which they were aimed.

Did you know?

Communism is associated with the colour red. One symbol of communism is the red star and the flag of the Soviet Union was red. Throughout the Cold War period Americans often referred to communists as 'reds'.

American B52 bombers.

Did you know?

The largest nuclear bomb ever tested was detonated in 1961. The Russian *Tsar Bomba* was eight metres long and weighed 27 tons. The bomb was more than 100 times more powerful than the American weapons detonated in Japan at the end of the Second World War. When it was tested, it created a fireball 8 kilometres (5 miles) in diameter.

The Tsar Bomba.

The table below gives statistics that are widely used for arms holdings in 1960. However, some historians think that the USSR's figures are overestimated. Nonetheless, the table shows what many people in the USA and the USSR believed the situation was at the time.

Nuclear capacity in 1960	USA	USSR
Inter-continental ballistic missile (long-range airborne)	450	76
Mid-range airborne ballistic missile	250	700
Nuclear submarine	32	12
Long-range bombers able to carry nuclear weapons	2,260	1,600

Each country had particular areas of concern.

- The USA's biggest concern was the rate at which the USSR was building nuclear weapons – and the size of those weapons. The *Tsar Bomba*, detonated in 1961, was the most powerful, and therefore most destructive, bomb ever.
- The USSR's biggest concern was that US missiles were much closer to the USSR than its missiles were to the US. In 1958, the USA arranged to have nuclear missiles at their UK bases. In 1961, their bases in Italy and Turkey received nuclear weapons too. These could easily be fixed on specific targets, such as Moscow. The USSR could fire missiles at the USA, but the missiles had to travel further, which meant they could not be targeted anywhere near as accurately.

What is more, America had specially equipped **B52 bombers** that were capable of dropping nuclear weapons on the Soviet Union.

The USSR had relatively few missiles and no way of dropping them accurately on American soil. Nonetheless, the US government was extremely worried about the Soviet Union's nuclear capabilities.

Activities

1 Copy the table below.

2 Use the information in 'The arms race' section of this chapter to complete the second column of the table, explaining why America was in a stronger position than it thought.

America is worried that...	But the real situation is that...
... Sputnik 1 proves that the USSR has very powerful missiles.	
... the USSR can land a spaceship on the moon, therefore it could put nuclear missiles in space.	
... Khrushchev has said that the USSR is producing missiles as fast as it is producing sausages.	

In 1957, Russian scientists launched Sputnik 1 – the world's first man-made satellite. By 1960, the Russians had even landed a robotic spacecraft on the moon. Khrushchev boasted that the Americans were 'sleeping under a red moon'. This demonstrated the sophistication of Soviet technology, and many Americans believed that the rockets used to put satellites in space could be used to launch nuclear missiles at America.

However, the USSR was simply not wealthy enough to mass-produce missiles and Khrushchev's claim that the USSR was 'producing missiles like we are producing sausages' was an empty boast.

The Cuban Revolution

Cuba had traditionally been an ally of the USA. American presidents believed that Cuba's friendship was important because it was only 145 kilometres (90 miles) away and therefore part of the American sphere of influence.

Much of the land in Cuba was owned by American businesses. According to a report by the US Department of Trade in 1956, US companies ran:

- 90% of the phone and electric supply
- 50% of the railways
- 40% of all sugar production
- all the oil refineries were US owned and supplied.

The Cuban Revolution of 1959 overthrew Cuba's pro-American government. The new revolutionary regime, led by Fidel Castro, wanted greater independence from the United States. As part of this policy, Castro's new government took over American property located in Cuba. In response, America banned the import of Cuban sugar. This threatened to bankrupt the Cuban economy.

January 1959	Castro went to the USA. President Eisenhower refused to see him or accept his government as the rightful government of Cuba.
May 1959	Castro's Land Reform Act banned foreign ownership of land. Other countries that owned land in Cuba accepted payment for this. The USA did not, because they did not accept that Castro's government had the right to pass laws.
January 1960	Castro took the land the USA would not take payment for.
February 1960	Castro made an agreement to sell the USSR sugar and buy its oil.
March 1960	Oil from the USSR arrived. The US-owned refineries refused to take it. Castro nationalised the oil refineries.
July 1960	The USA banned all trade with Cuba. Castro nationalised all US businesses in Cuba. The USSR agreed to buy more sugar, and provide more goods and loans.

Cuba turned to the USSR for help. Khrushchev was delighted to have an ally deep in America's sphere of influence. Consequently, he agreed to offer economic aid to Cuba in order to help his new ally industrialise.

The Bay of Pigs incident

John F. Kennedy became president of the USA in January 1961. By this point, the CIA had tried, and failed, to assassinate Castro several times and were increasingly concerned over Cuba's ties with the USSR. Americans did not want a communist country on their doorstep; certainly not one that had the USSR as an ally. The CIA persuaded Kennedy to launch an invasion of Cuba to dislodge Castro's government and put Batista (the old, corrupt ruler of Cuba who had been a US ally) back in charge. This invasion had been planned for over a year. They assured Kennedy that:

- they could make it look like a Cuban revolt, not a US invasion, as they had been training Cuban exiles in guerrilla fighting and they could disguise old US planes to look like Cuban ones for bombing
- Castro's hold on the country was weak
- most Cubans would join in against Castro once the invasion began.

Kennedy agreed to the plan. But the invasion was a disaster.

- The plan, supposedly secret, was known to Castro's government.
- Most Cubans did not want Batista back.
- The first strike by the disguised planes, on 15 April, missed most of its targets, including Castro's air base. The planes were photographed and US involvement was made public. Kennedy cancelled a planned second airstrike.

- The Cuban-exile army of about 1,400 invaded at the Bay of Pigs on 17 April. It was soon facing heavy air attacks and about 20,000 of Castro's troops. Kennedy sent in planes, but too late. The Cuban exiles, with not enough US help and no support from other Cubans, surrendered.

The Bay of Pigs ended any chance that the USA and Cuba might negotiate a friendly relationship. Castro declared himself a communist. The Americans began making fresh plans to overthrow Castro, and the USSR began to negotiate with Castro to provide military 'protection' that would, for the first time, place Soviet nuclear missiles very close to the USA.

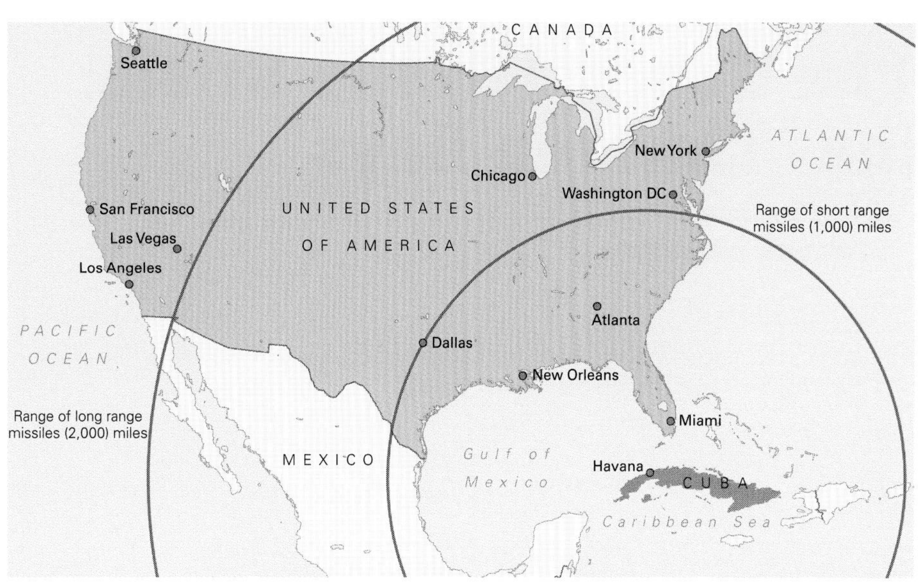

Map showing Cuba in relation to the USA.

Missile bases

In spite of his victory, Castro felt vulnerable and feared another American attack. He therefore asked Khrushchev to help him defend Cuba. In August 1961, Khrushchev devised a plan that would solve the problems of both Cuba and Russia. He decided to station Russian nuclear weapons on Cuban soil. He claimed this would deter America from attempting another invasion. It would also place Russian nuclear missiles within striking range of America, balancing the US presence in Turkey. This meant that Khrushchev could attack America without spending large amounts of money developing inter-continental ballistic missiles.

ResultsPlus

Build Better Answers

Exam question: Describe the key features of the arms race. (6 marks)

You need to make two or three developed statements that answer the question, not simply write all you know. For example, a key feature of the arms race at this time is that it was a race about nuclear weapons.

A basic answer (level 1):

One key feature of the arms race was that both sides developed nuclear weapons. Another feature was that the USA was winning the arms race until the mid-1960s.

A good answer (level 2):

One key feature of the arms race was that both sides developed nuclear weapons. For example, America was the first superpower to develop the atomic bomb and by the early 1960s they had modified B52 bombers so they were capable of dropping these bombs on the USSR. Another key feature was that the USA was winning the arms race until the mid-1960s. For example, the USA had 20 times more nuclear warheads than the Soviet Union.

Activity

Use the information in this chapter to draw a timeline of the key events of 1957–61, showing the build up to the Cuban Missile Crisis.

The Cuban Missile Crisis: the 'Thirteen Days'

Learning objectives

In this chapter you will learn about:

- how America learned of Khrushchev's plan
- the 'hawks and the doves'
- the events of the 'Thirteen Days'.

Did you know?

Robert McNamarra, the Secretary of Defence, when asked how close to war the USA and the USSR came over Cuba, said: 'I thought I might never live to see another Saturday night'.

The Thirteen Days

The 'Thirteen Days' was the period in 1962 at the height of the Cuban Missile Crisis during which there seemed to be the greatest threat of nuclear war.

The events of the 'Thirteen Days' of 1962:

16 Oct	Kennedy is informed of Khrushchev's plans to place nuclear missiles on Cuba.
20 Oct	Kennedy decides to impose a naval **blockade** around Cuba to prevent further missiles reaching Cuba.
22 Oct	Kennedy gives a public address officially declaring the blockade and calling on Khrushchev to recall his ships.
23 Oct	Khrushchev sends a letter to Kennedy stating that Soviet ships will break through the blockade.
24 Oct	Soviet ships approach the line of blockade (500 miles from Cuba). At 10.32am the closest ships suddenly stop or turn around. Khrushchev issues a statement that the USSR is prepared to launch nuclear weapons if America goes to war.
25 Oct	American and Soviet armed forces are on the highest level of alert – they are told to prepare for war. Kennedy writes to Khrushchev asking him to withdraw missiles from Cuba.
26 Oct	Khrushchev responds to Kennedy's letter, saying that he will withdraw Soviet missiles in return for a guarantee that the USA will not invade Cuba.
27 Oct	Khrushchev receives intelligence that the USA is planning to invade Cuba in 24 hours. He proposes a deal: the USSR will withdraw missiles from Cuba if the USA will agree never to invade Cuba and withdraw its nuclear missiles from Turkey. An American spy plane is shot down over Cuba. American 'hawks' demand **retaliation**. Robert Kennedy (Kennedy's brother and chief advisor) approaches the Russian ambassador accepting Khrushchev's deal but demands that the withdrawal of American missiles from Turkey is kept secret.
28 Oct	Khrushchev accepts this secret deal.

Khrushchev's plan is revealed

On 25 September 1962, Khrushchev sent 114 Soviet ships to Cuba. The ships carried a secret cargo, including nuclear warheads and long-range missiles, that would be used to construct nuclear bases on Cuba. For a long time, Khrushchev's plan remained secret. But by mid-October American spy planes had discovered what was going on. On 22 October Kennedy addressed the American people and told them of the Soviet plans to build nuclear missile bases on their doorstep.

Kennedy's news shocked the world. Many Americans panicked and started building nuclear shelters in preparation for nuclear war. A fleet of nuclear submarines was prepared by the US Navy and 156 ICBMs were primed for launch.

'Hawks and doves'

During the crisis, Kennedy and Khrushchev's advisors were split into two groups: hawks and doves. The 'hawks' on both sides wanted an aggressive policy. Some American generals, for example, believed that a nuclear war between the USA and the USSR was inevitable and therefore Kennedy should go to war because, as things stood, America had a good chance of winning. The 'doves', on the other hand, advised caution, recommending diplomatic strategies, which they felt offered the best chance of peace.

Images taken by US spy planes of nuclear missile bases being built in Cuba. The images were released in 1962.

ResultsPlus
Top Tip

When answering a question about *key features* of an event, such as the Cuban Missile Crisis, avoid telling the story. It is important to answer the question and focus on the key features rather than narrating events from the beginning to the end.

ResultsPlus
Build Better Answers

Exam question: Describe the key features of the Cuban Missile Crisis. (6 marks)

■ **A basic answer (1–3 marks)** contains simple statements that are accurate but contain no supporting examples.

▲ **A better answer (4–6 marks)** contains detailed statements. Each statement makes a relevant point and is backed up with specific examples to show that it is a key feature.

Before answering this question, think how you would develop the following key features of the Cuban Missile Crisis:

- the Crisis was caused by Khrushchev's decision to put Soviet missiles on Cuba
- the Crisis was resolved by a compromise between the two superpowers
- the Crisis nearly started a nuclear war.

Activities

1 Copy and complete the table below, explaining how the statements apply to the USA, the USSR or both.

	USA	USSR	Both
Cuban Missile Crisis was a success			
Cuban Missile Crisis was a failure			

2 Write a paragraph that explains who gained most from the Cuban Missile Crisis. Make sure that you back up your point with detailed examples.

The Cuban Missile Crisis: immediate and long-term consequences

Learning objectives

In this chapter you will learn about:

- the immediate consequences of the Cuban Missile Crisis, including the creation of the 'hotline', the Test Ban Treaty and *détente*
- the long-term consequences of the Cuban Missile Crisis, including the doctrine of Mutually Assured Destruction (MAD) and the French decision to leave NATO.

The immediate consequences of the Cuban Missile Crisis

The first consequence of the Cuban Missile Crisis was the reduction in Khrushchev's authority. Because the removal of American missiles from Turkey remained secret, it seemed to many that he had backed down and betrayed his allies in Cuba.

The Cuban Missile Crisis had highlighted the fragility of international peace and the difficulties of negotiation between Russia and America in a crisis situation. As a result, the superpowers agreed to the introduction of the following measures:

- the 'hotline' – in June 1963, a direct communications link was set up between the American President in Washington and the Russian Premier in Moscow
- the Limited Test Ban Treaty – in August 1963, the USA and USSR agreed to ban the testing of all nuclear weapons in space, in the sea and above ground. Underground nuclear tests were still permitted.

The Test Ban Treaty was the first step taken to control the use of nuclear weapons. Once there was agreement on this, the way was open to discuss limiting weapon production and cutting down stockpiles.

President Kennedy signalled his commitment to working with the USSR in a speech of June 1963, in which he argued that both superpowers needed to focus on their 'common interests'. This speech was the beginning of a policy called 'détente': a relaxing of tension in the relationship between the USA and the USSR. Initially, moves to détente were slow but détente became a key feature of superpower relations during the 1970s.

Cartoon of Khrushchev and Kennedy, trying to keep the 'monster' of nuclear war contained.

The long-term consequences of the Cuban Missile Crisis

The leaders of the Soviet Union were determined never again to be pushed around by America. Therefore, the Soviet government made every effort to catch up with America in the arms race. By 1965, the USA and the USSR were on an equal footing in terms of their nuclear capability. This created greater stability in the relationship between the two superpowers. American and Russian leaders realised that any nuclear war was bound to destroy both countries. This idea, known as the **doctrine** of Mutually Assured Destruction (MAD), gave both superpowers an excellent reason for avoiding war.

Another long-term consequence of the Cuban Missile Crisis was the French decision to leave NATO. In the event of a nuclear war between America and Russia, the members of NATO would be obliged to fight alongside America. French President Charles de Gaulle was appalled at the thought that France would be destroyed in this way. Therefore, in 1966, France ended its military **alliance** with America and began to develop its own nuclear missiles.

Did you know?

The 'hotline' between the American President and the Soviet Premier is sometimes known as the 'red telephone'. Despite this, it was originally a teleprinter system. It was first used in 1967, and in 1971 it was upgraded and became an actual telephone. It is still used today, and is tested every hour of every day.

Activities

1. Divide the class into two groups. One group should study the immediate consequences of the Cuban Missile Crisis. The other group should study the long-term consequences of the Cuban Missile Crisis.
2. Divide each group into pairs. Each pair should produce a ten-minute lesson designed to teach a pair from the other group about the topic they have been studying.

   Each lesson should include:

   - an interesting activity to enable the 'students' to learn about the topic
   - an activity designed to assess what the 'students' have learned
   - feedback, based on the assessment, explaining what the 'students' know well and targets for improvement.
3. Join with a pair from the other group, and take it in turns to teach your lesson.

Czechoslovakia: 'Prague Spring'

Learning objectives

In this chapter you will learn about:

- Czechoslovakian opposition to Soviet control
- Dubcek's attitude to communism
- the events of the 'Prague Spring'.

Czechoslovakian opposition to Soviet control

There are strong similarities between what happened in Hungary in 1956 and events in Czechoslovakia 12 years later.

Czechoslovakia was a Soviet satellite state. Communism had had few benefits for the Czech people. In the mid-1960s, Czechoslovakia was still run by the secret police, which brutally crushed all political opposition. At the same time, the Czechoslovakian economy was struggling. Therefore the majority of Czech people suffered a declining standard of living during the 1960s.

Political repression and economic problems made Communist Party leader Antonin Novotny highly unpopular, and as a result his leadership was challenged. On 5 January 1968, Alexander Dubcek became the Communist Party leader: the most powerful man in Czechoslovakia.

Dubcek

Dubcek was the natural choice to lead Czechoslovakia. He was a committed communist who was on friendly terms with Leonid Brezhnev (the Russian leader following Khrushchev's fall from power in 1964). Dubcek's aim was to create a genuinely popular form of communism. He described this as 'socialism with a human face'. Essentially, Dubcek wanted to get rid of the most repressive aspects of communist rule, to reform the economy and to allow more cultural freedom. In this way, he hoped to revitalise Czechoslovakian politics, economics and social life.

Czechoslovakia and the USSR.

The events of the 'Prague Spring'

'Prague Spring' is a phrase used to describe the liberal changes brought about by Dubcek from April 1968. It was named after the city of Prague, which is the Czechoslovakian capital. As part of his plan to create 'socialism with a human face', Dubcek introduced the following reforms:

- a relaxation of press **censorship**
- the legalisation of political opposition groups
- official government toleration of political criticism
- more power given to regional governments
- more power given to the Czech parliament
- 'market socialism' – the reintroduction of capitalist elements into the Czech economy.

Dubcek said that his aim was to allow 'the widest possible democracy in the social and political life of Czechoslovakia'. Dubcek's reforms were welcomed enthusiastically by students, intellectuals, workers and younger members of the Czech Communist Party. Artists and writers such as Milan Kundera and Vaclav Havel took full advantage of the reforms, writing books, plays, and essays critical of Soviet-style communism.

Older Czechoslovakian communists were shocked by the 'Prague Spring' and their horror was shared by Soviet Premier Brezhnev and his allies across Eastern Europe.

ResultsPlus

Build Better Answers

Exam question: Describe one reason why Dubcek introduced reforms in Czechoslovakia. (2 marks)

■ **A basic answer (level 1)** is accurate but lacks detail.

● **A good answer (level 2)** is accurate and includes supporting information.

The following is a basic level 1 answer to the exam question above. Add supporting information to turn it into a good answer.

Dubcek introduced reforms because he wanted to solve Czechoslovakia's economic problems.

Activity

Imagine that you are one of Dubcek's speechwriters. Write a speech for him to deliver to the Czechoslovakian Communist Party, introducing his reforms and explaining why the 'Prague Spring' will help the Party to become more popular.

You may wish to refer to the problems experienced in other communist countries, for example East Germany and Hungary.

Czechoslovakia: the Brezhnev Doctrine

Learning objectives

In this chapter you will learn about:

- the re-establishment of Soviet control in Czechoslovakia
- the Brezhnev Doctrine
- the Soviet invasion of Czechoslovakia.

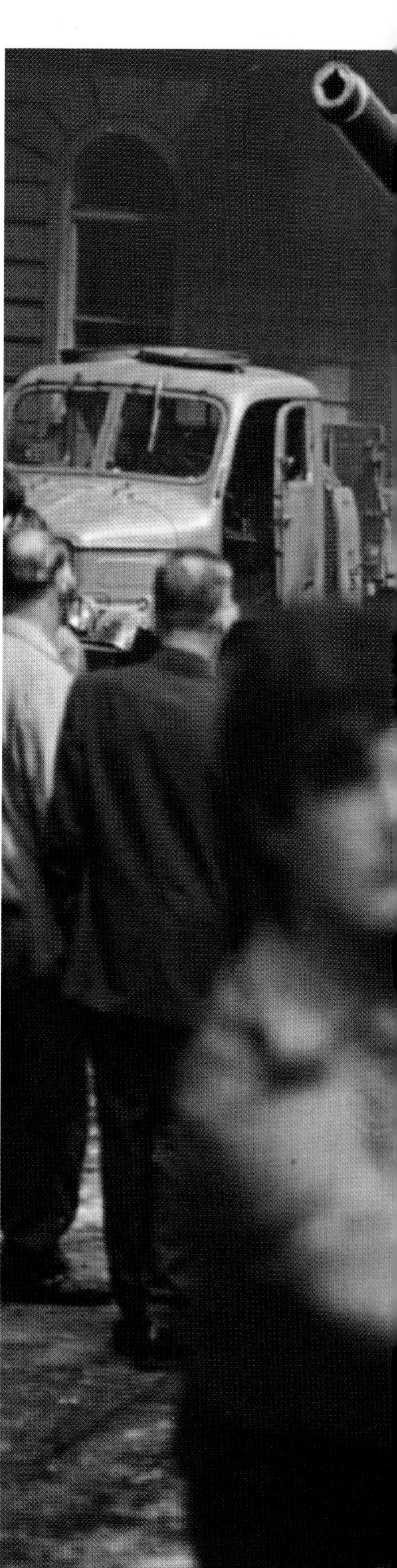

Brezhnev's dilemma

The 'Prague Spring' made life very difficult for Soviet Premier Brezhnev. On the one hand, he regarded Dubcek as a friend, and Dubcek had made no attempt to leave the Warsaw Pact or damage the USSR. On the other hand, secret Soviet intelligence reports suggested that Dubcek's reforms would lead to a weakening of Soviet control over Czechoslovakia and, in the long run, the break-up of the Eastern Bloc.

From April through to July, Brezhnev was in constant contact with Dubcek and attempted to persuade him that the reforms had gone too far. However, Dubcek failed to take the hint and took little action to control political opposition in Czechoslovakia. By late August, Brezhnev had had enough and ordered a full-scale invasion of Czechoslovakia in order to overthrow Dubcek.

The Brezhnev Doctrine

Throughout August 1968, the Soviet media portrayed Czechoslovakia as a massive threat to the USSR. Brezhnev went further and put forward a justification of the invasion, which became known as the 'Brezhnev Doctrine'. According to this doctrine, the USSR had the right to invade any country in Eastern Europe whose actions appeared to threaten the security of the whole Eastern Bloc. Brezhnev argued that Dubcek's actions threatened to undermine the Warsaw Pact and communist control in Eastern Europe, and therefore the Soviet Union had to invade.

The Soviet invasion of Czechoslovakia

Soviet tanks rolled into Czechoslovakia on the evening of 20 August 1968. Dubcek ordered the Czech people not to respond with violence. Nonetheless, there was a great deal of non-violent civil disobedience. For example, many students stood in the way of tanks holding anti-invasion banners.

Dubcek was arrested and taken to Moscow where Brezhnev tearfully told him that he had betrayed socialism. Dubcek was forced to sign the Moscow Protocol, which committed the Czech government to 'protect socialism' by reintroducing censorship and removing political opposition.

People in Prague on 21 August 1968, holding up the Czechoslovakian flag and throwing burning torches in an attempt to stop a Soviet tank.

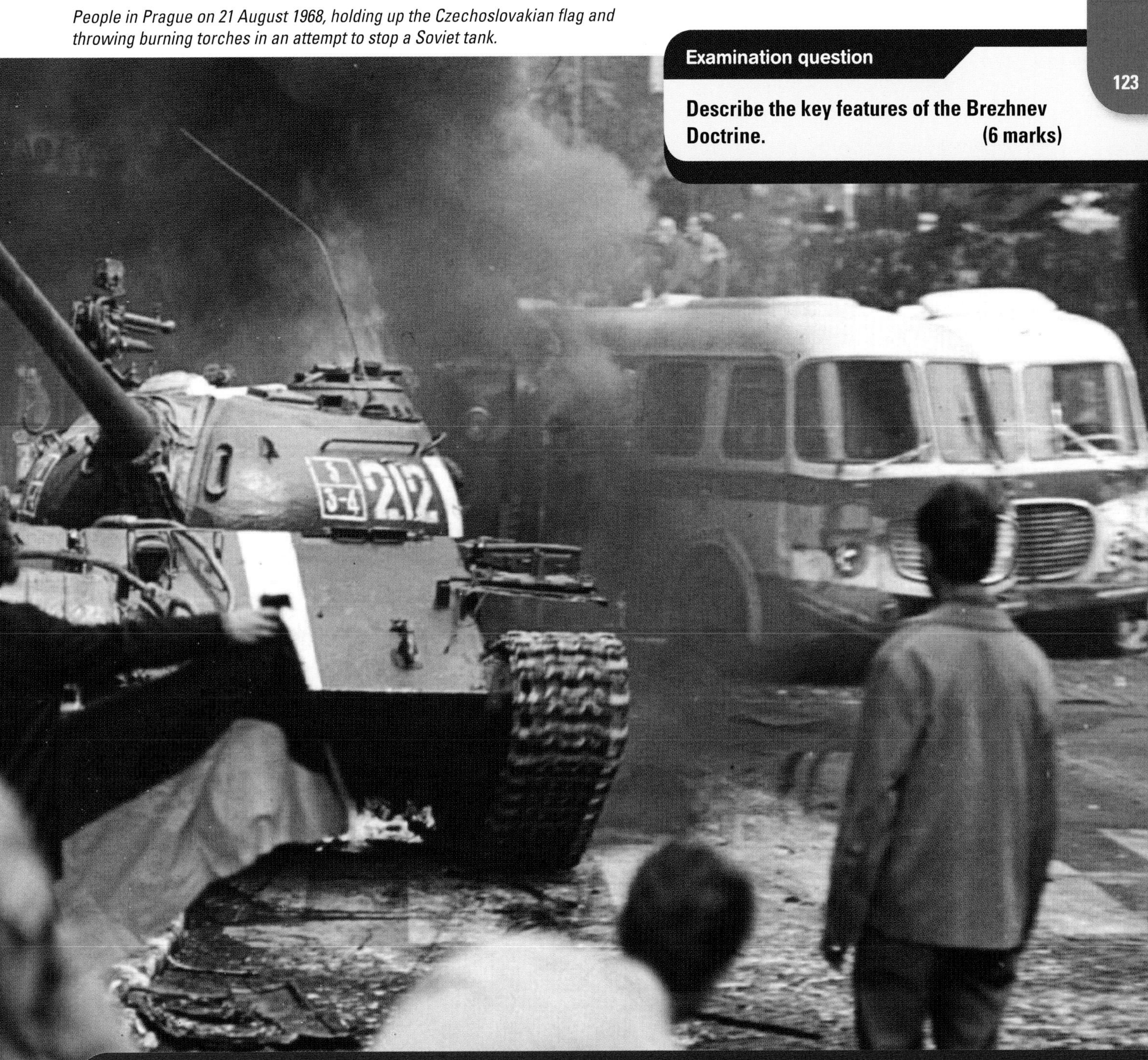

Examination question

Describe the key features of the Brezhnev Doctrine. (6 marks)

Activity

Imagine you are a reporter working in Moscow in 1968. You must prepare a telegram to send back to your newspaper in London explaining what the Brezhnev Doctrine is and why it has been introduced.

Each word of a telegram costs money, so you need to summarise this information in as few words as possible. However, you mustn't miss out any key pieces of information.

Write your telegram, trying to use as few words as possible. Compare your telegram to that of the person next to you. Have they used fewer words than you? Have they covered all of the key points? Together, produce another version of the telegram, trying to reduce your word count even further.

Czechoslovakia: international reaction

Learning objectives

In this chapter you will learn about:

- America's reaction to the Soviet invasion of Czechoslovakia
- the divisions in European communism created by the invasion.

America's response

Brezhnev believed that America would do nothing to help the Czechoslovakian people. America was already fighting a bloody war against communism in Vietnam. Brezhnev was confident that America wanted to avoid a further military entanglement. Therefore, while America publicly condemned the invasion, it offered no military support against it.

Western European response

Western European governments followed America's lead – they condemned the invasion but provided no military help. The reaction of Western European Communist Parties was more surprising. Communist Parties in Italy and France, for example, were outraged by the Soviet invasion. Therefore, they formally declared themselves independent of the Soviet Communist Party. This created rival forms of European communism – Soviet communism in the East, and Eurocommunism in the West. This was very important because it showed the extent to which Soviet communism had lost authority and support as a result of the invasion.

ResultsPlus
Top Tip

Timing is very important in the exam. Before you start writing, make a brief note of the timings for each question. We suggest spending roughly:

- 2-3 minutes on the question on page 107
- 7 minutes on the question on page 115
- 15 minutes on the question on page 125.

If you qualify for extra time, remember to include this when you work out your timings.

Eastern European response

The Soviet invasion also led to discontent in Eastern Europe. Significantly, the Yugoslavian and Romanian governments both condemned the invasion and distanced themselves from the Soviet Union. Following 1968, Yugoslavian and Romanian communists formed alliances with China, the world's other major communist power, further dividing the communist world. However, the East German and Polish governments welcomed the Soviet response – as they were concerned that Czechoslovakia was being too liberal. These pro-Moscow leaders might lose their jobs if Czech reforms were allowed to spread to other Eastern Bloc countries.

The Czech people demonstrate against the Russian presence in Prague.

ResultsPlus

Build Better Answers

Exam question: Explain why relations between the Soviet Union and the USA changed in the years 1957–69. (12 marks)

You need to make relevant points, supported by specific examples, with a clear focus on how each factor led to the situation described.

In each level, the number of statements you make will affect your mark. For example, in level 2, a single developed argument is unlikely to get more than 5 marks, whereas three developed arguments will achieve 8 or 9 marks.

■ **A basic answer (level 1)** is correct, but does not have details to support it (for example, *One reason why the relationship between the Soviet Union and the USA changed is because of the Cuban Missile Crisis*).

● **A good answer (level 2)** provides the details as well (for example, *One reason why the relationship between the Soviet Union and the USA changed is because of the Cuban Missile Crisis. Following the Cuban Missile Crisis, the USA and USSR negotiated a Test Ban Treaty (August 1963), which banned all nuclear tests except those carried out underground*).

▲ **A better answer (level 3)** shows the links between reasons or shows why one is more important (for example, *One reason why the relationship between the Soviet Union and the USA changed is because of the Cuban Missile Crisis. Following the Cuban Missile Crisis, the USA and USSR negotiated a Test Ban Treaty (August 1963), which banned all nuclear tests except those carried out underground. This was the most important reason why the relationship between the USA and the USSR changed, because this was the first time since the beginning of the Cold War that the two superpowers had tried to limit the arms race. Before this, the arms race was very competitive and there was a continuous threat of nuclear war*).

▲ **An excellent answer (full marks)** shows how three reasons are linked and reaches a judgment about their relative importance.

Now write another paragraph in answer to this question. Choose one of the following points, add examples and explain how important this factor was:

- disagreements over the future of Berlin
- the creation of the Washington–Moscow hotline
- the effects of the Soviet invasion of Czechoslovakia.

Activity

Complete the speech bubbles below to show the different reactions to the Soviet invasion of Czechoslovakia.

Lyndon B. Johnson, president of the USA.

Josip Broz Tito, communist leader of Yugoslavia.

Jacques Duclos, leader of the French communists.

Know Zone Unit 1 - section 5

In the Unit 1 exam, you will be required to answer questions from three sections. In each of those sections you will have to answer three questions: Part (a), Part (b) – where you have to do one of the two questions set – and Part (c).

You have about 25 minutes to answer the three questions on each section. Use the number of marks available for each question to help you judge how long to spend on it and how much to write.

Here we are going to look at questions for Parts (b) and (c) of Section 5.

ResultsPlus
Build Better Answers

Question (b)

Tip: Part (b) questions will usually ask you to describe the 'key features' of a major policy or an event. This question is worth 6 marks. Make sure that when you describe you don't just tell the story: think about the information and organise it as if you were putting it under headings. Let's look at an example.

Describe the key features of the Berlin Crisis. (6 marks)

Student answer	Examiner comment
One key feature of the Berlin Crisis was refugees leaving Eastern Germany. Another key feature was that it led to many meetings between leaders. A final key feature was the building of the Berlin Wall.	This answer lists three relevant points. It would therefore receive 3 marks. However, in order to get full marks, you need to provide supporting evidence for each point.

Let's rewrite the answer to mention these three points, but also provide evidence to support them. So that you can spot it easily we will put the supporting evidence in bold.

The first key feature of the Berlin Crisis was refugees leaving Eastern Germany. **Between 1949 and 1961, almost three million Eastern German citizens fled to the west looking for a better life. Many of these were highly skilled.** The next key feature of the Berlin Crisis was that it led to many meetings between leaders. **There were four summits at which Khrushchev, the Russian leader, met the American Presidents Eisenhower and Kennedy. These took place in Geneva, Paris, Vienna and America and attempted to find a peaceful solution to the crisis.** The third key feature was the building of the Berlin Wall. **In 1961, Khrushchev ordered the creation of a wall dividing East and West Berlin. The wall prevented refugees leaving East Germany and meant that Khrushchev could look strong without going to war.**	This answer makes three points and backs them up with examples. It would therefore receive full marks.

Question (c)

Tip: Part (c) questions require extended writing. They will ask you to use your knowledge to explain why something happened. You should try to find three reasons and explain them. Remember that you will have only about 15 minutes to answer this question and so you need to get straight to the point.

Explain why relations between the Soviet Union and the USA changed in 1962. (12 marks)

Student answer	Examiner comment
In 1962, relations between the Soviet Union and the USA changed because the Soviet Union placed missiles on Cuba. Cuba was only 90 miles from the coast of America and because of this the Americans felt very threatened by the arrival of Russian nuclear weapons, which were capable of destroying whole American cities. This made the relationship worse because the Americans thought that this was a very aggressive thing to do.	This answer is good, but it only gives one reason why the relationship changed. Better answers will contain three reasons.

Let's rewrite the answer to provide examples and explanation. So that you can spot them easily we have put the causes in bold.

In 1962, the relationship between the Soviet Union and the USA changed a great deal. At first it got much worse. But by the end of the year, the relationship had improved. **The first reason for the change was that the Soviet Union placed missiles on Cuba.** Cuba was only 90 miles from the coast of America and because of this the Americans felt very threatened by the arrival of Russian nuclear weapons, which were capable of destroying whole American cities. This made the relationship worse because the Americans thought that this was a very aggressive thing to do. **This led to the second reason for change, Kennedy's first reaction to the missiles on Cuba.** Kennedy publicly demanded that the USSR remove its weapons and ordered a naval blockade of Cuba. This made the relationship even worse because it looked like both sides were preparing for nuclear war. **Thirdly, both sides wanted to avoid nuclear war and so Kennedy sent his brother to do a deal with the USSR.** In the deal the USSR agreed to remove the missiles from Cuba, and the USA agreed to remove the missiles they had in Turkey. This made the relationship better because the two sides agreed a private deal, which stopped a nuclear war. Overall, the most important factor that changed the relationship between the USA and the USSR in 1962 was Khrushchev's decision to place missiles on Cuba because without this, none of the other changes would have happened.	This answer is an improvement on the previous answer because it makes three points and links these points together, showing how each point led to the next. It achieves top marks because it also prioritises the factors, explaining which is the most important.

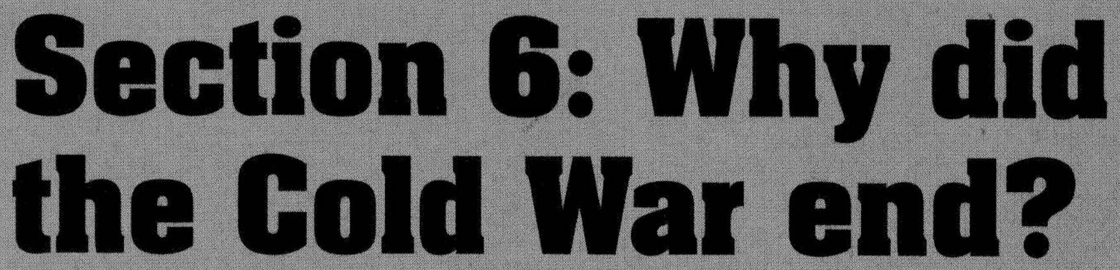

Section 6: Why did the Cold War end?

Following the Cuban Missile Crisis, relations between the two superpowers mellowed, leading to a period of relative stability and peace. However, good relations were undermined by the Soviet invasion of Afghanistan and the election of a new American president who believed that the Cold War was a moral mission: a fight between good and evil. As a result, the 1980s witnessed renewed hostility between the superpowers during an era known as the Second Cold War.

In this section you will study:

- détente and its collapse
- President Reagan and the Second Cold War
- Premier Gorbachev, the fall of the Berlin Wall, and the collapse of the Soviet Union.

You will consider how the Soviet invasion of Afghanistan led to a breakdown in the relationship between the USA and the USSR. You will also study the impact of the last two 'Cold Warriors': American President Ronald Reagan and Russian Premier Mikhail Gorbachev. Finally, you will examine the reasons for the end of the Cold War and the collapse of the Soviet Union.

Détente – the search for peace

Learning objectives

In this chapter you will learn about:

- the treaties in 1967 and 1968 which began détente
- the SALT I Treaty, the Helsinki Conference and the Apollo–Soyuz mission, which marked the high point of détente.

The Cuban Missile Crisis of 1962 brought the world to the brink of a **nuclear holocaust**. During the late-1960s and 1970s, Soviet and American leaders tried to ease the tensions in their relationship. In the West, this policy was known by the French word *détente*; the Russians called it *razryadka*. Russia and America signed two important treaties at the end of the 1960s that are good examples of the détente relationship. The treaties were important because they limited the possibility of further conflict between the superpowers.

- The 1967 Outer Space Treaty stopped the **arms race** spreading to outer space as it pledged that no nuclear weapons would be placed in space by either superpower.
- The 1968 Nuclear Non-Proliferation Treaty agreed that neither superpower would supply nuclear weapons to other states or help other states to develop nuclear weapons. This stopped superpower conflict engulfing other areas of the world.

The high point of détente was reached in the mid-1970s, with three important statements of the new understanding between the two superpowers.

The Strategic Arms Limitation Treaty (SALT I), 1972 imposed limits on the nuclear capability of Russia and the USA.

- The USA and USSR agreed that there would be no further production of strategic ballistic missiles (short-range, lightweight missiles).
- Both powers agreed that submarines carrying nuclear weapons would only be introduced when existing stocks of intercontinental ballistic missiles became obsolete.

SALT I was signed by the American president and the Soviet premier in 1972. It was significant because it was the first agreement between the superpowers that successfully limited the number of nuclear weapons they held. It also showed that détente had created an environment in which the two sides could co-operate on important issues.

Examination question

Describe the key features of détente. (6 marks)

Astronauts from the Apollo–Soyuz mission, 1975. The two crews sit in front of their flags. In front of the two crews is a model showing the docking of the two spacecraft.

The Apollo–Soyuz mission, 1975 was a joint space mission in which an American Apollo spacecraft and a Russian Soyuz spacecraft docked high above the Earth. The 1960s had been dominated by an extremely competitive race to the moon, but this marked the beginning of superpower co-operation in space.

The Helsinki Agreements, 1975

The Helsinki Conference had representatives from 35 countries. They came from all of Europe, except Andorra and Albania. There were also representatives from the USSR, the USA and Canada. They discussed an agreement that had taken two years to draft. The terms of the agreement applied to everyone. There were three main issues: security, co-operation and human rights.

Security

- All country boundaries were accepted (so East and West Germany accepted each other's existence for the first time).
- All disputes were to be settled peacefully (if necessary through the UN), not by use of threats or force.
- No country would interfere in the internal affairs of another country.
- Countries would inform each other about any big military manoeuvres and would accept representatives from other countries to observe them.

Co-operation

Countries agreed to co-operate on many different levels. For example:

- economic co-operation through trade (so the USA would buy oil from the USSR, whilst the USSR would buy wheat from the USA)
- industrial co-operation through setting the same standards and running joint industrial projects
- scientific co-operation through sharing information and research (for example, in medicine or space research)
- educational co-operation (for example, learning languages, student exchanges).

Human Rights

Countries should respect human rights, including:

- freedom of speech
- freedom of movement
- freedom of religion
- freedom of information.

The Helsinki Agreements stabilised the situation in Europe by agreeing greater co-operation between the superpowers and their European allies in terms of trade and fighting international terrorism. This limited the possibility of superpower conflict by creating a stable relationship between the USSR and America in Europe.

Activity

In groups choose one of these five key events of the détente period:

- Outer Space Treaty
- Nuclear Non-Proliferation Treaty
- SALT I
- Helsinki Conference
- Apollo–Soyuz mission.

Imagine it is the time of this event. Present a news report to the rest of the class explaining what has happened and why it is important.

The collapse of détente: the Soviet invasion of Afghanistan

Learning objectives

In this chapter you will learn about:

- the Kabul Revolution
- the establishment of a communist regime in Afghanistan
- the reasons for the Soviet invasion of Afghanistan.

The Kabul Revolution: April 1978

Even détente could not stop superpower competition over the developing world. Indeed, Soviet leader Brezhnev saw the communist revolution in Afghanistan as an opportunity to extend his power in the oil-rich Middle East. The Kabul Revolution of April 1978 witnessed the dramatic overthrow of the government. The new government, based in the Afghan capital of Kabul, was determined 'to build socialism in Afghanistan'. The new communist president, Mohammed Taraki, quickly became an ally of the USSR.

However, the revolutionary government of Afghanistan was far from stable. It suffered from personal rivalries and disagreements. Moreover, many Muslim leaders across the country were angered by the socialist reforms the government introduced. By the spring of 1979 this anger had caused a civil war to break out across the country between government and Islamic fighters. President Taraki was forced to accept Hafizullah Amin, the head of the army, as prime minister. But the two men quickly became bitter rivals. In October 1979, Amin supporters assassinated Taraki and Amin claimed presidency of the country.

The Soviet invasion: December 1979

Following Amin's seizure of power, Brezhnev ordered the Soviet invasion of Afghanistan. Brezhnev took the decision for the following reasons.

- Although Amin was a communist, the USSR did not trust him. The Soviet secret police reported that he was an American spy. He was also unpopular with a large number of Muslims in the country and Brezhnev feared that Muslim groups were planning to take control of the country.
- The USSR was concerned that, as a result of the civil war, Afghanistan would become an Islamic state and influence nearby Soviet republics to do the same. The Islamic states were not communist and therefore any countries that became Islamic would have no reason to make alliances with Russia.
- Babrak Karmal, an Afghani communist, argued that he had enough popular support to form a new government but needed Soviet help to defeat Amin's military.
- Brezhnev believed that America would tolerate the invasion, as it had done in Czechoslovakia following the 'Prague Spring' to avoid war.

Soviet troops killed Amin along with many of his supporters, and Karmal was declared president (a post he retained until 1986). Yet the invasion proved to be a disaster both for Afghanistan and the Soviet Union. It lasted ten years and around 1.5 million people died, including almost 15,000 Russian soldiers.

ResultsPlus

Build Better Answers

Exam question: Describe one cause of the Soviet invasion of Afghanistan. (2 marks)

You need to make a developed statement that both answers the question and provides some detailed support.

■ **A basic answer (level 1):**

Brezhnev ordered the invasion of Afghanistan because he believed that the new president was an American spy.

● **A good answer (level 2):**

Brezhnev ordered the invasion of Afghanistan because he believed that Hafizullah Amin, the new president, was an American spy. Russian intelligence reports suggested that Amin was trying to do a deal with America.

Activities

The Soviet invasion of Afghanistan might seem to be a quite complicated topic. You must produce *A Beginner's Guide to the Soviet Invasion of Afghanistan* so that people can understand this important event.

1 Copy the table below.

A Beginner's Guide to the Soviet Invasion of Afghanistan		
Who?	**What?**	**Why?**

2 Now add relevant information in each column.

- In the first column, list the key people mentioned in this chapter and provide brief details about their role – you may choose to find pictures to illustrate this part of your guide.
- In the second column, describe the key events of the invasion. (The second column below has been started for you as an example.)
- In the final column, explain in your own words the reason why the invasion was launched – you may choose to do this as a diagram.

A Beginner's Guide to the Soviet Invasion of Afghanistan		
Who?	**What?**	**Why?**
	In December 1979, Brezhnev ordered Soviet troops to invade Afghanistan. The war that followed this invasion lasted ten years and 1.5 million people were killed.	

The collapse of détente: the American reaction to the Soviet invasion of Afghanistan

Learning objectives

In this chapter you will learn about:

- President Carter's immediate reaction to the invasion of Afghanistan
- the failure of the SALT II Treaty
- the American boycott of the Moscow Olympic Games.

President Carter and Afghanistan

Brezhnev's invasion was a severe miscalculation. The American president, Jimmy Carter, was appalled at the Soviet aggression. Consequently, he made a statement that became known as the Carter **Doctrine**. Essentially, he argued that the USA would not allow the USSR to gain control of territory in the oil-rich Middle East. He also immediately took a number of steps to try to remove Soviet troops from Afghanistan.

1 He formed an alliance with China and Israel to support Afghan rebels, who were opposed to the Soviet invasion and the Afghan communist government. America's Central Intelligence Agency **(CIA)** provided weapons and funds for the Mujahideen – an Islamic organisation which was fighting to free Afghanistan from Soviet control.
2 He imposed **economic sanctions** (restrictions), stopping virtually all trade with the Soviet Union.
3 He ended diplomatic relations with the Soviet Union.

US President Jimmy Carter and Soviet leader Leonid Brezhnev arrive outside the Soviet Embassy in Vienna, Austria, for the SALT II Treaty talks, June 1979.

The end of détente

Carter's actions did not force Soviet troops to withdraw from Afghanistan. However, they did effectively end détente. Indeed, Carter took two further steps that showed that détente was over.

The end of Salt II

First, Carter withdrew his support for the SALT II agreement. Negotiations for the Treaty had been running since 1972. SALT II would have reduced stocks of nuclear missiles to 2250 warheads for each superpower. Carter's withdrawal meant that the Treaty never became law. (Carter later signed the treaty but, after the Soviet invasion of Afghanistan, he no longer believed in it and increased US defence spending. The Senate never ratified the treaty.)

The Olympic boycott

Secondly, Carter led a **boycott** of the 1980 Moscow Olympic Games. Around sixty countries, including China, Malawi, West Germany and Zaire, followed the American lead and refused to attend the games in protest at the Soviet invasion of Afghanistan. The American government set up an alternative Olympics, called the Olympic Boycott Games, which was held in Philadelphia. The American press ridiculed the official Olympic Games and nicknamed Misha Bear, Russia's Olympic mascot, Gulag Bear – a reference to Soviet prison camps, which were known as *gulags*.

The 1984 Los Angeles Olympic Games was also highly political. In **retaliation** for the 1980 boycott, the USSR and 14 communist countries refused to attend the Los Angeles Olympic Games. The USSR organised the Friendship Games as a communist alternative.

By 1980 détente was dead. The invasion of Afghanistan and the American response meant that superpower relations were at their lowest point since the Cuban Missile Crisis of 1962.

Did you know?

During the 1984 Los Angeles Olympic Games, McDonalds ran a campaign called 'When the US Wins, You Win'. Customers were offered free food every time America won a medal: a Coca-Cola for a bronze medal, fries for a silver medal and a Big Mac for a gold medal. The campaign was a financial disaster for McDonalds, as the Soviet boycott of the Olympics led to many more American medals than expected.

ResultsPlus
Build Better Answers

Exam question: Describe one factor that led to the end of détente. (2 marks)

■ **A basic answer (level 1)** is accurate but lacks detail.

● **A good answer (level 2)** is accurate and includes supporting information.

Look at the question above. Take one of the following factors:

- the Soviet invasion of Afghanistan
- the Carter Doctrine
- American withdrawal from the SALT II negotiations.

What supporting information would you use to develop your point?

Activity

Imagine you are part of the committee organising the Olympic Boycott Games in Philadelphia in 1980. You must design a mascot for these Olympics. The mascot should in some way represent the values that President Carter was defending when he chose to boycott the Moscow Olympic Games. Draw a picture of your mascot and label the key features, linking them to the reasons for the boycott.

Ronald Reagan and the Second Cold War: 'Evil Empire'

Learning objectives

In this chapter you will learn about:

- what is meant by the Second Cold War
- President Reagan's attitude to the Cold War
- the 'Evil Empire' speech.

The Second Cold War

The 'Second Cold War' is a phrase used to describe the period between 1979 and 1985, which marked a new low in superpower relations. As in the late 1950s and early 1960s, the public was extremely concerned about the possibility of nuclear war. This anxiety was reflected in popular culture, particularly in television shows such as the American TV movie *The Day After* (1983) and the British TV drama *Threads* (1984).

President Reagan

Détente had fallen apart under President Carter. Ronald Reagan, who became the new American president in 1981, had no intention of putting it back together. Indeed, he believed it was time for America to start fighting again: Reagan wanted to win the Cold War.

The American media were not convinced that Reagan was suitable to be president. He was famous for starring in low-budget 1950s movies. His most famous role was in the film *Bedtime for Bonzo* (1951), in which he starred alongside a chimp. Reagan was portrayed as a modern-day cowboy, who knew nothing of world affairs and was totally unqualified to be American president. French and British commentators were also worried by Reagan, particularly when he stated that he could imagine 'a limited nuclear war in Europe'.

Nonetheless, Reagan had strong ideas on the future of the Cold War. For example, he believed that détente had been a disaster for the USA. He thought the policy had made the USA weak while allowing the USSR to grow strong. Reagan rejected the idea of peaceful co-existence with the USSR, believing that it was America's destiny to fight for individual freedom in the Cold War.

'Evil Empire'

Reagan made his view of the Soviet Union plain in his famous 'Evil Empire' speech in March 1983. Reagan was a committed Christian and gave this speech at a meeting of the National Association of Evangelicals, a Christian organisation. Reagan argued that the Cold War was a fight between good and evil, and that America fought with God's blessing.

Reagon urged Americans not to: 'ignore the facts of history and the aggressive impulses of an evil empire' and to 'remove yourself from the struggle between right and wrong and good and evil'. Reagan's point was that the Cold War was a moral war and that America had a moral duty to invest in new nuclear weapons in order to defend liberty from the 'evil' Soviet Union.

A number of years ago, I heard a young father give a speech in which he said, 'I love my little girls more than anything'. He went on: 'I would rather see my little girls die now; still believing in God, than have them grow up under communism and one day die no longer believing in God'. There were thousands of young people in that audience. They came to their feet with shouts of joy. They had instantly recognised the profound truth in what he had said.

An extract from President Reagan's 'Evil Empire' speech given in March 1983. Adapted from www.americanrhetoric.com/speeches/ronaldreaganevilempire.htm

This cartoon appeared in The Sun newspaper on 21 October 1981. Reagan is dressed as a cowboy in the foreground, while Brezhnev is the figure in the background. Both are trying to destroy Europe.

Did you know?

In the 1980s, the British government had a plan for surviving a nuclear war. The British army would surround all the cities that were bombed to ensure that survivors could not leave. The government worked out that the survivors in the cities would die within two weeks due to radiation sickness. They believed that they would cause fewer problems if they all died in one place rather than escaping to the countryside.

Activity

Imagine you are a freelance journalist writing for newspapers in the United Kingdom. It is the day after Reagan's 'Evil Empire' speech. You have been asked by two newspapers to write a report on the speech.

The first newspaper requires a balanced report on the speech. Your report must explain what was said in the speech and why this is important in the context of the Cold War. It must not reveal your opinion about the speech.

The second newspaper requires a highly opinionated report on the speech. You must state clearly if you agree or disagree with Reagan's opinion, and you must explain how the speech has changed your opinion of President Reagan.

You may choose to use the text from Reagan's speech in either or both of your reports.

Reagan and the Second Cold War: 'Star Wars' – America strikes back

Learning objectives

In this chapter you will learn about:

- Reagan's vision of SDI
- the problems created by SDI
- the shift in the arms race.

Reagan's vision

Many of Reagan's closest advisors misunderstood him. They thought that when he talked about victory in the Cold War, he was only trying to win support from the American people. But Reagan had a bold vision: he was determined to win the Cold War. He honestly believed that the USA should fight to win. Specifically, Reagan believed that the USSR could be forced to disarm by his new initiative: SDI (Strategic Defence Initiative).

SDI – 'Star Wars'

Reagan's plan for winning the Cold War involved taking the arms race to a new level. He proposed a 'nuclear umbrella', which would stop Soviet nuclear bombs from reaching American soil. Reagan's plan was to launch an army of satellites equipped with powerful lasers, which would intercept Soviet missiles in space and destroy them before they could do America any harm. For obvious reasons, Reagan's scheme soon became known as 'Star Wars'. Reagan believed that his 'Star Wars' technology would make Soviet nuclear missiles useless and therefore force the USSR to disarm.

SDI was a turning point in the arms race. During détente, the superpowers had been evenly matched and had worked together to limit the growth of their nuclear stockpiles. SDI was a complete break from this policy. In fact, SDI broke the terms of the Outer Space Treaty of 1967 (see page 129), which was signed during détente and had committed the superpowers to use space technology for peace alone.

Examination question

Describe one feature of SDI.
(2 marks)

ResultsPlus
Top Tip

Structure is really important when answering a question such as the one on page 139 (about how SDI affected the superpowers' relationship). Rather than writing everything you know, break down your answer into three key points. Ensure that you back up each point with examples before moving on to the next point.

The Soviet response to SDI

SDI presented enormous problems for the Russians. Soviet leaders knew perfectly well that they could not compete with Reagan's 'Star Wars' plan.

First, America had won the race to the moon in 1969, and by the early 1980s it had developed the next generation of spacecraft: the space shuttle.

Secondly, the Soviet economy was not producing enough wealth to fund consumer goods, conventional military spending and the development of new space-based weapons.

Finally, the USSR was behind America in terms of its computer technology. During the 1980s, the American computer market boomed. Prior to the SDI, however, Soviet leaders were highly suspicious of computers because they were concerned they might be used to undermine the power of the Communist Party. For example, computers with word processors and printers could be used to produce anti-government **propaganda**, or computers linked to telephones could be used to leak secrets to governments in the West. Computers were essential for the development of a 'Star Wars'-type programme.

For these reasons, Reagan's proposals meant that the USSR could no longer compete in the arms race.

Activity

In the exam, it is important that you support your general points with specific examples. Complete the following spider diagram by adding specific examples from this chapter.

SDI broke from détente.

SDI turned the **space race** into an 'arms race'.

How did SDI affect the relationship between the USA and the USSR?

SDI ensured that the USSR could no longer keep up in the arms race.

ResultsPlus
Build Better Answers

Exam question: Describe how SDI affected the relationship between the USA and the USSR. (6 marks)

■ **A basic answer (level 1)** contains simple statements that are accurate but contain no supporting examples.

● **A good answer (level 2)** contains statements that are accurate and are developed with specific information.

▲ **An excellent answer (full marks)** includes two or three detailed statements. Each statement must make a relevant point, backed up with specific examples and an explanation of how this affects the relationship between the USA and the USSR.

For the question above, you can use the notes you made on your spider diagram. How would you develop and explain the following effects of SDI?

- SDI broke from détente.
- SDI turned the space race into an arms race.
- SDI ensured that the USSR could no longer keep up in the arms race.

Gorbachev and the end of the Cold War: 'new thinking' in Russia

Learning objectives

In this chapter you will learn about:

- Gorbachev's vision for communism
- Gorbachev's relationship with the West
- Gorbachev's 'new thinking'.

The Chernobyl nuclear power plant after it exploded in April 1986.

Gorbachev and communism

Mikhail Gorbachev was the last leader of the Soviet Union, serving from 1985 until its collapse in 1991. He oversaw the end of the Cold War, the fall of the Berlin Wall and the end of communism in Russia. However, it was never his intention to undermine communism. Rather, he hoped to be communism's saviour.

Gorbachev's relationship with the West

Gorbachev had very little foreign policy experience prior to becoming the leader of Russia. At first, he viewed the relationship with America in rather simplistic terms. For example, following his first meeting with President Reagan in 1985, he commented that 'Reagan is not just a class enemy; he is extremely primitive. He looks like a caveman and is mentally retarded.'

Gorbachev's relationship with the West was tested over the Chernobyl crisis. In April 1986, the nuclear reactor in the Chernobyl nuclear power plant in the Ukraine went critical and exploded. Initially, Gorbachev authorised a cover story that denied there had been a release of dangerous radiation. The Western media were unconvinced by the Soviet cover story and Western governments put pressure on Gorbachev to tell the truth about the scale of the disaster. Chernobyl became an international symbol of the crisis in Soviet communism.

Gorbachev's 'new thinking'

Gorbachev himself recognised that communism in Russia faced many problems.

- The Soviet economy was not nearly as efficient as the American economy. While Americans in the 1980s enjoyed an excellent standard of living, everyday life in Russia was dominated by shortages. For example, it was not uncommon for housewives in Moscow to queue for up to five hours simply to get a packet of sausages.
- Many of the Soviet people had lost faith in the Communist Party.

Gorbachev's plan for reviving communism involved a radical programme of reform. This was often summarised in two words:

- *perestroika* (restructuring) – economic reforms designed to make the Soviet economy more efficient
- *glasnost* (openness) – **censorship** of the press was to be relaxed.

Gorbachev assumed that *perestroika* and *glasnost* would strengthen the power of the Soviet Communist Party. Indeed, although Gorbachev talked about reform, he was very slow to allow democratic elections in Russia.

> The main reason for Gorbachev's popularity was the visible signs that Russia was changing. He made it possible to buy Western newspapers and magazines; the cloak of government secrecy was slowly lifted; and the press began publishing sensational articles on Stalin and past Soviet leaders. He enabled the people to gain a sense of themselves as individuals, and in so doing he accelerated the decline of the Soviet system.

Adapted from Dimitri Volkogonov, The Rise and Fall of the Soviet Empire, 1999.

Perestroika and *glasnost* are probably words you have not heard before. Try not to get their definitions confused. For example, think about the similar sounds of 'stroika' and 'structure' to remember that *perestroika* means restructuring.

Activity

1 Copy the following cards describing some of Gorbachev's early attitudes and measures.

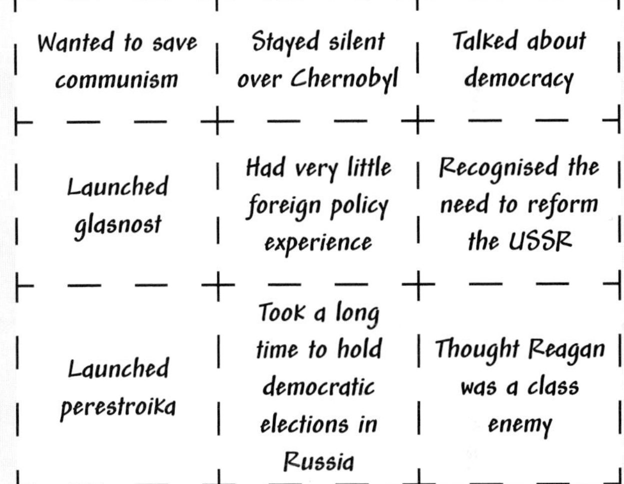

Wanted to save communism	Stayed silent over Chernobyl	Talked about democracy
Launched glasnost	Had very little foreign policy experience	Recognised the need to reform the USSR
Launched perestroika	Took a long time to hold democratic elections in Russia	Thought Reagan was a class enemy

2 On a large sheet of paper, draw the following scale.

Strengthened relationships with the West ———————— *Weakened relationships with the West*

Read each card. Decide how this factor changed Russia's relationship with the West. Place each card in an appropriate place on the scale.

3 Use your completed scale to write a paragraph in answer to the following: *Describe how Gorbachev's early attitudes and measures strengthened Russia's relationship with the West.*

Gorbachev and the end of the Cold War: Reagan and Gorbachev's changing relationship

Learning objectives

In this chapter you will learn about:

- the strengths and weaknesses of the superpowers in 1985
- three summits and the INF Treaty
- the reasons for the changing relationship between the USA and the USSR.

The positions of the superpowers in 1986

When Gorbachev became leader of Russia in 1985, it was clear that the USA was in a much stronger position than the USSR.

	USA	USSR
Strengths	• booming economy • excellent computer technology • excellent space technology • highly equipped conventional military forces • international reputation as 'leaders of the free world' • NATO allies	• Warsaw **Pact** allies • greater number of nuclear missiles than the USA
Weaknesses	• fewer nuclear missiles than the USSR	• committed to an expensive war in Afghanistan • failing economy • old-fashioned technology • reputation ruined by the Chernobyl crisis

Geneva and Reykjavik

The first meeting between President Reagan and Premier Gorbachev occurred at the Geneva **Summit** in November 1985. Reagan was clearly in the stronger position. Nonetheless, his aims were fairly limited.

Reagan's aim for the conference was to persuade Gorbachev that he sincerely desired peace between the two superpowers. Gorbachev, although in a weaker position, was hoping to persuade Reagan to drop his plans for SDI.

Gorbachev was also keen to establish a working relationship with the American president. Indeed, prior to the meeting, he sacked the long-serving Soviet foreign minister, Andrei Gromyko, and appointed Eduard Shevardnadze as his replacement. This move signalled an end to the aggressive foreign policy that had been pursued by Gromyko.

The Geneva meeting was significant because the two leaders were able to talk face-to-face and develop a personal relationship. However, no formal agreement on arms control was reached.

The Reykjavik meeting of October 1986 was much more ambitious. Reagan proposed scrapping all **ballistic nuclear missiles**. Gorbachev, however, was unwilling to agree to these proposals because Reagan refused to drop his SDI project.

Reagan and conciliation

Why did Reagan later change his mind about the USSR to the extent of wanting to resume détente with the 'Evil Empire'? Several things changed his mind.

- He could see public opinion was against another arms race. He wanted to save the money that an arms race would cost the USA. He also did not want the USA to be seen as a brutal bully. There had been large scale demonstrations across Western Europe against the siting of US missiles there. In 1984, before Gorbachev came to power, Reagan had stopped using phrases such as 'Evil Empire' and begun to use phrases such as 'mutual compromise' and calling 1984 'a year of opportunity for peace'.
- He could see there was widespread approval of Gorbachev and his changes in the USSR. There was such enthusiasm for Gorbachev's reforms that a new word was invented to describe it: 'Gorbymania'. This spread from the USSR through the Eastern European states to many other countries, including the USA. Gorbachev was the first ruler of the USSR to gain significant public approval in the USA. He had also won the approval of other heads of state, including the British prime minister, Margaret Thatcher.
- He got on with Gorbachev and seems to have believed that Gorbachev wanted reforms in the USSR and an end to the Cold War. Once Reagan had decided to try for détente, he made sure that he got the publicity right. For example, when he and Gorbachev met, he made sure that they, and their wives, looked as if they genuinely got on.

INF Treaty

Following the Reykjavik meeting, American and Soviet diplomats continued to try to draft an arms-reduction treaty. The result was the Intermediate-Range Nuclear Forces (INF) Treaty, signed in Washington in December 1987. The treaty eliminated all nuclear missiles with a range of 500–5500 kilometres (310–3400 miles).

The INF Treaty was significant because it was the first treaty to reduce the number of nuclear missiles that the superpowers possessed. It therefore went much further than SALT I, which simply limited the growth of Russian and American nuclear stockpiles. During the next four years, the two sides destroyed hundreds of missiles and strict procedures were put in place to task inspectors to ensure the treaty was followed. It was a great breakthrough.

Premier Gorbachev (sitting on the left) and President Reagan sign the INF Treaty, Washington, December 1987.

Why did Gorbachev sign the INF Treaty?

Gorbachev had refused to agree to an arms treaty in Reykjavik because Reagan refused to drop his plans for SDI. Nonetheless, a year later he signed the INF Treaty in spite of the fact that Reagan was still committed to SDI. Why did Gorbachev change his mind?

- Gorbachev came to see that nuclear weapons were highly expensive but added nothing to Soviet security.
- Reagan persuaded Gorbachev that the USA had no intention of invading the USSR.
- Gorbachev realised that the Soviet economy could never recover as long as it was spending so much money on nuclear weapons.
- Gorbachev believed that disarmament would win him popularity in the West and that this would allow him to make profitable trade deals between the USSR and the West.
- Gorbachev believed that political and economic measures would be more effective in guaranteeing Russia's security than military strength.

Summit conferences after Reagan

In 1988, Ronald Reagan went to Moscow for the first time for a summit conference. They agreed to work towards disarmament of both nuclear and conventional arms. The summit fixed no targets, but it eased the tensions created by Afghanistan and opened the way to the agreements that took place after Reagan left the presidency.

The Malta Summit, 1989

The summit was a meeting between US President George Bush and President Gorbachev. This meeting began work on the agreements that were to be CFE (1990) and START I (1991), below.

The CFE Agreement, 1990

This agreement, signed by Bush and Gorbachev, set limits to the non-nuclear forces that the Warsaw Pact and NATO could have in Europe. Negotiations for this began in 1989 and the process was made difficult because the USSR was beginning to break up at the time. This meant that, for example, Hungary was part of the Warsaw Pact when negotiations began, but had left by the time the Treaty was ready to be signed.

START I, 1991

Signed by Bush and Gorbachev, with pens made from scrapped nuclear missiles, this set limits to the numbers of nuclear weapons. Both sides agreed to reduce their holdings of nuclear warheads by about a third, by destroying them. It also agreed that both sides would continue to reduce. It did not agree on all kinds of nuclear weapons (the agreement did not cover some nuclear submarines or space weapons), but covered most of them.

Activities

1 Use the information in this chapter to complete the following table.

Summit	Gorbachev's aims	Degree of success for Gorbachev	Reagan's aims	Degree of success for Reagan
Geneva				
Reykjavik				
Washington				

2 Choose one of the summits. Imagine you are either Premier Gorbachev or President Reagan. Write a brief note to your advisors explaining what has been achieved at the summit and how you feel about the outcome of the meeting.

Gorbachev and the end of the Cold War: the break-up of Eastern Europe and the fall of the Berlin Wall

Learning objectives

In this chapter you will learn about:

- Gorbachev's attitude to Eastern Europe
- the break-up of the Eastern Bloc
- the fall of the Berlin Wall and the end of the Warsaw Pact.

Gorbachev's attitude to Eastern Europe

Gorbachev's attitude to Eastern Europe can be summarised in the following way:

- In December 1988, he announced that ideology should play a smaller role in Soviet foreign affairs. In practice, this meant that the USSR would no longer favour trade with communist states over trade with capitalist countries.
- Gorbachev was keen for Eastern European states to enjoy *perestroika* and *glasnost*.
- Gorbachev withdrew Soviet troops from Eastern European bases in order to save money.

The break-up of the Eastern Bloc

Gorbachev had never intended to weaken communist control of Eastern Europe. Once again, his desire was to strengthen communism by reform. However, once reform had started in the **Eastern Bloc**, he was unable to contain it. The Eastern Bloc had previously relied on the Soviet army to prop up their pro-Moscow regimes. There would not be another invasion of Hungary or Czechoslovakia, so the Eastern European governments were weakened.

A German celebrates the fall of the Berlin Wall, 12 November 1989. There were days of jubilant celebrations at the uniting of East and West Berlin.

The fall of the Berlin Wall

The fall of the Berlin Wall has come to symbolise the end of the Cold War. However, it would be wrong to confuse the fall of the wall with the end of the war.

The fall of the Berlin Wall is an excellent case study of the effects of reform in Eastern Europe. East Germany was slow to embrace *perestroika* and *glasnost*. Indeed, the East German government even banned Russian publications during the 1980s because they were too liberal. However, the communist government was unable to contain its citizens' desire for freedom once neighbouring states had abandoned communism.

As soon as democratic elections were announced in Hungary there was a mass movement of East German citizens through Hungary to West Germany. As a result, the East German government was forced to announce much greater freedom of travel for East German citizens. As part of this decision, on 9 November the East German government announced that East Germans would be allowed to cross the border with West Berlin. On hearing this news, thousands of East Berliners flooded the checkpoints in the wall, demanding entry into West Berlin. The border guards let them pass – the Berlin Wall had fallen. Many people started to chip away and dismantle parts of the wall, and ten new border crossings were created by the East German government in the following days. Many people were reunited with friends and relatives thay had been separated from since the wall had been built 30 years before. The opening of the Berlin Wall was the first step towards the reunification of Germany.

The end of the Warsaw Pact

As the Eastern Bloc disintegrated, it became obvious that the Warsaw Pact could not survive. The Pact was an alliance that united the communist states of Eastern Europe against the capitalist states in the West. However, as first Poland, then Hungary and finally East Germany all rejected communism, the Pact no longer served any purpose. Military co-operation ceased in early 1990 and the Warsaw Pact was formally dissolved in July 1991.

ResultsPlus

Top Tip

Detailed answers will score more highly in the exam. The use of dates is a good way to make your answer more detailed. For example, when writing about the break-up of the Eastern Bloc, try to include the dates on which the different Eastern European countries rejected communism.

Activity

You have been asked to design a museum exhibit on the break-up of the Eastern Bloc. You must produce a proposal for your exhibit. This could be in the form of a poster or a booklet.

Your proposal must include:

- information about how the exhibit would be laid out and how much space should be given to each section of the exhibit
- examples of pictures and documents that could be included in the exhibit (you may need to do some independent research to find these)
- details of the text that you would like to accompany the exhibit.

In your proposal you must explain why you have chosen this layout and defend your choice of pictures and documents.

Gorbachev and the end of the Cold War: the fall of the Soviet Union

Learning objectives

In this chapter you will learn about:

- the overthrow of President Gorbachev
- Gorbachev's final days in office and the fall of the Soviet Union
- the end of the Cold War.

Soviet reaction to the fall of the Berlin Wall

Gorbachev was undoubtedly the 'darling of the West'. Indeed, British Prime Minister Margaret Thatcher described him as 'a man I can do business with'. He was widely respected for his willingness to reform and the fact that his policies had led to the break-up of Eastern Europe.

At home in Russia, however, Gorbachev was treated with suspicion and cynicism. Leading members of the Communist Party believed that *perestroika* and *glasnost* had weakened communism rather than reviving it. Consequently, on 19 August 1991 a group of senior communist government officials – known as the 'Gang of Eight' – organised a coup which removed Gorbachev from power.

Initially, the coup was successful. Gorbachev, who was away from the capital at the time, was prevented from returning to Moscow. The new government declared a state of emergency, which overturned the freedoms gained during *perestroika* and *glasnost*. The new government's goal was to restore the power of the Soviet Union and secure the future of the communist government.

The new government lasted for three days. Boris Yeltsin, the future president of Russia, played a crucial role in defeating the coup. Yeltsin described the new government as 'illegal' and called on the people of Moscow to resist the new regime.

A group of people sit on top of a tank following the failed coup against Gorbachev, August 1991.

Boris Yeltsin (standing on tank holding papers) prepares to speak to the crowds in Moscow following the failed coup against Gorbachev, August 1991.

Gorbachev's final days as president and the fall of the Soviet Union

On 21 August Gorbachev returned to Moscow and resumed his position as leader of Russia. Immediately following his return, Gorbachev announced that it was still his intention to save Soviet communism. However, the coup had damaged Gorbachev's authority, while it had made Yeltsin a popular hero.

Gorbachev's final attempt to save the Soviet Union was the introduction of a new constitution, which was designed to give the Soviet republics, such as Latvia and the Ukraine, much greater independence. The leaders of these countries, however, wanted full independence, and for this reason the new constitution was never accepted. As a result, Gorbachev officially announced the dissolution of the Soviet Union and his resignation as president on 25 December 1991. The Cold War had ended.

> The process of renovating the country and radical changes in the world turned out to be far more complicated than could be expected. However, work of historic significance has been accomplished. The totalitarian system, which deprived the country of an opportunity to become successful and prosperous long ago has been eliminated. Free elections, freedom of the press, religious freedoms, representative organs of power, a multiparty system became a reality; human rights are recognised as the supreme principle.

Extract from Mikhail Gorbachev's resignation speech, December 1991.

The end of the Cold War

American President George Bush had declared that the Cold War was over at the Malta Conference in 1989. However, communism was still undefeated and the coup of August 1991 raised the prospect of another standoff between East and West. The Baltic States (Estonia, Latvia and Lithuania) declared themselves independent in 1990 and this was accepted by the USSR the following year. This led to copy-cat demands within the Soviet Union.

The USSR before its collapse.

The individual states which emerged after the collapse of the USSR.

It seemed that the country was on the brink of collapse. It was the fall of the Soviet Union in December 1991 that finally ended the ideological battle between the capitalist West and the communist East. The dissolution of the Soviet Union also ended superpower conflict, because once the USSR was dissolved, America became the world's only superpower.

ResultsPlus
Watch out

Throughout your study of the Cold War you have come across a number of acronyms, such as SALT, SDI, INF, the USSR and NATO. If you only learn the letters, it can be easy to get these confused. Make sure you know what the acronyms stand for.

Activities

You have been commissioned to write a biography of Mikhail Gorbachev, focusing on his role as Russian leader and his contribution to ending the Cold War. You must complete this task in four stages.

1. Write a table of contents with titles for each of the chapters that you are going to write.
2. Write a 20-word summary of the contents of each of the chapters.
3. You have a budget of £2,000 to spend on pictures to illustrate the book. Choose a series of pictures to accompany your chapters. Write a sentence justifying why each picture you have chosen should be in the book. Pictures cost:
   - £250 for a black and white image
   - £500 for a colour image.
4. Choose a title for the biography that accurately reflects the contents of the book.

ResultsPlus
Build Better Answers

Exam question: Explain why relations between the Soviet Union and the USA changed in the years 1979–91. (12 marks)

You need to make relevant points supported by specific examples, with a clear focus on how each factor led to the situation described. To reach the highest level, you must show how the factors are linked to each other and reach a judgment about their relative importance.

In each level, the number of statements you make will affect your mark. For example, in level 2, a single developed argument is unlikely to get more than 5 marks, whereas three developed arguments will achieve 8 or 9 marks.

■ **Level 1 – a paragraph from a basic answer:**
One reason why the relationship between the Soviet Union and the USA changed is because of the end of détente.

● **Level 2 – a paragraph from a good answer:**
One reason why the relationship between the Soviet Union and the USA changed is because of the end of détente. During détente the superpowers worked together and signed SALT I, which limited their nuclear capabilities. However, when détente broke down, the USA pulled out of SALT II negotiations and therefore the two sides never formally agreed the treaty.

▲ **Level 3 – a paragraph from an excellent answer:**
One reason why the relationship between the Soviet Union and the USA changed is because of the end of détente. During détente the superpowers worked together and signed SALT I, which limited their nuclear capabilities. However, when détente broke down, the USA pulled out of SALT II negotiations and therefore the two sides never formally agreed the treaty. This shows that the relationship had changed because during détente the USA and the USSR worked together, but after the end of détente they were no longer willing to co-operate. The end of détente is the most important factor because it allowed the Cold War to spread to outer space with SDI, which in turn forced Gorbachev to negotiate with the West.

Know Zone Unit 1 - section 6

In the Unit 1 exam, you will be required to answer questions from three sections. In each of those sections you will have to answer three questions: Part (a), Part (b) – where you have to do one of the two questions set – and Part (c).

You have about 25 minutes to answer the three questions on each section. Use the number of marks available for each question to help you judge how long to spend on it and how much to write.

Here we are going to look at questions for Parts (b) and (c) of Section 6.

ResultsPlus

Build Better Answers

Question (b)

Tip: Part (b) questions will usually ask you to describe the 'key features' of a major policy or an event. This question is worth 6 marks. Make sure that when you describe you don't just tell the story: think about the information and organise it as if you were putting it under headings. Let's look at an example.

Decribe the key features of the détente. (6 marks)

Student answer	Examiner comment
In the 1960s there were a few times when it looked like Russia and America would start a nuclear war, such as the Cuban Missile Crisis of 1962. However, after this, Russian and American leaders decided that this was too dangerous and therefore they would have a different relationship, which was called détente. At first, détente went really well and the two countries made a treaty called SALT I. They also had a space mission together, which was very different to the space race to the moon. However, by 1980, détente had broken down and the two countries started the Second Cold War.	This answer shows a lot of knowledge about détente. However, this knowledge is not organised and therefore does not effectively answer the question. A better answer would contain two or three points with supporting evidence.

Let's rewrite the answer to make three points and provide accurate examples to develop them. So that you can spot them easily we will put the points in bold.

The first key feature of détente was co-operation between the superpowers to limit nuclear weapons. For example, they signed the Nuclear Non-Proliferation Treaty in 1968 and SALT I in 1972. Both of these treaties restricted the number of nuclear weapons that each country could control. **A second key feature of détente was co-operation in space.** The Outer Space Treaty of 1967 said that neither superpower could place nuclear weapons in space, and the Apollo-Soyuz mission marked a highpoint of the superpowers working together. **Finally, a third key feature of détente was co-operation in Europe.** At the Helsinki Conference of 1975, Russia and America agreed to work together to fight terrorism in Europe.	This answer makes three points and backs them up with examples. It would therefore receive full marks.

Question (c)

Tip: Part (c) questions require extended writing. They will ask you to use your knowledge to explain why something happened. You should try to find three reasons and explain them. Remember that you will have only about 15 minutes to answer this question and so you need to get straight to the point.

Explain why relations between the Soviet Union and the USA changed between 1979 and 1985. (12 marks)

Student answer	Examiner comment
Between 1979 and 1985, the relationship between the USSR and the USA changed for three reasons. The first reason was because the Russian leader, Brezhnev, ordered the invasion of Afghanistan. The second reason was because the American President Carter decided to boycott the Moscow Olympic Games in 1980. The final reason was because of new leaders in America and the USSR, who were able to work together.	This answer lists three valid reasons why the relationship changed in this period. However, the answer is just a list and does not provide any detail to support these points, or any explanation of how they changed the relationship.

Let's rewrite it to mention three clear causes of change, but also include examples and explanation. We have put the causes in bold to make them easy to spot.

Between 1979 and 1985, the relationship between the USSR and the USA changed for three reasons. **The first reason was because the Russian leader, Brezhnev, ordered the invasion of Afghanistan.** The American president was unhappy with the invasion because Afghanistan was in the Middle East and he believed that America should stop communism spreading to areas of the world which had natural resources, like oil, that America needed. The invasion changed the relationship between the USSR and the USA because the USA began funding rebel fighters to try and overthrow the communist regime in Afghanistan. **The second reason was because the American President Carter decided to boycott the Moscow Olympic Games in 1980.** This was the president's response to the Soviet invasion of Afghanistan, and made the relationship even worse. America did not attend the games, and instead held their own Olympics. **The final reason was because of new leaders in America and the USSR, who were able to work together.** President Reagan's 'Star Wars' policy forced the Soviet leader, Gorbachev, to hold talks with America. This resulted in a better relationship because Reagan persuaded Gorbachev that the USA had no intention of invading the USSR.	This is a much better answer because instead of listing points, it adds detail to them, explaining how each event changed the relationship between the two superpowers. To get full marks this answer would have to give three reasons and prioritise them by making links between them.

Welcome to examzone

Revising for your exams can be a daunting prospect. Use this section of the book to get ideas, tips and practice to help you prepare as well as you can.

Zone In!

Have you ever become so absorbed in a task that it suddenly feels entirely natural? This is a feeling familiar to many athletes and performers: it's a feeling of being 'in the zone' that helps you focus and achieve your best.

Here are our top tips for getting in the zone with your revision.

- **Understand the exam process** and what revision you need to do. This will give you confidence but also help you to put things into proportion. Use the Planning Zone to create a revision plan.
- **Build your confidence** by using your revision time, not just to revise the information you need to know, but also to practise the skills you need for the examination. Try answering questions in timed conditions so that you're more prepared for writing answers in the exam.
- **Deal with distractions** by making a list of everything that might interfere with your revision and how you can deal with each issue. For example, revise in a room without a television, but plan breaks in your revision so that you can watch your favourite programmes.
- **Share your plan with friends and family** so that they know not to distract you when you want to revise. This will mean you can have more quality time with them when you aren't revising.
- **Keep healthy** by making sure you eat well and exercise, and by getting enough sleep. If your body is not in the right state, your mind won't be either – and staying up late to cram the night before the exam is likely to leave you too tired to do your best.

Planning Zone

The key to success in exams and revision often lies in the right planning, so that you don't leave anything until the last minute. Use these ideas to create your personal revision plan.

First, fill in the dates of your examinations. Check with your teacher when these are if you're not sure. Add in any regular commitments you have. This will help you get a realistic idea of how much time you have to revise.

Know your strengths and weaknesses and assign more time to topics you find difficult – don't be tempted to leave them until the last minute.

Create a revision 'checklist' using the Know Zone lists and use them to check your knowledge and skills.

Now fill in the timetable with sensible revision slots. Divide your revision into smaller sections to make it more manageable and less daunting. Make sure you give yourself regular breaks and plan in different activities to provide some variety.

Keep to the timetable! Put your plan up somewhere visible so you can refer back to it and check that you are on track.

Know Zone

In this zone, you'll find some useful suggestions about how to structure your revision, and checklists to help you test your learning for each of the main topics. You might want to skim-read this before you start your revision planning, as it will help you think about how best to revise the content.

Revision techniques

Remember that different people learn in different ways – some remember visually and therefore might want to think about using diagrams and other drawings for their revision, whereas others remember better through sound or through writing things out. Think about what works best for you by trying out some of the techniques below.

- **Summaries**: writing a summary of the information in a chapter can be a useful way of making sure you've understood it. But don't just copy it all out. Try to reduce each paragraph to a couple of sentences. Then try to reduce the couple of sentences to a few words!
- **Concept maps**: if you're a visual learner, you may find it easier to take in information by representing it visually. Draw concept maps or other diagrams. These are particularly good at showing links. For example, you could create a concept map which shows the effects of the Versailles Treaty on Germany, with arrows pointing to such things as 'land losses', 'military losses' etc.
- **Mnemonics**: this is when you take the first letter of a series of words you want to remember and then make a new word or sentence.
- **Index cards**: write important events and people on index cards then test yourself on why they were important.
- **Timelines**: create a large, visual timeline and annotate it in colour.
- **Quizzes**: let's face it, learning stuff can be dull. Why not make a quiz out of it? Set a friend 20 questions to answer. Make up multiple-choice questions. You might even make up your own exam questions and see if your friend can answer them!

And then when you are ready:

- practice questions – go back through the sample exam questions in this book to see if you can answer them (without cheating!)
- try writing out some of your answers in timed conditions so that you're used to the amount of time you'll have to answer each type of question in the exam.

If you are sitting your exams from 2014 onwards, you will be sitting all your exams together at the end of your course. Make sure you know in which order you are sitting the exams, and prepare for each accordingly – check with your teacher if you're not sure. They are likely to be about a week apart, so make sure you allow plenty of revision time for each before your first exam.

Know Zone Unit 1 Section 1

You should know about the following things. If you can't remember any of them, just look at the page number and re-read that chapter.

- ❏ How the alliance system developed up to 1914 **(pages 8–9)**
- ❏ The role of Germany in creating tension in Europe **(pages 8–9)**
- ❏ The importance of colonies to the Great Powers **(pages 10–11)**
- ❏ How the Kaiser's actions threatened Britain and France **(pages 10–11)**
- ❏ The importance of the navy to Britain **(page 12)**
- ❏ How Germany was threatening British naval supremacy **(pages 12–13)**
- ❏ The economic background to the First World War **(pages 14–15)**
- ❏ The importance of industrialisation **(pages 14–15)**
- ❏ The importance of the decline of Ottoman power **(pages 16–17)**
- ❏ The importance of the Balkans to different countries **(pages 16–17)**
- ❏ The impact of the Bosnian Crisis **(pages 18–21)**
- ❏ How the Balkan Wars increased tension **(pages 18–21)**
- ❏ The events of the Sarajevo assassination **(pages 22–23)**
- ❏ The role of chance in history **(pages 22–23)**
- ❏ The impact of the Sarajevo assassination **(pages 24–25)**
- ❏ How Austria-Hungary intended to take revenge on Serbia **(pages 24–25)**
- ❏ Why war broke out in August 1914 **(pages 26–27)**
- ❏ How the alliances and ententes contributed to the outbreak of war **(pages 26–27)**

Key people

Do you know why these people are important?

Otto von Bismarck

Kaiser Wilhelm (William) II

David Lloyd George

Edward Grey

Emperor Franz Joseph

Tsar Nicholas

Archduke Franz Ferdinand

Gavrilo Princip

Colonel Apis

Key events

Do you know why these events are important? If not, go back to the page and look them up!

1882 Triple Alliance signed **(page 8)**

1894 Dual Entente signed **(page 8)**

1904 Entente Cordiale signed **(page 9)**

1905 Morocco Crisis **(page 11)**

1906 Launch of first dreadnought **(page 12)**

1907 Triple Entente signed **(page 9)**

1908 'Young Turk' uprising **(page 19)**

1911 The Agadir Crisis **(page 11)**

1912 Outbreak of Balkan Wars **(page 20)**

1914 Assassination at Sarajevo **(page 22)**

1914 Outbreak of the First World War **(page 26)**

Know Zone Unit 1 Section 2

You should know about the following things. If you can't remember any of them, just look at the page number and re-read that chapter.

- ❑ Why Germany wanted an armistice **(page 31)**
- ❑ The terms of the armistice **(page 31)**
- ❑ The aims of the 'Big Three' **(pages 32–35)**
- ❑ How these aims affected the terms of the treaties **(pages 32–35)**
- ❑ Why the European powers were so determined to punish Germany in the peace treaty **(pages 32–35)**
- ❑ The terms of the Treaty of Versailles **(pages 36–39)**
- ❑ How Europe was politically divided after the war **(pages 40–43)**
- ❑ The terms of the treaties other than Versailles **(pages 40–43)**
- ❑ The new Europe in 1926 **(pages 44–45)**
- ❑ How the Big Three felt about the decisions made at Versailles **(pages 46–47)**
- ❑ The German reaction to the Versailles treaty **(pages 46–47)**
- ❑ How international relations deteriorated in 1923 **(pages 48–49)**
- ❑ The importance of the Locarno and Kellogg–Briand Pacts **(pages 48–49)**
- ❑ How the League of Nations was organised **(pages 50–51)**
- ❑ How the work of the League extended beyond peace-keeping **(pages 50–51)**
- ❑ The political actions of the League in the 1920s **(pages 52–53)**
- ❑ The valuable work of the commissions **(page 53)**
- ❑ The weaknesses of the League of Nations **(pages 54–55)**
- ❑ How those weaknesses hindered the work of the League **(pages 54–55)**

Key events

Do you know why these events are important? If not, go back to the page and look them up!

1918 Armistice and end of the war **(page 31)**

1919 Treaties of Versailles, St Germain, Neuilly signed **(pages 36–42)**

1919 League of Nations established **(page 38)**

1920 Treaties of Sèvres and Trianon signed **(pages 42–43)**

1923 Treaty of Lausanne signed **(page 43)**

1923 French occupy Ruhr **(page 48)**

1924 Dawes Plan **(page 48)**

1925 Locarno Pact **(page 48)**

1928 Kellogg-Briand Pact **(page 49)**

Key people

Do you know why these people are important?

Marshall Foch

Woodrow Wilson

David Lloyd George

Georges Clemenceau

Gustav Stresemann

Fridtjof Nansen

Know Zone Unit 1 Section 3

You should know about the following things. If you can't remember any of them, just look at the page number and re-read that chapter.

- ❑ Why the Great Depression began in 1929 **(page 59)**
- ❑ How economic depression affected relations between the Great Powers **(page 59)**
- ❑ The impact of the Great Depression on Germany **(pages 60–61)**
- ❑ The impact of the Great Depression on Japan **(pages 62–63)**
- ❑ How the League failed to stop Japanese aggression in Manchuria **(page 63)**
- ❑ The ambitions of Mussolini **(pages 64–65)**
- ❑ How the League failed to stop Italian aggression in Abyssinia **(pages 64–65)**
- ❑ The impact of the Treaty of Versailles on Germany **(pages 66–67)**
- ❑ Whether the Treaty of Versailles was fair on Germany **(pages 66–67)**
- ❑ The steps by which Hitler developed German foreign policy **(pages 68–69)**
- ❑ The British and French reactions to Hitler's actions **(pages 68–69)**
- ❑ How appeasement affected Hitler's actions **(pages 70–71)**
- ❑ How Austria was absorbed into Germany **(pages 70–71)**
- ❑ How Hitler acquired the Sudetenland **(pages 72–73)**
- ❑ The strength of anti-war feelings, particularly among the British **(pages 72–73)**
- ❑ The importance of the Nazi–Soviet Pact **(pages 74–75)**
- ❑ The events that resulted in Europe going to war in 1939 **(pages 74–77)**
- ❑ How to take an overview of Britain's reaction to German foreign policy 1933–39 **(pages 78–79)**
- ❑ How to make a historical judgment based on a series of events **(pages 78–79)**

Key people

Do you know why these people are important?

Pu Yi	Pierre Laval	Edvard Benes
Lord Lytton	Adolf Hitler	Joseph Stalin
Benito Mussolini	Neville Chamberlain	Edouard Daladier
Haile Selassie	Kurt Schuschnigg	
Samuel Hoare	Arthur Seyss-Inquart	

Key events

Do you know why these events are important? If not, go back to the page and look them up!

1929	Wall Street Crash **(page 59)**
1931	Mukden Incident and Japanese invasion of Manchuria **(pages 62-63)**
1932	Lytton Commission reports **(page 63)**
1933	Hitler comes to power in Germany **(page 68)**
1935	Italian invasion of Abyssinia **(pages 64-65)**
1935	Hoare–Laval Pact leaked to press **(page 65)**
1935	Saar rejoins Germany **(page 68)**
1936	Remilitarisation of Rhineland **(page 68)**
1936	Rome–Berlin Axis **(page 69)**
1937	Anti-Comintern Pact **(page 69)**
1938	Anschluss **(pages 70-71)**
1938	Sudeten Crisis **(page 72)**
1938	Munich Conference **(page 72)**
1939	Pact of Steel **(page 69)**
1939	German occupation of Moravia, Bohemia and Memel **(page 74)**
1939	Nazi–Soviet Pact **(page 74)**
1939	Outbreak of Second World War **(page 75)**

Know Zone Unit 1 Section 4

You should know about the following things. If you can't remember any of them, just look at the page number and re-read that chapter.

- ❑ The difference between communism and capitalism **(pages 84–87)**
- ❑ The three key meetings of the Grand Alliance **(pages 84–87)**
- ❑ The difficult relationship between Russia and America before the Cold War began **(pages 84–87)**
- ❑ The breakdown of trust between Russia and America **(pages 88–89)**
- ❑ How Russia and America viewed each other in 1946 **(pages 88–89)**
- ❑ The key features of the Truman Doctrine and Marshall Aid **(pages 90–91)**
- ❑ America's reasons for offering Marshall Aid **(pages 90–91)**
- ❑ Stalin's control of the satellite states **(pages 92–94)**
- ❑ Why Stalin established Cominform and Comecon **(pages 94–95)**
- ❑ How the 'spheres of influence' became 'two camps' **(pages 92–95)**
- ❑ The division of Germany into East and West **(pages 96–99)**
- ❑ The impact of the Berlin Blockade **(pages 97–99)**
- ❑ The formation of NATO and the arms race **(pages 98–99)**
- ❑ The effect of Soviet rule on Hungary **(pages 100–103)**
- ❑ The causes and consequences of 'de-Stalinisation' **(pages 100–103)**
- ❑ The impact of the Hungarian revolt of 1956 **(pages 100–103)**

Key people

Do you know why these people are important?

Franklin D. Roosevelt	Matyas Rakosi
Winston Churchill	Nikita Khrushchev
Joseph Stalin	Dwight D. Eisenhower
Harry S. Truman	Janos Kadar

Key events

Do you know why these events are important? If not, go back to the page and look them up!

- 1941 Grand Alliance created **(page 84)**
- 1943 Teheran Conference **(page 84)**
- 1945 Yalta Conference **(page 85)**
- 1945 Potsdam Conference **(page 86)**
- 1946 Churchill's 'Iron Curtain' speech **(page 88)**
- 1946 Long Telegram sent **(page 88)**
- 1946 Novikov's Telegram sent **(page 88)**
- 1947 Truman Doctrine announced **(page 90)**
- 1947 Marshall Plan announced **(page 90)**
- 1947 Cominform created **(page 94)**
- 1948 Paris Conference **(page 91)**
- 1948–9 Berlin Blockade **(page 97)**
- 1949 Comecon created **(page 95)**
- 1949 West Germany and East Germany created **(page 97)**
- 1949 Formation of NATO **(page 98)**
- 1955 Warsaw Pact established **(page 98)**
- 1956 Krushchev's 'Secret Speech' **(page 100)**
- 1956 Soviet invasion of Hungary **(page 101)**

Know Zone Unit 1 Section 5

You should know about the following things. If you can't remember any of them, just look at the page number and re-read that chapter.

- ❏ The refugee problem facing the East German government **(page 107)**
- ❏ Krushchev's response to this crisis **(page 107)**
- ❏ The failure of negotiations with Khrushchev over the future of Berlin **(pages 108–109)**
- ❏ Khrushchev's ultimatum and Kennedy's preparation for war **(pages 108–109)**
- ❏ The reasons for the creation of the Berlin Wall **(pages 110–111)**
- ❏ Kennedy's response to the building of the Berlin Wall **(pages 110–111)**
- ❏ The development of the arms race between 1945 and 1961 **(pages 112–115)**
- ❏ The effects of Cuba's revolution **(pages 112–115)**
- ❏ Khrushchev's decision to build missile bases on Cuba **(pages 112–115)**
- ❏ How America learned of Khrushchev's plan **(pages 116–117)**
- ❏ The 'hawks and the doves' **(page 117)**
- ❏ The events of the 'Thirteen Days' **(pages 116–117)**
- ❏ The immediate consequences of the Cuban Missile Crisis, including the creation of the 'hotline', the Test Ban Treaty and détente **(page 118)**
- ❏ The long-term consequences of the Cuban Missile Crisis, including the doctrine of Mutually Assured Destruction (MAD) and the French decision to leave NATO **(page 119)**
- ❏ Czechoslovakian opposition to Soviet control **(pages 120–121)**
- ❏ Dubcek's attitude to communism **(pages 120–121)**
- ❏ The events of the 'Prague Spring' **(pages 120–121)**
- ❏ The re-establishment of Soviet control in Czechoslovakia **(pages 122–123)**
- ❏ The Brezhnev Doctrine **(page 122)**
- ❏ The Soviet invasion of Czechoslovakia **(pages 122–123)**
- ❏ America's reaction to the Soviet invasion of Czechoslovakia **(page 124)**
- ❏ The divisions in European communism created by the invasion **(page 124)**

Key events

Do you know why these events are important? If not, go back to the page and look them up!

- 1957 Russian scientists launch Sputnik 1 **(page 114)**
- 1959 Geneva Summit **(page 108)**
- 1960 Paris Conference **(page 108)**
- 1961 Vienna Conference **(page 108)**
- 1961 East German troops erect a barbed wire fence around West Berlin **(page 110)**
- 1961 Bay of Pigs invasion **(page 114)**
- 1962 Premier Khrushchev sends nuclear missiles to Cuba **(page 115)**
- 1962 Cuban Missile Crisis **(page 116)**
- 1963 President Kennedy visits Berlin **(page 111)**
- 1963 'Hotline' between Washington and Moscow created **(page 118)**
- 1963 Limited Test Ban Treaty **(page 118)**
- 1968 'Prague Spring' **(page 121)**
- 1968 Soviet invasion of Czechoslovakia **(page 122)**

Key people

Do you know why these people are important?

John F. Kennedy	Dwight D. Eisenhower	Leonid Brezhnev	Josip Broz Tito
Nikita Khrushchev	Alexander Dubcek	Lyndon B. Johnson	

Know Zone Unit 1 Section 6

If you can't remember any of the following things just look at the page number and re-read that chapter.

- ❑ The treaties in 1967 and 1968 which began détente **(page 129)**
- ❑ The SALT I Treaty, the Helsinki Conference and the Apollo–Soyuz mission **(page 129–131)**
- ❑ The Kabul Revolution **(pages 132–133)**
- ❑ The establishment of a communist regime in Afghanistan **(pages 132–133)**
- ❑ The reasons for the Soviet invasion of Afghanistan **(pages 132–133)**
- ❑ President Carter's immediate reaction to the invasion of Afghanistan **(pages 134–135)**
- ❑ The failure of the SALT II Treaty **(page 135)**
- ❑ The American boycott of the Moscow Olympic Games **(page 135)**
- ❑ What is meant by the Second Cold War **(pages 136–137)**
- ❑ President Reagan's attitude to the Cold War **(pages 136–137)**
- ❑ The 'Evil Empire' speech **(pages 136–137)**
- ❑ Reagan's vision of SDI **(pages 138–139)**
- ❑ The problems created by SDI **(pages 138–139)**
- ❑ The shift in the arms race **(pages 138–139)**
- ❑ Gorbachev's vision for communism **(pages 140–141)**
- ❑ Gorbachev's relationship with the West **(page 140)**
- ❑ Gorbachev's 'new thinking' **(page 141)**
- ❑ The strengths and weaknesses of the superpowers in 1985 **(pages 142–145)**
- ❑ Three summits and the INF Treaty **(pages 142–145)**
- ❑ The reasons for the changing relationship between the USA and the USSR **(pages 142–145)**
- ❑ Gorbachev's attitude to Eastern Europe **(pages 146–147)**
- ❑ The break-up of the Eastern Bloc **(pages 146–147)**
- ❑ The fall of the Berlin Wall and the end of the Warsaw Pact **(page 147)**
- ❑ The overthrow of President Gorbachev **(pages 148–149)**
- ❑ Gorbachev's final days in office and the fall of the Soviet Union **(pages 148–151)**
- ❑ The end of the Cold War **(pages 150–151)**

Key events

1967 Outer Space Treaty **(page 129)**

1968 Nuclear Non-proliferation Treaty **(page 129)**

1972 SALT I **(page 129)**

1975 Helsinki Conference **(page 130–131)**

1975 Apollo–Soyuz mission **(page 130)**

1978 Kabul Revolution **(page 132)**

1979 Soviet invasion of Afghanistan **(page 132)**

1980 Moscow Olympic Games **(page 135)**

1983 Reagan's 'Evil Empire' speech **(page 136)**

1983 Reagan proposes SDI **(page 138)**

1984 Los Angeles Olympic Games **(page 135)**

1985 Geneva Summit **(page 142)**

1986 Chernobyl disaster **(page 140)**

1986 Reykjavik Summit **(page 142)**

1987 INF Treaty **(page 143)**

1989 Communist government falls in Poland, Hungary and Czechoslovakia **(page 146)**

1989 Fall of the Berlin Wall **(page 147)**

1991 Warsaw Pact dissolved **(page 147)**

1991 'Gang of Eight' remove Gorbachev from power **(page 148)**

1991 Gorbachev resigns and announces the fall of the Soviet Union **(page 149)**

Key people

Do you know why these people are important?

Ronald Reagan
Jimmy Carter
Mikhail Gorbachev
Boris Yeltsin
Leonid Brezhnev

Don't Panic Zone

As the day of the exam gets closer, many students tend to go into panic mode, either working long hours without really giving their brain a chance to absorb information, or giving up and staring blankly at the wall.

Look over your revision notes and go through the checklists to remind yourself of the main areas you need to know about. Don't try to cram in too much new information at the last minute and don't stay up late revising – you'll do better if you get a good night's sleep.

Exam Zone

What to expect in the exam paper

You will have 1 hour and 15 minutes in the examination. There will be six sections in the Unit 1 exam paper and you have to answer questions from three of these sections. That gives you 25 minutes on each section, so you are not expected to write huge amounts.

In each section there are three questions and you should answer all three – though you will get a choice on Part (b). You might want to spend about 2–3 minutes on Part (a), about 7–8 minutes on Part (b) and about 15 minutes on Part (c).

Part (a) is worth 2 marks.

It has a photograph to help you remember the topic and then a question which asks you to describe one action, event, way, reaction etc. You need to identify the action, event, way, reaction etc. and then add some detail to get the second mark.

So if the question says, 'Describe one way in which Germany's land size was reduced by the Treaty of Versailles' you can say:

'Its colonies were taken away. These were ...'.

Page 7 has an example of this type of question.

Part (b) is worth 6 marks.

Part (b) is divided into two parts. You should answer **either** Part b (i) **or** Part b (ii).

It asks you to describe how something happened or what the key features were. So if you are asked *how* Germany was punished in the Treaty of Versailles, make sure you don't write about *why* it was punished.

Sometimes the question asks about 'key features', which means you need to group your facts under headings (although you don't actually write the headings).

So if you are asked for the key features of the Prague Spring, you ought to think:

'Czechs want more freedom', 'Russians resist', 'West fails to support'.

Then you give some facts about each of these key features.

You can see an example of this type of question explained on page 91.

Part (c) is worth 12 marks.

It asks you to explain why something happened. You have to think of a number of reasons (at least three is recommended) and use your knowledge to explain why those reasons brought about the outcome mentioned in the question.

So if you are asked 'Why did war break out in 1914?' you might think the following were some of the reasons:

'colonial rivalry, economic rivalry, the assassination of the Archduke'.

You then have to show why each one led to war.

Then, if you can do the clever bit and make a case for any reason or reasons being more important than the others, you will get top marks.

You can see an example of this type of question explained on page 63.

Meet the exam paper

In this exam you will write all of your answers in the spaces provided on the exam paper. It's important that you use a black pen and that you indicate clearly which questions you have answered where a choice is provided – instructions will be given on the paper. Try to make your handwriting as legible as possible.

This diagram shows the front cover and two pages from a sample exam paper. These instructions, information and advice will always appear on the front of the paper. It is worth reading it carefully now as well as in the exam. Check you understand it and ask your teacher about anything you are not sure of.

Because there are six sections and lots of space provided for writing, the exam booklet can seem a bit daunting when you first see it. Remember that you're only answering on three of the six sections, and that you don't need to fill all of the space allowed for answers. If possible, ask your teacher to show you an example of a past paper before your exam so that you know what to expect before you go in.

Print your surname here, and your other names afterwards. This is an additional safeguard to ensure that the exam board awards the marks to the right candidate.

Here you fill in the school's exam number.

The Unit 1 exam lasts 1 hour 15 minutes. Plan your time accordingly.

Make sure that you understand exactly which questions from which sections you should attempt.

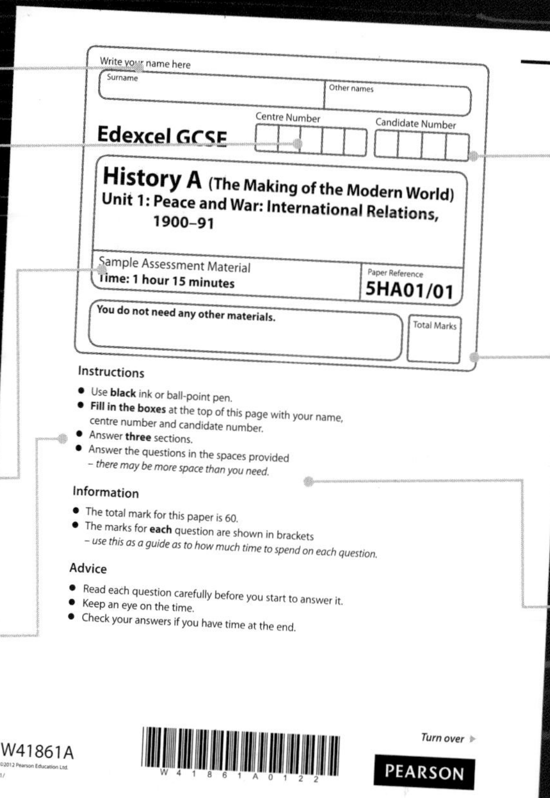

Write your name here

Surname | Other names

Edexcel GCSE | Centre Number | Candidate Number

History A (The Making of the Modern World)
Unit 1: Peace and War: International Relations, 1900–91

Sample Assessment Material
Time: 1 hour 15 minutes

Paper Reference
5HA01/01

You do not need any other materials.

Total Marks

Instructions

- Use **black** ink or ball-point pen.
- **Fill in the boxes** at the top of this page with your name, centre number and candidate number.
- Answer **three** sections.
- Answer the questions in the spaces provided
  – *there may be more space than you need.*

Information

- The total mark for this paper is 60.
- The marks for **each** question are shown in brackets
  – *use this as a guide as to how much time to spend on each question.*

Advice

- Read each question carefully before you start to answer it.
- Keep an eye on the time.
- Check your answers if you have time at the end.

W41861A
©2012 Pearson Education Ltd.
1/

W 4 1 8 6 1 A 0 1 2 2

Turn over

PEARSON

Here you fill in your personal exam number. Take care to write it accurately.

In this box, the examiner will write the total marks you have achieved in the exam paper.

Don't feel that you have to fill the answer space provided. Everybody's handwriting varies, so a long answer from you may take up as much space as a short answer from someone else.

If you answer Section 1 put a cross in this box ☐ .

SECTION 1
Why did war break out? International rivalry, 1900–14

Answer Part (a), EITHER Part (b)(i) OR Part (b)(ii) AND then Part (c).

The photograph below shows the British battleship H.M.S. Dreadnought in 1906.

Question 1

Answer Part (a).

(a) Describe **one** action taken by Britain and Germany in relation to their navies in the years 1900–14. (2)

3

Turn over

W 4 1 8 6 1 A 0 3 2 2

Check that you are answering the right number of questions in the right section. In Unit 1 you should answer questions from **three sections**.

Each section in Unit 1 opens with a photograph. The caption above the photograph tells you what it depicts.

Pay attention to words in bold, especially numbers. Make sure you give the number of features the question asks for.

Read dates in questions carefully.

The number of marks available for each question is given on the right.

Pay careful attention to which sub-questions and question parts you are required to answer. Mark the relevant box as instructed on the exam paper.

Answer EITHER Part (b)(i) OR (b)(ii).

EITHER

(b) (i) Describe the key features of the Moroccan Crisis (1905). (6)

OR

(b) (ii) Describe the key features of the Bosnian Crisis (1908–09). (6)

Indicate which question you are answering by marking a cross in the box ☒. If you change your mind, put a line through the box ☒ and then indicate your new question with a cross ☒.

Chosen Question Number: **Part (b)(i)** ☐ **Part (b)(ii)** ☐

The live question paper will contain one further page of lines.

4

W 4 1 8 6 1 A 0 4 2 2

Zone Out

This section provides answers to the most common questions students have about what happens after they complete their exams. For more information, visit www.examzone.co.uk.

When will my results be published?

Results for GCSE summer examinations are issued on the third Thursday in August. January exam results are issued in March and March exam results are issued in April. If you are sitting your exams from 2014 onwards, there will no longer be January sittings: you will sit all of your exams in June.

Can I get my results online?

Visit www.resultsplusdirect.co.uk, where you will find detailed student results information including the 'Edexcel Gradeometer' which demonstrates how close you were to the nearest grade boundary.

I haven't done as well as I expected. What can I do now?

First of all, talk to your teacher. After all the teaching that you have had, and the tests and internal examinations you have done, he/she is the person who best knows what grade you are capable of achieving. Take your results slip to your subject teacher, and go through the information on it in detail. If you both think that there is something wrong with the result, the school or college can apply to see your completed examination paper and then, if necessary, ask for a re-mark immediately.

Bear in mind that the original mark can be confirmed or lowered, as well as raised, as a result of a re-mark.

Can I resit this unit?

If you are sitting your exams before 2014, you may resit a unit once prior to claiming certification for the qualification. If you are sitting your exams from 2014 onwards, you will not be able to resit any of the exams.

Glossary

Term	Definition
alliance	A formal agreement between countries.
Anschluss	The formal union of Germany and Austria.
appeasement	A policy of maintaining peace by negotiation and making concessions.
armistice	A truce or agreement to stop fighting.
arms race	When countries compete to have the most effective armed forces.
atomic bomb	A highly destructive nuclear weapon.
B52 bomber	A heavy-duty military aircraft capable of crossing large distances and carrying heavy loads.
ballistic nuclear missiles	Nuclear missiles capable of being launched from one continent and hitting targets in another.
Big Three (after the First World War)	Clemenceau (France), Wilson (United States) and Lloyd George (Britain).
Big Three (after the Second World War)	Roosevelt (United States), Stalin (Soviet Union) and Churchill (Britain) – the original leaders of the Grand Alliance.
blockade	An attempt to prevent resources reaching their destination.
boycott	To refuse to take part in something.
censorship	Action by the government to prevent the publication of any material of which they disapprove.
CIA	Central Intelligence Agency – an American organisation designed to monitor foreign governments.
collective security	Nations acting together to maintain peace.
conscription	Compulsory service in the armed forces.
consolidated	United and strengthened.
dictator	A person who rules a country with total power, often using harsh or extreme methods.
diktat	An agreement forced on someone.
doctrine	A statement of ideas.
Eastern Bloc	The European countries within the Soviet sphere of influence.
economic sanction	A restriction on trade with another country.
entente	A friendly understanding between countries.

Term	Definition
fallout shelters	Buildings designed to protect people in the event of a nuclear attack.
Grand Alliance	A military pact between the USA, the USSR and Great Britain, in order to defeat Nazi Germany during the Second World War.
Great Depression	The world economic recession in the 1930s.
Habsburgs	The ruling family of Austria-Hungary.
imperial	Relating to empire-building and matters of empire.
isolationism	The policy of the US government in the 1920s and 1930s, which meant that the USA planned to keep out of international affairs.
liberation	Setting free. For example countries were liberated from German rule after the Second World War.
mandate	A country placed in the care of one of the victorious powers after the First World War.
mobilised	Got ready. When troops are mobilised they are ready to fight.
nationalism	A belief in your nation being independent.
nuclear arsenals	Stocks of nuclear weapons.
nuclear holocaust	The virtual destruction of the human race by nuclear weapons.
oppression	The removal of freedom and use of tyranny and cruelty.
Ottomans	The Muslim rulers of Turkey before 1918.
pact	An agreement.
plebiscite	A referendum or public vote.
propaganda	Information that is deliberately designed to win political support.
refugee	Someone fleeing from bad conditions.
reparations	Payments made in compensation for damage caused.
retaliation	An attempt to pay someone back for a wrongdoing.
self-determination	The right of nations to rule themselves.
space race	A period from the late 1950s to the early 1970s during which the USA and the USSR competed to achieve 'firsts' in space.
summit	A high-level meeting between government representatives.
totalitarian	A political system based on unlimited government control.
ultimatum	A demand.

Acknowledgements

Pearson Education Limited
Edinburgh Gate
Harlow
Essex
CM20 2JE
England

ISBN 978-1-44690-315-5

The publishers are grateful to Jenny Clifton, James Ellison and Andrew Lees for their contributions to the book.

Designed by eMC Design Ltd

Illustrations by Peter Bull Studio

15 14 13 12
10 9 8 7 6 5 4 3 2

Printed and bound in Malaysia (CTP-PPSB)

The publisher would like to thank the following for their kind permission to reproduce their photographs:

(Key: b-bottom; c-centre; l-left; r-right; t-top)

akg-images Ltd: 23; **Alamy Images**: The Print Collector 17, 83, Trinity Mirror / Mirrorpix 82; **Corbis**: 98, 106, Bettmann 35, 46, 85, 89, 103cl, 125c, 130, 144, epa / Libor Hajsky 123, Hulton-Deutsch Collection 103cr, Keystone 6, 27, Wally McNamee 128, Reuters 140, Sygma / J. L. Atlan 112, Peter Turnley 147, Underwood & Underwood 47tr, 58; **Getty Images**: Hulton Archive 59, 71, 97, 103l, Time & Life Pictures 22, 100, 103r, Topical Press Agency 12; **iStockphoto**: Ozgur Donmaz 30; **Mary Evans Picture Library**: 19, 47bl, Robert Hunt Library 10, Weimar Archive 39, 60-61; **nisyndication.com**: Zoke / Michael Attwell, The Sun, 21 Oct 1981 135; **Photoshot Holdings Limited**: UPPA 124; **Press Association Images**: AP 108, 149; **Punch Cartoon Library**: 55, 65, 66; **Rex Features**: Arthur Grace 134, Everett Collection / CSU Archives 125l, Poderni-White 148, Sipa Press 111, 117; **RIA Novosti Photo Library**: 113; **Solo Syndication / Associated Newspapers Ltd**: David Low, Evening Standard, 30 Sep 1938 73, David Low, Picture Post, 21 Oct 1939 75, David Low, The Bulletin (Sydney), 23 Jan 1919 32, Illingworth, Leslie Gilbert, Daily Mail, 14 February 1949, The National Library of Wales 99bl, Illingworth, Leslie Gilbert, Daily Mail, 20 April 1949, The National Library of Wales 99tl, Illingworth, Leslie Glibert, 30 June 1948, The National Library of Wales 91; **The Herb Block Foundation**: 118; **TopFoto**: RIA Novosti 113r, Topham Picturepoint 110

Cover images: Front: Pearson Education Ltd

We are grateful to Curtis Brown Group Ltd for a quote by Winston Churchill from The Iron Curtain Speech, copyright © Winston S. Churchill. Reproduced with permission of Curtis Brown Ltd, London on behalf of The Estate of Winston Churchill.

Every effort has been made to trace the copyright holders and we apologise in advance for any unintentional omissions. We would be pleased to insert the appropriate acknowledgement in any subsequent edition of this publication